THE CAMBRIDGE COMPANION TO SHELLEY

Percy Bysshe Shelley (1792–1822) was an extraordinary poet, playwright, and essayist, revolutionary both in his ideas and in his artistic theory and practice. This collection of original essays by an international group of specialists is a comprehensive survey of the life, works, and times of this radical Romantic writer. Three sections cover Shelley's life and posthumous reception; the basics of his poetry, prose, and drama; and his immersion in the currents of philosophical and political thinking and practice. As well as providing a wide-ranging look at the state of existing scholarship, the Companion develops and enriches our understanding of Shelley. Significant new contributions include fresh assessments of Shelley's narratives, his view of philosophy, and his role in emerging views about ecology. With its chronology and guide to further reading, this lively and accessible Companion is an invaluable guide for students and scholars of Shelley and of Romanticism.

THE CAMBRIDGE
COMPANION TO
SHELLEY

EDITED BY
TIMOTHY MORTON
University of California, Davis

CAMBRIDGE
UNIVERSITY PRESS

CAMBRIDGE UNIVERSITY PRESS
Cambridge, New York, Melbourne, Madrid, Cape Town, Singapore, São Paulo

Cambridge University Press
The Edinburgh Building, Cambridge CB2 2RU, UK

Published in the United States of America by Cambridge University Press, New York

www.cambridge.org
Information on this title: www.cambridge.org/9780521533430

© Cambridge University Press 2006

First published 2006

Printed in the United Kingdom at the University Press, Cambridge

A catalogue record for this book is available from the British Library

ISBN-13 978-0-521-82604-4 hardback
ISBN-10 0-521-82604-7 hardback
ISBN-13 978-0-521-53343-0 paperback
ISBN-10 0-521-53343-0 paperback

CONTENTS

NOTES ON CONTRIBUTORS

JEFFREY N. COX is Professor of English and of Comparative Literature and Humanities at the University of Colorado, Boulder, where he is also Associate Vice Chancellor for Faculty Affairs. His work on Shelley and on Romantic drama includes *In the Shadows of Romance: Romantic Tragic Drama in Germany, England and France* (1987), *Poetry and Politics in the Cockney School: Keats, Shelley, Hunt and Their Circle* (1998), and the *Broadview Anthology of Romantic Drama* (2003), edited with Michael Gamer.

JACK DONOVAN teaches in the Department of English and Related Literature at the University of York. He edited Shelley's *Laon and Cythna* for the second volume of the Longman Annotated English Poets edition of *The Poems of Shelley* (2000) and is currently part of the team preparing the third volume of Shelley's poems in the same series.

PAUL HAMILTON is Professor in the School of English and Drama at Queen Mary University of London. He is the author of several books on Romanticism and historicism, including *Metaromanticism* (2003).

JERROLD E. HOGLE is Professor of English, University Distinguished Professor, and Vice Provost for Instruction at the University of Arizona. He is the author of *Shelley's Process* (1988) and *Evaluating Shelley* (1996), and co-editor of *Evaluating Shelley* (1996). He is also editor of *The Cambridge Companion to Gothic Fiction* (2002).

WILLIAM KEACH is Professor of English at Brown University. He is the author of *Shelley's Style* (1984). His most recent book is *Arbitrary Power: Romanticism, Language, Politics* (2004). His previous books include *Shelley's Style* (1984), and he has edited *Coleridge: The Complete Poems* for the Penguin English Poets series (1997).

THERESA KELLEY is Marjorie and Lorin Tiefenthaler Professor of English at the University of Wisconsin, Madison. She is the author of *Reinventing Allegory* (1997) and

Wordsworth's Revisionary Aesthetics (1988), and editor, with Paula Feldman, of *Romantic Women Writers: Voices and Countervoices* (1995).

TIMOTHY MORTON is Professor of Literature and the Environment at the University of California, Davis. He is the author of *Shelley and the Revolution in Taste* (1994) and numerous essays and books on Percy and Mary Shelley, including *The Poetics of Spice* (2000) and a Routledge textbook on *Frankenstein* (2002).

JEFFREY C. ROBINSON is Professor of English at the University of Colorado, Boulder. He is the author of *Reception and Poetics in Keats* (1998), *Wordsworth Day by Day: Reading His Work into Poetry Now* (2005), and editor, with Jerome Rothenberg, of *Poems for the Millennium 3: The University of California Book of Romantic and Post-Romantic Poetry* (forthcoming), and *Unfettering Poetry: Fancy and British Romanticism* (forthcoming).

KAREN WEISMAN is Associate Professor of English at the University of Toronto, where she teaches Romantic and post-Romantic culture. She is also cross-listed with the Jewish Studies Program. She is the author of *Imageless Truths: Shelley's Poetic Fictions* (1994), and many articles on Romanticism, contemporary poetry, and Anglo-Jewish literary history. She is currently completing a study of forms of subjectivity in the elegy.

ACKNOWLEDGEMENTS

I would like to thank all my contributors, who wrote, revised, and revised again to produce a stunning collection of essays that compellingly redis-covers Shelley for the twenty-first century. Thank you to David Simpson, who read and commented on my chapter on Shelley and ecology. I am very grateful to my wife Kate for reading through some of the chapters with me, and for accommodating my writing during the first year of our daughter Claire's life. I was lucky to have my research assistants, Seth Forrest and Christopher Schaberg, who worked on copy-editing and indexing. I am fortunate to have such a helpful and intelligent editor as Linda Bree. The University of California at Davis provided me with a Faculty Development Award and two Small Grants in aid of research to help with the publication of this volume.

A NOTE ON THE TEXT

The latest editions of Shelley were as yet unfinished as this book went to press. I have taken the liberty, therefore, of referring principally to Everest and Matthews's edition (Longman; abbreviated as *P*), with references to the prose coming from David Lee Clark's handy, though out-of-date, edition (abbreviated as *Pr*), barring a few occasional citations from E. B. Murray's or Ingpen and Peck's edition (the latter is abbreviated *IP*). The Companion cites Clark's edition because of the ease with which students may find a copy of this edition of the prose. Where the Longman edition is not yet completed (works written after *The Cenci* (1819)), I refer to the revised Norton edition edited by Donald Reiman and Neil Fraistat. References to this text are marked with an *N* in parenthesis after citations. The Companion refers to translations in principal from Hutchinson's Oxford edition (*H*).

CHRONOLOGY

1792   Percy Bysshe Shelley (PBS) born 4 August at Field Place, Warnham, near Horsham, West Sussex, the eldest child of Timothy Shelley, MP, and Elizabeth Pilfold Shelley, and eldest grandson of Bysshe Shelley.

1797   William Godwin marries Mary Wollstonecraft 29 March; she gives birth to their daughter Mary 30 August and dies 10 September.

1798   Studies with Warnham clergyman, Rev. Evan Edwards.

1802–4   Boards at Syon House Academy, Isleworth, on Great Western Road in the Thames Valley.

1804–10   PBS a student and boarder at Eton.

1806   Grandfather becomes Sir Bysshe Shelley, baronet. Earliest year in which PBS may have written poems in *The Esdaile Notebook*.

1808   Corresponds with his Wiltshire cousin Harriet Grove; she ends their informal engagement in late 1810.

1809   Writes several poems now gathered in *The Esdaile Notebook*.

1810   Writes and submits his first book-length poem *The Wandering Jew* for publication, which is rejected.
Gothic novel *Zastrozzi* (spring).

Poems by PBS and his sister Elizabeth, under the title *Original Poetry by Victor and Cazire* (autumn).

University College Oxford (October); meets Thomas Jefferson Hogg.

Gothic novel *St Irvyne* (December).

Posthumous Fragments of Margaret Nicholson (December).

1811   Meets Harriet Westbrook (January).

Writes and circulates *The Necessity of Atheism* with Hogg.

Expelled from Oxford (March).

Elopes with and marries Harriet Westbrook in Edinburgh on 29 August.

Meets Robert Southey in Keswick.

1812   Dublin; *Address to the Irish People*, *Proposals for an Association of Philanthropists*, *Declaration of Rights*.

Travels to Wales, then Devon; writes and circulates *Letter to Lord Ellenborough* in defence of the radical publisher Daniel Eaton, and the broadside ballad *The Devil's Walk*.

Flees to Tremadoc, North Wales, near Harlech, under government surveillance.

Raises funds for blocking an estuary to create more arable land.

Meets William Godwin during brief visit to London (autumn).

1813   The Shelleys leave Wales at short notice (February), pursued by creditors or robbers.

Dublin: retrieves the manuscript of *The Esdaile Notebook* from the printer.

London: PBS prints and privately circulates *Queen Mab* (between May and December).

Harriet and PBS's first daughter Ianthe born (23 June).

Publishes *A Vindication of Natural Diet*.

Joins expatriate, pro-revolutionary vegetarian French and English circle centered on Mrs Boinville.

1814   Early in the year publishes *A Refutation of Deism*.

(July) PBS and Mary Godwin elope to France, with her half-sister Claire Clairmont along as translator. Six weeks later they all return, out of funds.

Mary's and PBS's joint *History of a Six Weeks' Tour* is based on this honeymoon trip. Harriet's and PBS's first son, Charles, is born (30 November).

1815   Sir Bysshe Shelley dies (5 January).
Mary's first child, a daughter, is born prematurely and dies (6 March).
As part of settlement of his grandfather's estate, PBS receives money to pay his (and Godwin's) debts and provide an annual income for Harriet.
Writes *Alastor*.

1816   William Shelley born (January).
Alastor . . . and Other Poems (February), the first publication under his own name.
The Shelleys, Claire, Byron, and others settle in Switzerland for the summer.
Writes 'Hymn to Intellectual Beauty' and later 'Mont Blanc'.
Mary writes the first draft of *Frankenstein*.
Claire becomes pregnant by Byron.
Mary's other half-sister, Fanny Imlay, becomes despondent and commits suicide (London, October).
Harriet Shelley, abandoned by another lover and pregnant with another child, commits suicide by drowning sometime in early December.
Mary and PBS marry (30 December).

1817   Claire's daughter Alba/Allegra is born in secret in Bath.
The Lord Chancellor (Lord Eldon) denies PBS custody of his children by Harriet.
Habeas Corpus suspended, making the civil rights of radical journalists legally indefensible.
The Shelleys settle at Marlow outside London when his own anti-government pamphlet *A Proposal for Putting Reform to the Vote* is published.
(March until September) Writes *Laon and Cythna*. It is printed late in the year, but revised and reissued as *The Revolt of Islam* in December.
Clara born (September).
Drafts 'Essay on Christianity'.

Writes *An Address to the People on the Death of the Princess Charlotte* (November). *Frankenstein* published (December).

1818   Begins *Rosalind and Helen*.

The Shelleys and Claire, with their children and servants, leave for Italy in March.

PBS continues to negotiate Byron's acknowledgement and support for his and Claire's daughter.

Bagni di Lucca for the summer; translates Plato's *Symposium*; writes the essay 'On Love' and finishes *Rosalind and Helen* (published spring 1819).

PBS and Claire visit Allegra in Venice, although Claire stays nearby rather than at Allegra's home.

PBS and Byron become reacquainted.

During Mary's trip to Venice to join PBS, their daughter Clara becomes ill. She dies in September.

Lines Written among the Euganean Hills and *Julian and Maddalo*.

The Shelleys keep on the move, travelling to Rome, then Naples, Vesuvius, and other sites. They read Mme de Staël's *Corinne* together.

1819   They return to Rome (March); PBS completes a draft of the first three acts of *Prometheus Unbound*.

In June their son William dies; they leave immediately for Livorno.

The accumulated grief over the two children's deaths drives Mary into a deep depression.

PBS completes *The Cenci* and publishes it in Italy in 1819, in England a year later.

(August) Hearing news of the Peterloo Massacre of citizens listening to a speech about reform in a field outside Manchester, PBS writes *The Mask of Anarchy*.

(October) They move to Florence, where another child, Percy Florence, is born (12 November). *Peter Bell the Third*, 'Ode to the West Wind' (October–November).

PBS finishes *Prometheus Unbound* (published 1820); drafts the essays *A Philosophical View of Reform* and the brief 'On Life'.

British Parliament passes Six Acts collectively designed to suppress dissent still further.

1820	George III of England dies and is succeeded by his son George IV.
	Cato Street conspiracy to kill the English Prime Minister discovered and its plotters executed.
	The Shelleys move to Pisa. PBS writes 'Sensitive-Plant', 'Ode to Liberty', 'To a Sky-Lark', and 'Letter to Maria Gisbourne', who is visiting England at the time.
	(Autumn) *The Witch of Atlas*, 'Ode to Naples'. *Swellfoot the Tyrant* published and quickly suppressed (December).
	Prometheus Unbound published (September).
	Return to Pisa in October, where they meet Teresa 'Emilia' Viviani and the exiled Greek prince Alexander Mavrocordato.

1821	Edward and Jane Williams meet the Shelleys (January).
	The Williamses and Shelleys move to nearby residences at several different Italian locations.
	Writes *Epipsychidion* after visiting Teresa Viviani; published anonymously (May).
	In response to Thomas Love Peacock's *The Four Ages of Poetry*, writes *A Defence of Poetry*.
	Pirated editions of *Queen Mab* appear in England.
	Austrians crush the Neapolitan revolt and the Greeks rebel against Turkish rule.
	Learning of John Keats's death in Rome (23 February), writes *Adonais* (May–June; published July); it is printed in Pisa.
	Completes the drama *Hellas* in the autumn.
	Invites Byron, his lover the Countess Guiccioli, and her father and brother to Pisa.

1822	(January) Writes scenes for *Charles the First*; Edward John Trelawny arrives in Pisa.
	The group, but principally Shelley and Byron, plan theatricals.
	Writes several poems to or about Jane Williams, among them 'With a Guitar, to Jane'.
	Allegra Byron dies in a convent near Ravenna in April.
	(Summer) The Shelleys and the Williamses move to San Terenzo on the Bay of Lerici. PBS's boat arrives in May; PBS begins to write *The Triumph of Life*, unfinished at the time of his death.
	Mary miscarries (June).

Leigh Hunt and his family arrive; PBS invites Leigh Hunt to join, along with a more reluctant Byron, in a radical publishing venture, *The Liberal*.

Shelley and Edward Williams sail to Livorno (Leghorn) to meet the Hunts when they arrive. On the return trip (8 July), a sudden storm begins and PBS, Williams, and the boat boy are lost. Their bodies wash up later, and are cremated on the beach between La Spezia and Livorno; Shelley's ashes interred in the Protestant Cemetery in Rome in 1823.

1839   Percy Bysshe Shelley, *Poetical Works*, ed. Mary Shelley (London: Edward Moxon, 1839).

Arnold   Matthew Arnold, *The Complete Prose Works of Matthew Arnold*, ed. R. W. Super, 11 vols. (Ann Arbor: University of Michigan Press, 1960).

CH   *Shelley: The Critical Heritage*, ed. James E. Barcus (London and Boston: Routledge and Kegan Paul, 1975).

CP   *The Complete Poetry of Percy Bysshe Shelley*, ed. Donald H. Reiman and Neil Fraistat, 4 vols. (Baltimore and London: Johns Hopkins University Press, 2000–).

H   *Shelley: Poetical Works*, ed. Thomas Hutchinson, corrected by G. M. Matthews (London and New York: Oxford University Press, 1970).

Hogg   Thomas Jefferson Hogg, *The Life of Percy Bysshe Shelley*, 2 vols. (London: Edward Moxon, 1858).

IP   Percy Bysshe Shelley, *The Complete Works*, ed. R. Ingpen and W. E. Peck, 10 vols. (London and New York: Ernest Benn, 1926–30).

KSJ   *Keats-Shelley Journal*.

L   *The Letters of Percy Bysshe Shelley*, ed. F. L. Jones, 2 vols. (Oxford: Oxford University Press, 1964).

MSJ   *The Journals of Mary Shelley 1814–1844*, ed. Paula R. Feldman and Diana Scott-Kilvert, 2 vols. (Oxford: Clarendon Press, 1987).

N   *Shelley's Poetry and Prose*, ed. Donald Reiman and Neil Fraistat (2nd edn of Norton Critical Edition; 1st edn ed. Donald Reiman and Sharon B. Powers) (New York and London: Norton, 2002 (1977)).

P   *The Poems of Shelley*, ed. Kelvin Everest and Geoffrey Matthews (London and New York: Longman, 1989–).

Pr   *Shelley's Prose: Or The Trumpet of a Prophecy*, ed. David Lee Clark (1954, 1966; London: Fourth Estate, 1988).

RH   Richard Holmes, *Shelley: The Pursuit* (London: Weidenfeld and Nicolson, 1987).

W   Newman Ivey White, *Shelley*, 2 vols. (New York: Knopf, 1940).

TIMOTHY MORTON

Introduction

Contesting Shelley

'Shelley, the genius, the prophet, Shelley, and Byron, with his glowing sensuality and his bitter satire upon our existing society, find most of their readers in the proletariat; the bourgeoisie owns only castrated editions, family editions, expurgated in accordance with the hypocritical morality of today.'[1] Thus Friedrich Engels intones towards the end of his relentless excoriation of the condition of the working class in England, the double incantation of the writer's name charging the sentence with energy. Shelley continues to polarize people along class lines. I well remember, having been invited to present a BBC radio programme on Shelley's poetry in the early 1990s, being summarily informed after having assembled my list and my introduction that most of the poems I had chosen were not actually by him. My selections were from *Queen Mab*, *Alastor*, *Prometheus Unbound*, and some of the radical lyrics of 1819. It was the latter that were in dispute, ensuring that I did not get to do the show at all. To the blushing eyes of some liberal humanist editors, the representations of starving mothers asking for a bit of food must have been fakes. The idea that he could not have written such things persists two centuries after Shelley himself sent off his ballads and songs for publication, moved by the massacre of a huge crowd of protesters at St Peter's Fields in Manchester by those staunch relics of English hierarchy, the yeomanry cavalry.

Engels wrote his words four years before the adjective 'Shelleyan' came into circulation, though 'Shelleyite', perhaps denoting a stronger affiliation, appeared in the very year of Shelley's death, 1822.[2] The connotation of aesthetic effeteness inspired the name of the modern pop band, Shelleyan Orphan, but Engels had something more urgent in mind. Some circles have still not forgiven Percy Shelley for having been a class traitor. Shelley grew up in the ranks of the gentry (his grandfather had become a baronet during his childhood), but most of his life was spent in radical departures from upper-class norms. A glance at a Jane Austen novel will provide brilliantly convincing evidence of the painful world of the gentry from 1792 to 1822, between Shelley's birth and death. In order to retain one's status as a 'gentleman' or 'lady', one could not work for a living; one had to marry or inherit money. Like an English Marcel Proust, Austen systematically lacerates the upper class with 'remorseless gentleness', in the words of Theodor Adorno on Proust.[3]

Shelley rebelled in a more direct fashion. Like most rebels he became the family scapegoat, going into self-imposed exile in Italy, acting out foolhardily, and drowning at the age of thirty. Some of his surviving family members did their best either to ignore him or to turn him into a saint – to kick him upstairs to the great aristocracy in the sky, where he would be no more trouble. Almost two centuries later, I recall that doing a DPhil. on him at Oxford elicited funny comments. At University College, Weekes's Shelley Memorial draws a stone pall of Victorian cultural sainthood over his more colourful exploits. Whatever Shelley had to communicate, it is evidently still contagious.

Shelley was going to be a Member of Parliament, but the publication of his pamphlet on atheism sealed his fate as a figure on the margins of political legislation. Perhaps this is why in the *Defence of Poetry* he insists that poets are the 'unacknowledged legislators of the world' (*Pr* 297). Parliament's loss was culture's gain. Shelley was interested in all aspects of literary culture. He was not simply content to write and publish works: they had to be disseminated properly too. *The Necessity of Atheism*, written with Thomas Jefferson Hogg while Shelley was at Oxford, was scattered prominently at the front of Slatter and Munday's bookshop in the High Street (*RH* 50). A passing pastor noticed it and Shelley was swiftly expelled. Such acts of bravado in disseminating his work were not uncommon. Shelley penned a sonnet 'To a Balloon, Laden with *Knowledge*' and floated actual balloons, filled with actual knowledge in the form of radical pamphlets, across the Irish Sea. In Dublin he was said to slip such pamphlets into the cloak hoods of passing ladies (*RH* 119–20). He floated radical works down the Bristol Channel in bottles, an activity for which he attracted the interest of the secret service. He wrote poems about what we might call broadcasting, such as 'Ode to the West Wind', in which he prays that his words be 'scattered' across the earth like 'Ashes and sparks', or autumn leaves (63–7). Shelley would have loved the internet. He enjoyed playing with assumed personalities, signing a guest book in a Swiss inn as 'democrat, great lover of mankind, and atheist' (in Greek; *W* I.457). At Oxford, he had eagerly performed chemistry experiments (*W* I.79–80), and one imagines that he would have used computers both to disseminate knowledge and to hack into and undermine government systems.

Shelley lived in a time of terror. America and France had revolted. The British establishment had denounced the French revolutionaries as 'Terrorists' (the first usage of the word), and an oppressive counter-revolution was in full swing. In England, double agents infiltrated radical organizations and tried to undermine them from within. Shelley was a brave man whose bravery could teeter over the edge of recklessness. He had stood up to the despotic practices of 'fagging' at Eton (using younger boys as the servants of older ones, in a climate of punishment and physical abuse). Shelley did not change his habits much in adulthood. His life of escape and exile enabled him to observe at close range the different classes at work and play in England, Ireland, Wales, France, Switzerland, and Italy. Perhaps this is why he has been both so vilified and so beatified. He was a class traitor with attitude, blessed with privilege and armed with the philosophy of the radical Enlightenment, a radical cosmopolitan parody of the social butterfly.

Not surprisingly, Shelley's family almost disowned him. Moreover, he himself struggled with his resistance to being upper class, his transformation into something of a proto-socialist. At his most progressive, Shelley could be pro-feminist, proto-ecological, anti-slavery, anti-capitalist, antihomophobic, and against cruelty to animals, eating meat, and drinking alcohol. So keen was he in one sense to do no harm to sentient beings that he became a vegetarian. His interpersonal relationships, however, especially with women, were a disaster. He encouraged many women to believe that they could transcend their patriarchal conditions, throw off their chains, and become more independent. But he did so with the charismatic compulsion of a master seducer who, from an early 21st-century vantage point, resembles those hippies in the 1960s who confused sexual liberation with women's liberation. Shelley was capable of relapsing into the unfortunate condition of social privilege, pouring scorn on those beneath him in Wales, condemning the radical underground's pirating of *Queen Mab*, a poem that of all poems by members of the gentry looks as if it had been written with the underground explicitly in mind.

As an individual, Shelley may seem either a seraphic extraterrestrial or a militant proto-socialist crusader, unless one understands how he engaged with a variety of cultural communities. Research into Shelley's politics struggles through many arguments, including vegetarianism, quasi-feminism, anti-slavery, labour theories of value, psychology, philosophical anarchism, technological futurism, gradualist reformism, and triumphalism. But Shelley's analysis and critique of early capitalism also involved the establishment of *places from which* arguments could be launched, both figuratively (recurring poetic topoi) and materially (participation in subcultures).

Shelley's negotiations with several overlapping public 'circles' were complicated. The family and the domestic sphere were held in uneasy abeyance, though problematically reincorporated in Shelley's relationships with Harriet Westbrook, and later Mary Wollstonecraft Godwin and Claire Clairmont. The family was a touchstone of his poetic vision of social harmony. Shelley's reading with his tutors at Field Place and Eton was somewhat radical, with open access to the work of materialist philosophers. Shelley sidestepped his father's ambitions for a Parliamentary career through the publication of *The Necessity of Atheism* (1811), and was expelled from Oxford. Professed Deism was then a code for radical political sympathies; atheism was a serious offence. Shelley's break with his father was a crucial moment in terms of both family and literary work, and also of money, for which he struggled for much of his life. He often portrayed social tyrannies in terms of hateful father figures such as Jupiter and the incestuous Count Cenci, and used God's fatherhood as an analogue for earthly despotism in *Queen Mab*. Shelley was infamous for his views on the evils of marriage and the desirability of free love, and it is debated whether he practised the latter with Mary and Thomas Jefferson Hogg in 1815. *Laon and Cythna* depicts a love affair between a brother and sister who wage a war against a despotic government. The poem was retitled *The Revolt of Islam* when the incest of the protagonists became a scandal. Shelley was forcibly deprived of his children by Harriet after his elopement with Mary, and subsequently Harriet committed suicide, which may have been a factor in his leaving England for Italy.

Shelley's complex relationship with the first generation of poets who had responded to the French and American revolutions reconfigured the modes of radical behaviour and authorship which they established. Between 1811 and 1813 he corresponded vigorously with Godwin and Elizabeth Hitchener, trying to draw the latter into a circle with Harriet in Wales, where he also participated in what would now be called an experiment in social ecology. The intimidation tactics of the local squirearchy forced him from the land reclamation project in the new town of Tremadoc. He became involved in the growing insurgent tradition in Ireland (1812), distributing pamphlets in Dublin before a shocked Godwin dissuaded him.

Shelley participated in the radical community of Harriet Boinville at Bracknell in Windsor, which included the physicians William Lawrence (also a writer on evolution) and William Lambe, and experimented with vegetarianism. *Queen Mab* was published in 1813. Originally intended for ruling-class shelves and disguised as a philosophical fairy-story, it was a vision of past, present, and future society and an incitement to radical change. Detailed notes accessed scientific, philosophical, and political information from his extensive preparatory reading. *Queen Mab* was quickly pirated by the radical underground (Carlile, Clarke, Benbow, Canon, and others), in pocket-sized editions (easily hidden and transported). Shelley later objected to them, treating the self-taught publisher and *philosophe* Canon with considerable disrespect. *Queen Mab* was disseminated in Chartist discourse, and became significant for other writers from Marx to Shaw.

Shelley's ambiguous liaison with cultural groups is nowhere better exemplified. *Queen Mab* was the lasting influence on his later work, which ceaselessly unpacked and reformulated its figures, from the parallel prose/poetry project of 1814–16 (including *Alastor* and new work on diet, religion, and politics) to *The Triumph of Life* (1822). Despite his declared dislike of didacticism, the poem is remarkably and influentially didactic. On the other hand, Shelley shunned the countercultural spheres that would have enabled him to have 'somewhere to stand' from which to 'move the earth' (Archimedes' epigraph to *Queen Mab*). This distance often involved the adoption of satirical poetic and prose forms, despite the impression, again somewhat fostered by Shelley himself, that he was above such things.

Shelley ambivalently straddled crowd agitation politics and mass management strategies. *The Mask of Anarchy*'s (1819) famous appeal to the sleeping lions is an example of the former. The latter appears in Shelley's interest in efficient, 'globalizing' social plans. The 'Ode to Liberty' (1820), which presents an emancipatory theory of historical process in an allegory of its birth and growth in Greece, Rome, and revolutionary France, also discusses the relationship between sustainable ecologies and economic demand. Shelley's speculations on agricultural reform with his acquaintance G. W. Tighe employed the agricultural chemistry of Humphrey Davy to model a 'top down' approach. Shelley never separated poetry and politics, and the notes that he took during his acquaintance with Tighe were written in the same book in which he drafted 'Ode to the West Wind'. Shelley negotiated similarly ambivalent positions with regard to British imperialism and nationalism, torn in his poetry between Hellenizing and orientalizing discourses.

The cultivation of individual modes of 'active virtue', like the tutelage of Frankenstein's creature, continued to be a precarious affair. The ecstatic, Dionysian collective politics of *Prometheus Unbound* (1818–19) is predicated on the individual liberation of the ruling-class reformer, though there is a lack of critical consensus on the drama's purpose, and the role of the mysterious character Demogorgon. But in the unusually grotesque satire *Swellfoot the Tyrant* (1820), prosopopeia (putting words into the mouths of animals) and the use of the crowd as a protagonist generate a more populist appeal, in a play that alludes to the politics of the Queen Caroline affair, the rioting and satire that arose as a result of George IV's campaign against his wife to prevent her, commonly thought of as a 'people's Queen', from being crowned.

Shelley sought to establish a radical base in Italy, attempting to set up the journal *The Liberal* at Pisa. He became interested in the cultural history of Italy, intrigued by Renaissance Rome and reading the radical historian Sismondi for records of medieval republics, while expressing enthusiasm for the insurrection in Naples in 1820. Also in 1820 he met Prince Alexander Mavrocordato, the leader of the Greek patriots in Europe. Smitten by news of the Peterloo massacre (1819), he wrote a volume of popular songs and political prose which the essayist and publisher Leigh Hunt refused to publish, on the conservative grounds that its audience was not ready for it. Throughout his later years, Shelley collaborated significantly with Mary Godwin (the novelist), Byron the poet, and Peacock the novelist, maintaining strong relationships with figures as diverse as the poet Keats, Leigh Hunt, Godwin, Mary's philosophical anarchist father, and his friends Hogg, Medwin, and Trelawny.

The politics of time and the politics of dissemination were important for Shelley. When will the social change take place (in a sudden, violent revolution or more gradually), and to whom should revolutionary figuration be addressed? These questions run not only through the more obviously political writings, but also through works like 'Ode to the West Wind' which often receive attention as apolitical lyrics. Conversely, Shelley's political didacticism reconfigures the poetry of Milton and the eighteenth century.

It would take hundreds of pages to weigh the evidence and make a pronouncement on the more excruciating moments of Shelley's life. There are mitigating factors. Shelley was very young. He was fatally attracted towards his role as family scapegoat. His father could be extraordinarily hostile. And after all, he was in fact a member of the gentry, and any transition he could have made towards another way of being would have been painful. Such forensic rhetoric, however, would only reinforce the Romantic cult of the lone bardic genius, making it difficult to see the wider social implications and relationships within and around his writing. Moreover, the fact that Shelley was highly prepared to play to the interests of this cult only serves to redouble the problem. His biographers were by turns hagiographers and demonizers, another complicating factor that prevents us from assessing his life properly. In this volume, Theresa Kelley makes it clear that biographies are necessarily partial and that any decent attempt at one should squarely face this issue.

A brief history of Shelley scholarship

All of this brings us to the vexed and varied state of Shelley scholarship. A career so brief, so incendiary, was bound to attract both those who wished to fan the flames, and those who desired to dampen them. Mary Shelley was the first Shelley scholar. Her collaboration with Shelley is itself a remarkable and powerful contribution to Romantic poetry. It is, for example, hard to distinguish between the production of *Alastor* and that of *Frankenstein*: the themes and styles involved are so similar. Indeed, Percy collaborated with Mary on the latter. Mary's prefaces to the earliest editions of her late husband's work are remarkable for their tactful negotation between politics and poetics. Mary felt that audiences required persuasion that Percy's material was not too inflammatory. On the other hand, there are many points at which she sticks vigorously to the idea that Percy expressed his political ideals through his writings. After all, Mary was often the explicit addressee. Shelley scrawled 'Mary' on the top of one of the pages of his 'Essay on the Vegetable System of Diet' in 1814, perhaps as a marker, a request to do a spot of copy-editing.

Against his will, the Victorian establishment turned Shelley back into an effete upper-class poet. Matthew Arnold damned him with faint praise: to be 'beautiful' and 'ineffectual' at once is a tough spot for an activist (*Arnold* 1.237). Not that Shelley had lacked a share of prosodic inheritors. Elizabeth Barrett, Alfred Lord Tennyson, Robert Browning, and Algernon Charles Swinburne certainly learnt a few Shelleyan licks. Wordsworth praised Shelley for having one of the finest ears of his generation, which is as true a comment and as carefully delimited as claiming that Martin Luther King had a beautiful speaking voice. On the whole, middle- and upper-class nineteenth-century poets seemed unwilling to go the whole hog and start writing about mad monarchs, starving mothers, and the new aristocracy of commerce. A notable exception here must be made for William Michael Rossetti, whose edition of Shelley casts a net wider than the one Mary Shelley had dared to cast, and whose editorial principles updated Shelley rather than turning him into a relic of Romanticism.

Meanwhile, the first slew of biographies had emerged: by Thomas Medwin, Thomas Jefferson Hogg, and later Harry Buxton Forman and Newman Ivey White. They succeeded in mythologizing Shelley, who became too Romantic to be taken seriously. It became possible to write him off as a man 'wandering around Italy in a big shirt trying to get laid', in the words of a BBC comedy that picked up on the early cult of Shelley.[4] Palgrave's *Golden Treasury*, the major anthology of the age, canonized and deodorized Shelley's poetry, offering specimens of 'verse' seemingly unsullied by political interests. Thus began the entirely false division between Shelley the poet, who didn't care about politics, and Shelley the activist, who couldn't write a good line of verse if his life depended on it.

The radical working class claimed him as one of their own. Karl Marx was famous for declaring that had he lived longer, Shelley would have become a socialist, while Byron would have remained a mere stirrer of bourgeois sentiments.[5] The Chartists circulated copies of Shelley's political poems. Shelley's work, specifically *The Mask of Anarchy*, influenced Gandhi directly and Martin Luther King via Gandhi, in their promotion of nonviolent resistance. (See the chapter on Shelley's receptions.)

Along with this litany of radical appropriation, it is worth remarking, for the record, that what was considered radical poetry was not necessarily 'unpoetic' – whatever that means – or preoccupied with mundane things (mundane, that is, to the bourgeoisie) like grimy workplaces and poor diet. Radical working-class literature during Shelley's time was often coruscatingly psychedelic. The imagery of republicanism and democracy tended to defy gravity. It showed the extent of oppression in the negative, making it clear that a truly democratic society would regard contemporary England somewhat as would an extraterrestrial viewing the earth from the safety of outer space. It is a shame that current scholarship has so bought into the reactionary idea that the aesthetic is intrinsically a conservative thing, squishy, palpable, and endowed with dissent-silencing authority. Shelley wanted the aesthetic to make us think, not to put a stop to thinking.

The modernists were less happy with Shelley; though again, in this period, there is a striking difference between reactionary high modernist readings and the use of him by the radical avant garde, notably Bertolt Brecht and Walter Benajmin. Distinguishing himself even from Arnold on this score, F. R. Leavis had no time for him whatsoever. In Japan on the other hand, Shelley galvanized a generation of Romanticists.[6] In Italy Giosuè Carducci reappraised Shelley's revolutionary mix of idealism and classicism. Gabriele D'Annunzio, along with other Decadent poets, saw his work as an extending of nature beyond its normal bounds. André Maurois's *Ariel* (1923) painted Shelley as a bright young thing in an imaginative novelistic reconstruction (to say the least) of the poet's life. A major edition of Shelley had at last appeared, the ten-volume work by Roger Ingpen and Walter E. Peck which, in the absence of a complete new edition, is still, perhaps surprisingly, a reference work.

Shelley gradually drifted across the Atlantic, like one of his balloons, where his reception has been generally happier. His emergence in 1940s and 1950s America was fresh, lacking the explicit reference points of English politics and class. The American Shelley was from the start a Rip Van Winkle who had skipped a few generations of readers. He made quite a splash in the New Criticism thanks to Harold Bloom's *Shelley's Mythmaking* (1959). Shelley's prose became available in 1954 in the handy edition of David Lee Clark. American scholarship, more alive to the democratic expansiveness of a Whitman, was less likely than the British variety to accuse him of not being an Imagist. Thus it was that after a progress through New Criticism Shelley made some headway in phenomenological readings such as Earl Wasserman's (see Further Reading).

And so to Derrida. Shelley's American moment finally arrived in deconstruction, though that literary critical and philosophical mode was quite deaf to his political resonance – and especially to the ways in which his proto-deconstructive qualities often intertwined with his political interests. Harold Bloom edited a collection of essays on deconstruction whose sole exemplum was the poetry of Shelley; the collection included an essay by Derrida himself.[7] Paul De Man's essay 'Shelley Disfigured', which also appears in this volume, remains a classic of its genre and a major citation source for many critics still teasing out the finer nuances of his exacting reading of the way in which *The Triumph of Life* shoots itself in the epistemological foot, deconstructing itself before the reader has a chance to do it.

We must regret that poetics itself was not a firmer part of this project, despite the brilliant attention to single images, such as De Man's reading of the figure of the sun in *The Triumph of Life*. Shelley challenged Wordsworth's status as a 'poet of nature', that highly political word, in such poems as 'To Wordsworth', *Peter Bell the Third*, and *Alastor*. In particular, says Shelley, Wordsworth had failed in his presentation of intimate contact with other (sentient) beings. His work was not erotic enough. Communion with nature, as Shelley points out in 'On Love', is a function of our desire to reach out and touch something or someone, the nerve-tremblingly acute way in which our sensibility meets our conscious mind. It is thus not surprising that Shelley developed a whole range of figurative language that would somehow out-Wordsworth Wordsworth himself. Deconstructive readings have sometimes suffered from a tin ear for the ugly side of this sensibility, Shelley's intense awareness of blood and gore, his vegetarian's fantasies of raw flesh, and his meat and potatoes poetics of poverty and class struggle. Other scholars have begun to pay attention to the strangely self-referential way in which Shelley will talk of how 'the moving pomp might seem / Like pageantry of mist on an autumnal stream' (*Adonais*, 116–17). A pomp *is* a pageantry, so this image, an 'autophor' perhaps rather than a metaphor, is rather like a fractal, a repeating pattern that keeps ever so slightly exceeding its initial shape to produce a dazzling, jagged, zigzagging line. Other lines display Shelley describing the dream as being like an image of a dream of an idea of a dream of an image, in a dizzying spiral of hyperreal language, in which we begin not to be able to tell which level is the ground. There is Shelley the skilful poet of what classical rhetoric calls *obscurum per obscures*, an inverted metaphor that describes something concrete in terms of something abstract: the lightning bolt was like an idea. Consider the extraordinary lines about dew falling like 'silver music on the mossy lawn' in *The Triumph of Life* (355). Poetic dew is often silvery. But 'silver music' astonishingly displaces the colour into a hyperreal and synaesthetic realm.

The 1960s and 1970s witnessed the promise of the late G. M. Matthews's edition of Shelley. Kelvin Everest eventually assumed its mantle, and his edition (*P*) is due to be completed soon. At present, E. B. Murray is updating the prose for the Clarendon Press. A very valuable edition of Shelley's poetry and prose edited by Donald Reiman and Sharon Powers was published by Norton in 1977. And the Johns Hopkins University Press edition (*CP*) is appearing from Neil Fraistat and Donald Reiman. *P* and *CP* are highly significant editions: never before has Shelley been offered so completely. Moreover, they abide by quite different editorial principles, which makes for an illuminating clash. In the tradition of the press's editorial policy, the Longman edition (*P*) has been assembled according to classic textual critical principles. The 'best' text (judged according to various standards such as whether it was the latest possible version) is used, with modernized spelling and punctuation, and heavily annotated. The Johns Hopkins University Press edition (*CP*) has been produced in the wake of the postmodern critique of textual criticism, addressing such questions as the nature of literary authority. How can we tell what an author 'meant' anyway? In this edition the editors have preferred to publish the earliest 'issue' of a text, defining 'issue' quite broadly to catch the writer in the act of 'releasing' their work to an audience, however small.

Historicism has made us freshly aware that Shelley was deeply involved in the social and political events of his day, while providing fresh readings of his work that make us aware of how history and politics interweave with literary language in deep ways. When we consider the kind of dazzling variety that New Historical readings can produce, it is very enriching to know that Shelley was a committed vegetarian (Morton), that he participated actively in collaborations with numerous other Romantic circles (Cox), that he used the discourse of orientalism to undermine some of the emerging logics of imperialism (Leask), that he was an engaged satirist (Jones).[8] We now have a more complex picture of Shelley than ever.

Over the past four decades, scholarly studies of Shelley have emerged and taken shape. With the help of Harold Bloom, Carl Grabo, and others, Shelley took his place in New Criticism's approach to what they construed as the 'big six' (male) Romantic poets. The onset of deconstruction in the 1970s further propelled Shelley studies, as the poet's interest in epistemology and in the properties of figurative language inspired writers such as

Jacques Derrida to pay serious attention to his brilliantly problematic verse. Since the late 1980s, New Historicism and criticism influenced by cultural studies has found in Shelley a terrific source for the understanding of politics, history, and culture in the Romantic period; after all, this was the poet who declared that poets were the 'unacknowledged legislators of the world'. Even more recently, Shelley's poetics and politics have been freshly intertwined in studies of the avant-garde nature of his writing (Kaufman) and his investment in the figuration of diet (Morton) – see Further Reading for details.

Shelley studies have crystallized to the extent that distinct patterns of scholarship are visible: bibliography and textual criticism (in the old sense) have reached a state of reasonable solidity with the simultaneous publication of two sets of complete works (*P* and *CP*) on either side of the Atlantic; fairly strictly formal literary criticism, influenced principally by deconstruction and psychoanalytic approaches, has revealed the deliberate complexity and subtlety of Shelley's strikingly original poetics; and readings that consider contexts of all kinds have demonstrated Shelley's significant role in political debates and cultural configurations of his day, from atheism to vegetarianism.

The essays in this volume

Shelley was a protean writer, working in almost every corner of cultural and literary space in the Romantic period: from the upper class to the radical underground; from heterosexual love poetry to prose on homosexuality; from very subtle figurations to pugnacious political verse; from lyric to drama. The volume is thus in part organized thematically, on the basis of *intersections* between Shelley and his numerous interests: culture(s), nature(s), textuality, drama, philosophy, history (both politics and more general views of history and historicity), biography, and the literary–cultural 'afterlife' (posthumous reception). The Companion is not arranged chronologically to correspond with the genesis of his works: the shortness of his life and the continuity of his thought militate against this, despite attempts to read political disillusionment into his later work by scholars such as Harold Bloom. By including a generous section on Shelley's works that covers poetry, narrative, and drama, the Companion aims to orientate readers towards the issues that arise from his use of figurative language, in such a manner that the following more syncretic chapters will strengthen their view of Shelley and add some further subtle shading.

The first section of this Companion is devoted to Shelley's life and afterlife. Theresa Kelley opens the volume with a biography that illustrates

Shelley's short but intense engagement with the culture of his age. My essay on Shelley's posthumous reputation charts the development of numerous 'Shelleys', and the cults and cultures of reading that grew up around his work.

The second section provides the detailed work on Shelley's texts. Karen Weisman explores Shelley's work in lyric, that vast and slippery poetic genre derived from a metonymy for 'song'. She strongly rewrites Arnold's assertion that Shelley had a 'weak grasp on the actual'. Instead of damning Shelley for having his head in the clouds, Weisman insists that we pay attention to how Shelley expands the idea of the 'actual' in his work with lyrical forms. Jeffrey Cox shows that Shelley's interest in contemporary drama was matched by his drive radically to rethink what drama could encompass. In a highly original essay, Jack Donovan explores Shelley the storyteller, illuminating an aspect of Shelley's work that is too often neglected. Jeffrey Robinson accounts for the vital importance of translation in Shelley's poetic practice. William Keach demonstrates how Shelley puts politics at stake right down to the very level of individual phrases and single moments in his texts.

The third section investigates the manifold ways in which Shelley crosses boundaries between literature and other areas of culture. Always an inter-disciplinary writer who was not averse to the political tract, psychological exploration, and philosophical speculation, and to folding these into his literary texts, Shelley would, I feel, have wished this section to expand our view of him beyond the idea of a writer who appears in the poetry section of the bookshop. Jerrold Hogle traces Shelley's engagement with contemporary theories of language, and elaborates the ways in which his poetry is itself preoccupied with linguistic issues. Paul Hamilton shows that Shelley was significantly engaged with numerous currents in philosophy. The final chapter, by me, explores how the ideas of nature and culture are intertwined in Shelley's writing. It makes the case that Shelley was a proto-ecological thinker and poet.

NOTES

1. Friedrich Engels, *The Condition of the Working Class in England*, foreword by Victor Kiernan (Harmondsworth: Penguin, 1987 (German, 1845)), 245.
2. *OED*, 'Shelleyan', *a* and *sb*.
3. Theodor Adorno, 'Valéry Proust Museum', in *Prisms*, tr. Samuel and Shierry Weber (Cambridge, Mass.: MIT Press, 1983, 1997 (German, 1967)), 173–85 (181).
4. *Blackadder the Third*, episode 2 (BBC Productions, 1987).
5. Edward Aveling and Eleanor Marx Aveling, *Shelley's Socialism: Two Lectures* (London: private circulation, 1888; repr. London: Journeyman Press, 1979), 16.

6. Shigetoshi Ishikawa, 'Shelley Studies in Japan: With a Bibliography Compiled by Hiroshi Harata', *KSJ* 42 (1993), 142–55.

7. Harold Bloom et al., eds., *Deconstruction and Criticism* (New York: Seabury Press, 1979).

8. Nigel Leask, *British Romantic Writers and the East: Anxieties of Empire* (Cambridge: Cambridge University Press, 1992); Steven E. Jones, *Shelley's Satire: Violence, Exhortation, and Authority* (Dekalb: Northern Illinois University Press, 1994); Timothy Morton, *Shelley and the Revolution in Taste: The Body and the Natural World* (Cambridge and New York: Cambridge University Press, 1994); Jeffrey Cox, *Poetry and Politics in the Cockney School: Keats, Shelley, Hunt and Their Circle* (Cambridge and New York: Cambridge University Press, 1998).

PART I

Lives and afterlives

I

THERESA KELLEY

Life and biographies

> The figures of Victory with unfolded wings & each spurning back a globe with outstretched feet are perhaps more beautiful than those on either of the others. Their lips are parted; a delicate mode of indicating the fervour of their desire to arrive at their destined resting place, & to express the eager respiration of their speed.
>
> (Percy Shelley, letter to Thomas Love Peacock, *L* II.89)

Shelley's description of Roman statuary echoes the temper of his life, which was no less restless, no less impelled towards an ideal resting place, no less resistant to being sculpted into a single gesture or pose. As such, his life offers a pressing instance of the general problem of biography: how to capture a life that is lived not simply on a timeline but down through layers of being and action that are psychic, cultural, political, philosophical, and at times contradictory? As a poet, essayist, and celebrity whose Romantic notoriety is outdistanced only by Byron's, Shelley lived a life that was passionate, restless, and brief. He also left behind a remarkable body of poetry and prose. Even Wordsworth, who was no friend to Shelley's radical politics, praised Shelley as 'one of the best artists of us all . . . in workmanship of style' (*W* II.637). His prose is by turns astutely political and philosophically brilliant. The chronology presented at the beginning of this volume is an anchor but not an adequate measure of a life that was, as one of Shelley's recent biographers puts it, better characterized as 'a manuscript greatly over-scored and corrected than [as] . . . a clock or a calendar'.[1]

Michel Foucault's 'What is an Author' suggests how the identity of an author such as Shelley is also inextricable from his author function as a writer to whom readers late and soon attached concepts and no small degree of biographical notoriety.[2] But the question of Shelley's identity goes deeper. Indeed deciding who Shelley was requires some recognition of the post-structuralist notion of the subject as less a unified being than a psychic terrain where attitudes, reading, ideas, and actions repeatedly cross to create an identity that is not fixed over time but articulated in time, with all the possibilities for change and contradiction such a formulation implies. The welter of biographical opinion about Shelley witnesses the specific difficulty of fixing this biographical subject.

Take, for instance, Shelley's idealism – the conviction that the world should be grounded in or directed towards universal truths and ideas.[3] Early critical notice of this aspect of his character encouraged the reductive claim that Shelley imagined political change only in the abstract, that he was not of this world. In portraits completed during his life and soon after his death, some with a dubious relation to their declared subject (W II.518–38), the figure of a wispy, ethereal youth encouraged Victorian name-tags like 'ineffectual angel' (Matthew Arnold) or a 'child . . . gold dusty with tumbling amid the stars' (Francis Thompson).[4] Yet Shelley acted and wrote from a sharply political and material understanding of the world. He was a genuinely comprehensive (rather than simply anecdotal or local) critic of the economic and structural ills that patriarchal inheritance and government imposed. These constituted the pragmatic, material issues that he pursued in poetry and prose even as he kept ideal measures at hand to project what in his view society and human beings could become. It is no accident that he who wrote the idealist drama *Prometheus Unbound* soon afterward completed the more pragmatic political essay *A Philosophical View of Reform*; that the poet who imagined boats and chariots also drew them on the pages of his manuscript notebooks.[5] No biography of Shelley can afford to neglect these and other affiliations between his poetic idealism, sense of history, radical politics, and social vision.

Shelley's life is bound up with the Romantic cult of personality, in some measure because it was a life of scandal – scandalous to his comfortably Whig and Anglican father, but also scandalous to generations of readers. The list of scandals has something to outrage almost anyone. The young Shelley who rebelled against his father's authority and Whig politics may in some measure have gotten himself expelled from Oxford for atheism and married to someone of a respectable but not aristocratic family in order to reject his father in the most public manner possible. Shelley advocated free love and encouraged others to so experiment with his first and second wives, and may have so experimented with Claire Clairmont; he left his pregnant first wife to court his second; his constant tramping about Italy seeking companionship, happiness, and new vistas probably contributed to the deaths of his first two children with Mary; he was at the very least nervous and suggestible; at his worst he imagined being attacked and invented highly coloured events. He was also cosmopolitan, civil, generous, and capable of subtle kindness and tact, such as that he long exercised with Claire.

Indeed, what makes Shelley's life compelling is its restless complexity, geographical and emotional, fiscal and intellectual. Take, for example, the question of his sexual mores. For all the publicity that surrounds his free love pronouncements, what he probably longed for most was sexual and intellectual companionship that was not precisely heterosexual or homo-erotic, but somewhere out beyond the edge of a single-minded and biologic-ally driven theory of gender. If unfettered free love had been Shelley's project, he would not have established two successive households with a wife and unmarried sister that duplicated the sister surround of his early youth, nor would he have vested himself in a hefty set of competing domestic responsibilities in his union with Mary Godwin Shelley. Sexuality and domesticity were minefields for Shelley, yet he never steered clear of them. Like many aspects of his life, this one invites speculation, but resists biographical certainty.

Percy Bysshe Shelley was born 4 August 1792 in Sussex, England. The eldest son of a family of six, he was heir to a considerable estate which his grandfather had amassed by land acquisition, a financially advantageous marriage to a descendant of the Sidneys, and service to a Whig party aristocrat which was repaid with a baronetcy in 1806. Romantic Whigs were a minority party caught between the Tory ascendancy and rumblings from below for electoral and economic reform. Like their Whig compat-riots, Shelley's grandfather Bysshe and his father Timothy were committed to holding on to land and economic power.[6] Although he despised his father's politics, Shelley's revulsion was conflicted. He rebelled against inherited rank and wealth, particularly as guarantors of political power, yet he assumed that both would and should be his, even as he assumed that he would one day take his seat in Parliament. At home Shelley was the admired older brother whose Gothic tales of horror, alchemy, the grotesque, and the occult delighted and terrified his sisters. As an adult he recreated versions of this domestic and psychic configuration with wives, sisters, and other unrelated women.

As a young boy Shelley studied with a Welsh parson, the Reverend Mr Edwards, who recognized his pupil's talent for Latin and Greek. As a boarding student at Syon House Academy, Shelley became a victim and an underling, after years of being the brother whose tales had made him the imaginative command centre of the Shelley siblings. Small and feminine in appearance, he was an easy target. His cousin Thomas Medwin recalled that the academy was 'a perfect Hell' for Shelley (W 1.20). He responded in kind, with a violence that stood out in marked contrast to his capacity for kindness to friends. He wrote verse and engaged in pranks and experi-ments, including one that accidentally poisoned the headmaster's pigs, and others that involved gunpowder, all of which made it impossible not to notice him. A visiting science teacher, Dr Adam Walker, lectured on astronomy, magnetism, electricity, and how to use the telescope and microscope; he also introduced Shelley to cosmological hypotheses, among them the plurality of co-existing worlds in the universe. The dexterity with which Shelley conducted experiments with explosives suggests practical knowledge as well as his conceptual fascination with science.

Shelley's early years at Eton were miserable. At the time notorious for its lack of supervision (in 1809 there were 515 boys enrolled and just seven assistant masters under the headmaster), Eton institutionalized bullying: hazing was severe, as it was at the poet Robert Southey's Westminster School.[7] In this atmosphere, which condoned acts of violence and ignored sexual intimidation, younger and smaller boys were in for it and Shelley got it. He was harassed by numerous boys on an almost daily basis for at least a year. Someone would spot him and call out 'Shelley, Shelley, Shelley!' Others would join in, attacking his books and tearing his clothes. According to one witness, he stood 'baited like a maddened bull'.[8] As an older Eton boy, Shelley beat up a smaller boy when challenged to do so. As a microcosm of an institutional, systematic tyranny that makes bullies powerful and the victims eager to change places, Eton taught lessons that became the core of Shelley's political radicalism.

Although Eton offered no regular instruction in science, Walker lectured there on chemistry. With equipment purchased from Walker's assistant, Shelley blew up a tree with gunpowder, a focusing glass, and the sun, and may have electrified the door handle of a housemaster who got a shock when he touched it. This activity, Gilmour suggests, conveys less a systematic study of chemistry than the desire, which Mary Shelley later reproduces in the young Victor Frankenstein, to produce the quasi-magical effects identified with alchemy.[9] Yet the cumulative record of Shelley's youthful attraction to science suggests a double regard pitched towards the theoretical as well as the experimental. As he had done at home, at Eton Shelley wrote more gothic tales, looking for supernatural thrills, as he later acknowledged in 'Hymn to Intellectual Beauty' (1816), from 'ghosts' or 'the departed dead' (49–52). There he also met Dr James Lind, Fellow of the Royal Society and physician to the royal household. Lind took Shelley's learning in hand, directing him towards Plato, Voltaire, and French revolutionary philosophers, among them Condorcet. Shelley later declared that he owed more to Lind than to his own father.[10] The turn towards philosophy was crucial to Shelley's intellectual formation; in time it partially replaced his gothicism with the desire for ideals that might drive political and cultural change.

A year before he entered Oxford, Shelley was writing fiction and poetry and falling in love, this first time with his cousin Harriet Grove. He published a gothic novel *Zastrozzi* the next spring. Then and now, critical notices have not been glowing. The *Critical Review* (1810), for example, fumed that the work's hero 'is one of the most savage and improbable demons that ever issued from a diseased brain'.[11] Cameron notes that in *St. Irvyne* Gothic fantasy becomes at once more sexual, more political, and more philosophical (Cameron, *Young Shelley*, 29). Throughout the spring and early summer, Shelley's relation to Harriet Grove intensified until she and her parents distanced themselves from a suitor whose radical politics and anti-religious proclamations made them exceedingly uncomfortable. Infuriated, he wrote feverish letters to Hogg; in one he contemplated suicide and reported sleeping one night with poison and a loaded pistol.[12] He sent Harriet a copy of *Original Poetry by Victor and Cazire*, pseudonyms for Shelley and his sister Elizabeth, who had not given him permission to publish her work. Shelley's first long verse poem, *The Wandering Jew*, was rejected.

A month after he became a member of University College, Oxford, Shelley advertised the publication of his anonymous *Posthumous Fragments of Margaret Nicholson*. This odd assemblage of verses he offered as the work of the madwoman Margaret Nicholson who in 1786 attacked George III with a dessert knife. Part sexual raving, part critique of the government, the *Fragments* attracted some attention in Oxford, as did Shelley's decision to contribute proceeds from its sale to the support of the radical journalist Peter Finnerty, then imprisoned for having attacked Lord Castlereagh in print for his brutal management of Ireland.[13] Soon afterwards Shelley published a second Gothic novel, *St Irvyne*. His request that his publisher send him a copy of William Godwin's *Political Justice* suggests the role Godwin would play in Shelley's political education. At Oxford he became close to Thomas Jefferson Hogg, hinting for a time that a match could be made between him and Shelley's sister Elizabeth. Shelley's erotic triangulation of Hogg with Elizabeth, later with Harriet Shelley, and finally with Mary Shelley, suggests the sexual complexity of this friendship, at least until Shelley left for Italy.

During his first year at Oxford, Shelley's fiercely anti-Christian declamations alienated his father and soon afterwards alienated Oxford officialdom. When Shelley's and Hogg's pamphlet *The Necessity of Atheism* was advertised in early 1811, Shelley distributed copies, then had copies sent to all heads of colleges and many bishops. One Oxford don and minister burned a copy on the spot. To this first salvo against Anglican Oxford, Shelley added others: a named contributor to a public subscription for the Irish radical Peter Finnerty, Shelley also wrote to Leigh Hunt to congratulate him on being acquitted of libel against the government. By March Oxford officials had had enough. They summoned both Shelley and Hogg, who refused to answer questions. Both were expelled. Writing to Godwin in

January 1812, Shelley suggested that they shared the intellectual and social perspective of Godwin's *Political Justice* (*L* 1.25, 157).

Incensed by his son's political and religious unorthodoxy, his father banned him from home. In November 1811, Shelley completed his rebellion against his father's sense of family and inheritance by eloping with Harriet Westbrook, the daughter of a respectable merchant and barely sixteen (Shelley was nineteen). Thereafter Shelley repeatedly enraged his father with demands for money, coupled with reiterations of his atheist and radical views. This youthful rebellion achieved its implicit goal: Shelley freed himself sufficiently from the Whig and familial line to begin the work of his adult career. The domestic frame Shelley sought to create for doing that work at home and in public included Harriet, her much older sister Eliza, and for a time Elizabeth Hitchener, a Sussex schoolteacher whom Shelley addressed in a letter as a 'sister of my soul' (*L* 1.118; *W* 1.164–5). Soon after Hitchener joined the Shelleys, Shelley's idealized view of her gave way to relief when she chose to leave. White astutely notes that never again would Shelley be quite as unaware of the discrepancy between his ideal conceptions of another and the reality of that personality at closer range (*W* 1.202). For a time Shelley hoped to adopt two young females and rear them away from society (*RH* 69), a more radical version of an earlier social experiment by Thomas Day, a member of the Lunar Society near Birmingham (*L* 1.39). After Hogg tried to seduce Harriet while Shelley was away, the Shelleys quickly moved from York to Keswick without apprising Hogg of their departure or destination. Afterwards, Shelley defended Harriet's rejection in letters to Hogg, yet also insisted that the principle of free love trumped marital monogamy.

The public and political work involved Ireland and then Wales. In Dublin Shelley published three pamphlets. The first, his *Address to the Irish People*, emphasized their colonial status under the rule of England; the others, *Proposals for an Association of Philanthropists* and *Declaration of Rights*, urged consolidating different factions to create a base for political resistance and reform. As he would in *The Mask of Anarchy*, written in 1819 in response to the Peterloo Massacre, here Shelley argued against revolutionary violence, calling instead for a course of sobriety (against the usual identification of the Irish with drink) and planned resistance. Except for Catherine Nugent, whose artisan class background and republican views the Shelleys admired, the individual and collective Irish response to Shelley was mixed and at times fearful. The plans for a political association soon foundered.

The Shelleys travelled to Wales and then Devon, where Shelley wrote a public *Letter to Lord Ellenborough* in defence of Daniel Isaac Eaton, a liberal London bookseller and publisher who had published Part III of Thomas Paine's *Age of Reason*. Eaton was brought to trial and Ellenborough presided. He also published an anti-monarchy and anti-government broadside ballad titled *The Devil's Walk* (CP I.121–9, 281–93). The Shelleys and Elizabeth Hitchener circulated these works along with Shelley's *Declaration of Rights*. By now watched by government officials who had been tipped off by a worker in a post office where Hitchener had sent Shelley's Irish letters and pamphlets as per his request, the Shelleys slipped off to Tremadoc in north Wales, where Shelley worked hard to solicit funds for building a causeway across an estuary so that it might become agricultural land. The causeway and cultivated land still exist. Mounting personal debts prompted their departure for London, although Shelley claimed that they had to leave abruptly because an attacker with murderous intent had entered the house at night. Biographers have long debated evidence concerning the incident.[14]

In London, the Shelleys met Godwin, who had for some time been advising Shelley via correspondence about courses of action and reading; however, they soon left for Dublin with creditors at their backs. There they retrieved the manuscript of Shelley's early poems, *The Esdaile Notebook*, and returned to London, where they avoided creditors and enjoyed a radical, cosmopolitan London circle assembled by Mrs Boinville, widow of a French revolutionary. In late June 1813, the Shelleys' first child, Ianthe, was born. Some time before December, Shelley published and privately circulated *Queen Mab*, his first major poem and, with its appended notes, the first work to present the mix of political argument and poetic prophecy that is the signature of his mature poetics. Shelley had first planned to write such a poem late in 1811, shortly after his marriage to Harriet and expulsion from Oxford and the family circle. As the mediating figure between the divine and human realms, Shelley's Queen Mab teaches Ianthe the lessons of revolution from the past, for use in the present and the future. Although only about 90 of the 250 copies of *Queen Mab* were circulated in 1813, the poem was by 1822 available in four different editions, a fact the older Shelley regretted. As such, the poem became, as Holmes puts it, 'the most widely read, the most notorious, and the most influential' of Shelley's works, particularly among middle- and working-class radicals who read it in cheap printed editions, not the edition on 'fine paper' that Shelley in 1813 requested to entice unwary 'sons and daughters of aristocrats' to buy and read it (L I.361; RH 208).

Eleven of the seventeen notes appended to *Queen Mab* are extended essays, supplemented by extensive quotation from classical and Enlightenment philosophers, on the labour theory of value ('There is no real wealth but the labour of man' (*P* 1.364)); free love as a social principle in opposition to the rigidity of marriage contracts; the role of necessity in the moral and material universe; atheism; Christ and Christian dogma; and vegetarianism.[15] Shelley published the last as a separate pamphlet titled *A Vindication of Natural Diet* (1813). In a development of the note on Christianity, *A Refutation of Deism* (1814), Shelley expanded the argument of *The Necessity of Atheism* and cast it in the form of a philosophical dialogue between pro- and anti-Christian antagonists, thereby minimizing the likelihood of being prosecuted for holding the anti-Christian views that he in fact held.

As Shelley gravitated increasingly towards the social and intellectual circle of Mrs Boinville and her married sister, he drifted from Harriet and their marriage, living in London while Harriet mostly lived elsewhere. Meeting Mary Wollstonecraft Godwin again in June 1814, Shelley fell in love. Precipitated by Mary's admission of feeling, the two declared their intention to elope. Godwin was furious. He forbade the two to meet; Shelley threatened suicide. Divorce was not a viable option at the time because every divorce required that a separate bill be presented and passed by majority vote in the House of Lords, with all imaginable scandals made available to the public. Shelley and Mary eloped in late July by catching the boat to Calais, with Mary's half-sister Claire (then Mary Jane) Clairmont in tow and the infuriated Godwins on dry land.

In his *Memoirs*, Thomas Peacock reports that Shelley explained his decision to leave his first wife, then pregnant with their second child, for Mary in these terms: 'Every one who knows me must know that the partner of my life should be one who can feel poetry and understand philosophy. Harriet is a noble animal, but she can do neither.' Although he defended Harriet's intelligence and amiability long after her death, Peacock acknowledged that Mary was a better intellectual match for Shelley (*W* 1.350).[16] The next years brought many travails that would darken this new, companionate union, among them losing two children who survived to be born and others who did not; the suicide deaths of Fanny Imlay, Mary's other half-sister, and Harriet Shelley; constant upheavals and frequent moves in England and then Italy; Mary's depressions, triggered by all too many real sorrows; and Shelley's various erotic and philosophical attractions to other women. Nonetheless, its complex intellectual and familial nature was set from the beginning. Its familial ties extended back a generation, to the living Godwin and the dead Mary Wollstonecraft, on whose grave Shelley and Mary read her mother's writing. Mary and Shelley read, lived, and wrote in various stages of harmony and disharmony with each other, with works by Godwin and Wollstonecraft, and with Godwin himself. Reading and writing along parallel as well as distinct lines were key constants in their joined existence despite more deaths and dislocation over the next six years than many people experience in a single lifetime.

The elopement trip, memorialized in Mary and Shelley's *History of a Six Weeks' Tour*, ended when the money (and credit) ran out and the three truants returned to London. There the two and Claire Clairmont established a moveable household, especially for Shelley, who was often obliged to sleep elsewhere to stay ahead of creditors. In November Harriet Shelley gave birth to their second child, Charles. As Shelley fended off Godwin's anger and requests for money, and tried to get funds from Shelley's family, he and Mary committed themselves to a daily life dominated by extensive reading and writing. Shelley failed, despite repeated efforts, to persuade Harriet that she remained the object of his steadfast friendship although not his love. Over the next year he wrote her obtusely worded requests for funds and complained about her injustice to him.

After the death of his grandfather in 1815, Shelley sued for, and got, annuities from the Shelley estate which he settled on himself, on Harriet, and, as the years went on, on Godwin, who never stopped dinning Shelley for funds. During that spring letters between Shelley, Mary, and others, together with excised journal pages or uncharacteristic journal silences, suggest that Mary and Hogg (with Shelley's encouragement) as well as Shelley and Claire may have become lovers. Whether this free love 'experiment' continued in later years for Shelley and Claire is less clear (it emphatically did not for Mary, who by 1817 actively disliked Hogg). Shelley wrote and published *Alastor*, a mythological narrative that critiques poets who seclude themselves from love and the world by embowering and embalming themselves in nature. Aimed at Wordsworth, the poem nonetheless presents its Shelleyan narrator as a Wordsworthian poet. In life and art, Shelley did not so easily cast off predecessors.

In May 1816, Mary, Shelley, and Claire travelled again to France and on to Switzerland, where they met Byron for the first time. The Shelley entourage and Byron rented houses near each other on Lake Leman, where they told stories, read, and talked. Claire became Byron's lover. Shelley wrote 'Hymn to Intellectual Beauty' and 'Mont Blanc'. A ghost-story telling competition became the origin for Byron's *Manfred*, and also for Mary Shelley's *Frankenstein*, whose publication Shelley cannily secured in 1818, with greater royalties than any he received for his own publications. The Shelley entourage returned to London in the fall. By that winter, first Fanny Imlay, and then Harriet Shelley – whose life post-Shelley had been miserable – committed suicide. Harriet walked into the Thames, pregnant with the child of another man who had also abandoned her. Shelley married Mary

Wollstonecraft Godwin two weeks later, and reported the event in a letter
to Claire that is bemused and ironic about Godwin's visible relief that
Mary was now legally married to a member of the aristocracy (*L* 1.525).
Early in 1817, Claire gave birth to her daughter by Byron, whom they
initially named Alba, but whom Byron later renamed Allegra, one of
several less-than-enthusiastic recognitions of his paternity which the Shelleys persuaded Claire was crucial to Alba/Allegra's future in a society
where illegitimate children of lords fared better than those born to an
unknown father and unmarried mother. Court proceedings, in which
Queen Mab was used as evidence against Shelley, denied his request for
custody of his children by Harriet.

During 1817, while Mary and Shelley lived mostly at Great Marlow on
the Thames, the cosmopolitan circle that Shelley had begun to create with
his first extended residence in London consolidated around a new set of
friends to whom the Shelleys remained close long after they had moved to
Italy, among them Leigh and Marianne Hunt, whose children delighted in
Shelley's games with them, John Keats, Thomas Peacock, J. H. Reynolds,
Charles Lamb, William Hazlitt, Keats's boyhood friend Cowden Clarke,
and, more occasionally, Hogg. By attending London concerts, opera, and
ballet, and enjoying the company of friends, in particular Peacock and the
Hunts (*RH* 361–3), the Shelleys helped to leaven the difficulties with God-
win and the negative press consequent to the scandal of Shelley's marriages.

Early in 1817, popular resentment of governmental politics erupted in
response to three events: the hanging of a sailor who had participated in the
Spa Field riots of December 1816; the trials of those arraigned for speaking
out against the government; and the government's suspension of Habeas
Corpus and passage of the Seditious Meetings Act (*RH* 363–4).[17] In this
climate Shelley published a pamphlet, *A Proposal for Putting Reform to the
Vote*. It begins by arguing that political reform is necessary to release the
English from slavery. Inasmuch as the prohibition against English involvement in the slave trade (1807) was not extended to ending the use of slaves
in the Caribbean colonies until 1837, Shelley's charge was deliberately
inflammatory. His *Proposal* begins: 'A great question is now agitating in
this nation which no man or party of men is competent to decide; indeed
there are no materials of evidence which can afford a foresight of the result.
Yet on its issue depends whether we are to be slaves or freemen.' Fearful of
what might result if the aristocracy were abolished before the 'public mind'
reached the requisite maturity to govern itself (*Pr* 159–62), Shelley's map for
reform is liberal and cautious rather than radical. The reasons behind his
circumspection were probably mixed: one part prudence, given the trigger-
happy government response to political resistance; the other part genuine,

and arguably elite, concern about what the uneducated masses would do if they suddenly achieved political freedom. The Reign of Terror in France from 1793 to 1794 had done much to encourage the anxiety that Shelley, the anti-aristocrat who nonetheless expected he would one day take his seat in Parliament, shared with many contemporaries about the eruption of chaotic violence in the revolutionary moment.

At Marlow, Shelley and Mary established their preferred rhythm of reading, writing, boating, and, in Shelley's case, assistance to the poor. Mary gave birth to a daughter, Clara, in September. Hunt later reported that at Marlow Shelley lived a life of near-monastic simplicity, rising early, eating no meat, writing, reading, boating, and giving genuine aid to those whose poverty or infirmity others ignored. Even Thomas Baxter, the father of Mary's friend Isabel whose husband had ended her friendship with Mary after she and Shelley eloped, commended Shelley's temperament and character when they met, although neither he nor the son-in-law were willing to extend the acquaintance beyond this point. Over roughly six months, Shelley composed *Laon and Cythna*, a mythological romance-epic of revolution written in Spenserian stanzas. It is Shelley's longest poem, extending to twelve cantos or 4,818 lines.

Dedicated to Mary and situated at the moment when the French Revolution failed and cascaded into the violence of the Reign of Terror, *Laon and Cythna* chronicles the lives and loves of its eponymous heroes, who are also brother and sister. The character of Cythna is a tribute to Mary Godwin Shelley and her mother Mary Wollstonecraft, whose programme for a revolution in women that would make them equal in mind and spirit to men Cythna embodies and eventually dies for. In the course of the poem, she and Laon lead a bloodless revolution against the Sultan of Turkey, who later invites reactionary forces to help him overthrow the two lovers and heroes. After both are martyred on a burning pyre, they are taken by sailboat to the 'temple of the Spirit'. Described by Shelley as 'an idealism of moral excellence' of the kind that had not existed during the French Revolution and its aftermath, the poem echoes Milton, Wordsworth, and Coleridge. It also inaugurates Shelley's mature poetics with its casually brilliant use of poetic form and a plot whose inventions rehearse the arguments of *Queen Mab* and its notes within the imaginative frame of Shelleyan love and revolutionary transformation. In late poems and essays, Shelley imagines different versions of this story, most notably in *Prometheus Unbound*, where the lovers are in the end united and survive. In that poem Demogorgon's warning that it may be necessary to repeat the overthrow of tyranny reiterates Shelley's earlier recognition in *Laon and Cythna* that revolutions, even bloodless ones, are not likely to go unchallenged. The challenge to *Laon and Cythna* came even sooner, before the printed text of the poem was circulated. Pressured by his publisher to revise the poem by removing its most incendiary features – the sibling incest and the anti-monarchy diatribes – Shelley spent two days making the changes and swore the poem was ruined. It was reissued as *The Revolt of Islam* in December 1817 (its imprint date is 1818).

During the same autumn Shelley drafted his 'Essay on Christianity' and his and Mary's *History of a Six Weeks' Tour* was published. In November Princess Charlotte, the highly popular daughter of the most unpopular and profligate Prince Regent, died in childbirth. Shelley responded with an *Address to the People* in which he makes the princess's death an occasion to lament the condition of the English poor and the fact that the English were now prohibited from writing and speaking about their government. The *Address* compares the nation's mourning for her to the grief it should feel for three poor labourers, whom the government identified as the Pentridge Revolution leaders, who were tried and executed (drawn and quartered) on what Shelley, following accounts in the radical journals, believed were trumped up charges (*Pr* 162–9). In December Mary Shelley's first novel *Frankenstein* was published with Shelley's preface. In the interstices between poetic and polemical writing, Shelley began translating the so-called 'Homeric Hymns' and Spinoza's philosophical writings (*W* 1.527). His enormous output between 1817 and 1818 signals Shelley's newly focused sense of his mission and career.

By 1818, Shelley and probably Mary were eager to leave England for Italy, although Mary, who had a sharper sense of their financial precariousness, urged caution. Shelley's health (he had been advised that he was tubercular), his ever-present restlessness, Godwin's demands, the political situation in England, and the need to get Claire's daughter to Byron – all these considerations urged Italy. In his negotiations with Claire and Byron, separately and on the subject of their daughter, from England and thereafter in Italy, Shelley exercised enormous tact. Claire's temper irritated Mary, making their continuous co-habitation impossible. Shelley dealt with Claire's ungoverned tongue and worked out temporary living situations for her in England and later in Italy. Byron wanted no part of Claire; she was in turn furious with him and worried about their child's future. The Shelleys passed the child off as belonging to someone else, not Claire, but were concerned that their household looked suspicious, that Shelley would be taken for Claire's lover and the father of Alba-soon-to-be-Allegra. On this point as well, the solution seemed to be Italy, where Byron had by now settled. The Shelley household (including Claire and the child) left for Italy in March. By this time, after Harriet's death and the recognition that his hero Godwin was no hero, friends reported that Shelley had sobered, his idealist perceptions of others tempered by greater understanding of human failing and suffering.

Getting to Italy was strenuous. Travelling overland, they waited at one stop for a carriage spring to be repaired while Shelley read Schlegel aloud. They were detained at the Swiss border because Shelley was carrying copies of works by Rousseau and Voltaire, proscribed authors. As they climbed up the pass of Mont Cenis to Italy, Shelley sang the whole way.[18] At Milan Shelley's spirits climbed again. The party headed for Pisa, then settled in Leghorn (Livorno) where they met Maria Gisbourne, who had taken care of Mary as a newborn after her mother's death. Italy's climate (political as well as meteorological) and its antiquity and subsequent eras invigorated Shelley's writing as no other landscape had done. In early 1819, he wrote Peacock a series of letters that brilliantly describe Rome and its environs, and their effect on his imaginative sensibility. They also suggest the tenor of his friendship for Peacock, whose pragmatism was ever a counterfoil to idealist hopes. The Shelleys' life in Italy was characteristically restless and emotionally draining: they moved or changed lodging at least seventeen times between 1818 and 1820. Their first two children died within a single year; a third, Percy Florence, was born and survived; and Claire's daughter Allegra died in the convent where Byron had placed her. The Shelleys were also solicited for blackmail in the murky affair of a child, Elena, born in 1818, whom Shelley registered as his own (he described her to others as his 'Neapolitan charge') (L II.206, 208; W II.607).

In Italy Shelley wrote much of the poetry and prose for which he is known today: *A Defence of Poetry, Prometheus Unbound, The Cenci, Julian and Maddalo, Adonais,* the bitterly elegiac *Lines Written among the Euganean Hills, The Mask of Anarchy,* the sonnet 'England in 1819', the unfinished *Triumph of Life,* and the final poems to Jane Williams, including 'With a Guitar, to Jane'. In addition, Shelley read Aeschylus, began a verse drama on Tasso's life, translated portions of Calderón's plays, and completed a translation of the banquet section of Plato's *Symposium,* to which he added a *Discourse* on homosexual love in ancient Greece.

During their first summer in Italy, Shelley swam daily, translated the section from Plato's *Symposium,* and made plans for poems. Prompted by the meditation on love given by Plato's Diotima, Shelley composed the prose fragment 'On Love', which argues for a relation between love, necessity, and moral action in which love embodies 'a universal thirst for communion not merely of sense, but of our whole nature, intellectual, imaginative, sensitive; and which, when individualised, becomes an imperative necessity'. Shelley argues that this desire constitutes the evolutionary ground of man's social being (Pr 169–71). Having sent Allegra with a servant to Byron in Venice, Shelley set out later with Claire to see the child. There Shelley renewed his friendship with Byron, then appealed to Mary to hurry to Este, where Byron offered the Shelleys a villa. Clara became quite ill on the journey and died that September in Este. In 'Stanzas Written in Dejection – Near Naples', Shelley registered his grief and marital isolation. Years later, Mary wrote a poem, 'The Choice', which conveys her recollection of this moment as one when she was closed, unavailable to Shelley despite her continued love for him (33–40).[19] The darkness of these months infects *Lines Written among the Euganean Hills* and the opening section of *Julian and Maddalo,* a dramatic 'conversation' in which Shelley works out his and Byron's philosophical and temperamental differences.

Thereafter, Fraistat argues, Shelley's composition of *Prometheus Unbound* was 'fluid, continuous, and revisionary' (N 202). Related in its choice of subject and mythological vehicle to *Queen Mab* and *Laon and Cythna* (aka *The Revolt of Islam)*, Shelley's drama insists that political revolution requires an interior swerve away from anger and tyranny towards forgiveness and a self-disciplined autonomy of spirit. Only in this way, Shelley implies, can the Lucretian necessity that governs the proliferation of evil in the world be diverted from its normal route. In *Prometheus Unbound*, the protagonist begins the poem's narrative of global revolution by renouncing his curse on Jupiter, thereby breaking free of the moment in history and his own psyche when Jupiter's can still torture him.

In June 1819 the Shelleys' son William died of malaria. Mary was inconsolable. They decamped for Livorno, hoping for a reprieve from grief. There Shelley wrote *The Cenci*, a bitter tragedy about patriarchal and state authority, parental incest, and their eventual contamination of the play's heroine Beatrice. When news reached Shelley of the Peterloo Massacre in England, in which several citizens who attended a reform rally were killed by British troops in August 1819, he wrote *The Mask of Anarchy* in response. The poem's brilliantly perverse allegory in which crimes such as murder are given the faces of English politicians ends not with a call to arms but with Shelley's idealist caution against the possibility of 'anarchy' breaking out, a position that echoes the call in *Laon and Cythna* for a 'bloodless revolution'. Urging the English to stand and face British troops, Shelley imagines that peaceful solidarity will ensure the return of Liberty to the English people. Leigh Hunt, to whom Shelley sent the poem, chose not to publish it, fearing government reprisal. Hunt finally published it in 1832, long after Shelley's death and soon after the passage of the first bill to inaugurate English political reform of its electoral politics and suffrage.

Shelley next wrote a long letter defending the radical publisher Richard Carlile, who was being tried in England for blasphemy on the grounds that he had published Thomas Paine's *Age of Reason*. He sent it to Hunt for publication in the *Examiner*, which Hunt chose not to do. Joining the publishing fray against Wordsworth's *Peter Bell*, Shelley wrote a satirical *Peter Bell the Third* in which he attacked Wordsworth for being both poetically dull and dangerous because of his reactionary politics. While the Shelleys were living in Florence in the fall of 1819, their last child Percy Florence was born.

Shelley's hope for viable political reform, kept half-alive in part by watching the ebb and flow of revolutionary activity in the Italian states, took another dive at the end of 1819, when the English Parliament passed its 'Six Acts', which imposed further restrictions on political dissent. Shelley pressed on, writing the prose fragment 'On Life', 'Ode to the West Wind', and the most extended political essay of his career, *A Philosophical View of Reform*, unpublished in his lifetime. Its practical and temperate argument for reform presents the other side of Shelley's idealist analyses of revolution and poetry in *Prometheus Unbound* and later in his *Defence of Poetry*. As pendant works, these essays and poem witness the poetic craft as well as the imaginative and political range of Shelley's mature writing. Even so, his reputation in the English reviews of the year before, the worst of which he did not read in Italy until a year later, was mixed: the *Quarterly Review* used the suppressed *Laon and Cythna* to show the depravity of its surrogate *The Revolt of Islam*. Hunt defended poet and poem in the *Examiner*; De Quincey deplored the Shelleyan doctrine of free love. *Blackwood's* looked back to *Alastor* to make a case for 'a mind destined, in our opinion, under due discipline and self-management, to achieve great things in poetry' (W II.160). Shelley was not consoled to learn of another failed anti-government conspiracy and series of executions in England, and the death in early 1820 of the old mad, bad George III, succeeded by his worthless son as George IV.

In Pisa, Shelley wrote poems that allegorized the poet's isolation or imagined the course available to liberty, including 'Sensitive-Plant', 'Ode to Liberty', 'To a Sky-Lark', 'Ode to Naples' (on the occasion of a constitutional revolution there), and *Swellfoot the Tyrant*, which was published, but then suppressed. There the Shelleys met Teresa Emilia Viviani, unmarried, incarcerated until marriage in a convent and the fictionalized heroine of Shelley's *Epipsychidion*. Shelley's idealist fantasies about Emilia ended with her marriage. Responding to Peacock's teasing but also serious claim in *The Four Ages of Poetry* that poetry no longer mattered in the industrial and experimental era of modern England, Shelley composed his *Defence of Poetry*. There he argued instead that without the imaginative and prophetic understanding poetry and the poet supply, culture will turn in the same dull, utilitarian round of industrial culture and an economics of scarcity and market powers. After the news that the Austrians had crushed the

Neapolitan revolt was succeeded by news of the Greek uprising against their Turkish oppressors, Shelley composed the drama *Hellas*, which conveys the uneven and ongoing work of global revolution. When he learned that Keats had died of tuberculosis in Rome, Shelley wrote *Adonais*, the great pastoral elegy that honours the younger poet who Shelley believed was killed by unfavourable reviews.

In 1821, the Shelleys met and shared their accommodations with Jane and Edward Williams. Urging Byron and his Italian lover Teresa Guiccioli and her brother to join the Shelleys and the Williams, Shelley wrote scenes for a drama titled *Charles the First* and the group planned theatricals. In April Claire and Byron's daughter Allegra died in the convent near Ravenna where Byron had placed her. Shelley's sense of personal constraint and marital isolation deepened throughout this period, but especially in 1822. When Mary miscarried again, Shelley insisted that she sit on a block of ice so that she would not haemorrhage, thereby probably saving her life (*MSJ* 1.412n). Peacock, whom Shelley asked about going to Asia as an East India Company official, quite practically discouraged the project (*W* II.327). Shelley dreamed of drowned infants and murderous acts that terrified him and Mary.

Settled at San Terenzo on the bay of Lerici, Shelley commissioned a 24-foot sailboat crafted according to a design that Williams favoured. Shelley wrote a number of carefully seductive poems to Jane Williams, one given to her with a guitar, and began to write the sardonic poetic history of modernity which he called, after the Roman triumphs in which the victors drove their fallen captives before them, *The Triumph of Life*. The poem registers the bitter paradox that Shelley repeatedly observed in contemporary Italy: surrounded by an artistic and architectural record of the greatness of Roman and Greek antiquity, most Italians were, Shelley insisted, servile and unconcerned about their political existence. He was fascinated by the exceptions: revolutionaries like the Countess Guiccioli's brother and, more ambivalently, the Greek patriot Prince Alexander Mavrocordato. By 1821, Shelley was bitter about Byron, in part because he had encouraged the rumour that Shelley and Claire were the parents of the mysterious, now dead, Elena. Shelley asked one of his last new English friends, Edward Trelawny (Byron and the Shelleys joked that he looked like Byron's Corsair) to get him some prussic acid so that he might have in his possession 'that golden key to eternal rest' (*L* II.714). Having cautioned Hunt not to expect a great deal of Byron, Shelley nonetheless invited Hunt and his family to relocate to Italy, so that the three of them could launch the *Liberal*, a magazine that would address English readers from Italy, beyond the reach of English censorship and prosecution.

Shelley, Williams, and their boat boy sailed to Leghorn to meet the Hunts when they arrived from England. On the way back, the three were drowned on their return trip to San Terenzo on 8 July 1822. The boat had an open deck and more masts and sails than one of its size could be expected to manage in high winds. This was probably the main reason the boat and its passengers were lost. Other causes have been suggested: the boat may have been rammed by a vessel that reported seeing them, or Shelley, who could not swim, wanted to drown and so refused suggestions on positioning one of the sails in order to weather the storm. The bodies were found a month later, temporarily buried on the seashore as Italian law required, then later cremated.

Shelley's contemporaries produced a number of biographies, some less reliable than others. The prize for the most unreliable goes to Hogg: although his life of Shelley contains a great deal of information, much of it has to be sifted, given Hogg's tendency to present himself favourably. Trelawny provides crucial information and some exaggeration about those last months and the circumstances surrounding Shelley's death. Peacock's *Memoirs* is astute and balanced on those aspects of Shelley's life he found most sympathetic. Hunt defended Shelley during his life in the *Examiner*, and after his death in *Lord Byron and Some of his Contemporaries*. Thomas Medwin, Shelley's cousin and Syon House schoolmate, published a life in 1847 that is at times confused about dates and some facts. The letters and journals of Shelley, Mary Shelley, Claire Clairmont, and Byron are essential reading. Mary's lists of their reading for many of the years they were together witness the intellectual tenor of their lives together.

The chief of Shelley's modern biographers is Newman Ivey White, whose two-volume biography remains the most detailed and indispensable. Cameron's biographies foreground the radical Shelley whom the Victorians did not see or never knew, as does Foot's *Red Shelley*. Holmes's biography presents an acerbic but often acute portrait. Gilmour's biography of the young Shelley and Byron gives an astonishing view of Eton during Shelley's time there. Shelley's editors, past and present, provide indispensable information about his life and art. Students of Shelley's work and life will find much to consider regarding both in these editions and biographies. The questions that linger even in this superb body of scholarship register the complexity of Shelley's life and art, indeed of life and art in general.

NOTES

1. Ivan Roe, *Shelley: The Last Phase* (London: Hutchinson, 1953), 12.
2. Michel Foucault, 'What is an Author?', in *Language, Counter-Memory, Practice*, tr. Donald F. Bouchard and Sherry Simon, ed. Donald F. Bouchard (Ithaca, N.Y.: Cornell University Press, 1977), 124–7.

3. Seamus Perry, 'Hail, Muse!', *London Review of Books*, 6 February 2003, 31–2 (31).

4. Quoted by Neville Rogers, *Shelley at Work* (Oxford: Clarendon Press, 1956), vi.

5. Nancy Moore Goslee, 'Shelley at Play: A Study of Sketch and Text in His Promethean Notebooks', *Huntington Library Quarterly* 48 (Summer 1985), 211–55.

6. Kenneth Neill Cameron, *The Young Shelley: Genesis of a Radical* (New York: Macmillan, 1950), 42. Subsequent references to this work are given parenthetically in the text.

7. Ian Gilmour, *The Making of the Poets: Byron and Shelley in their Time* (London: Chatto and Windus, 2002), 72.

8. *Ibid.*, 96.

9. *Ibid.*, 99.

10. *Ibid.*, 101.

11. *Critical Review* 21 (November 1810), 329–31; W I.57.

12. Shelley to Hogg, 3 January 1811, in *Shelley and His Circle*, ed. K. N. Cameron and D. Reiman, 8 vols. (Cambridge, Mass.: Harvard University Press, 1961–86), II: 684; quoted in Gilmour, *Making of the Poets*, 137.

13. CP, editors' notes I.235–48; W I.107–8.

14. See, for example, W I.280–5.

15. P I.360–423 (the quotation on value is from I.364).

16. Thomas Love Peacock, *Memoirs of Shelley, with Shelley's Letters to Peacock*, ed. H. F. B. Brett-Smith (London: Henry Frowde, 1909), 336, 338.

17. E. P. Thompson, *The Making of the English Working Class* (Harmondsworth: Penguin, 1968), 773–5.

18. Claire Clairmont, *The Journals of Claire Clairmont*, ed. Marion K. Stocking (Cambridge, Mass.: Harvard University Press, 1968), 88.

19. Mary Shelley, *Mary Shelley's Literary Lives and Other Writings*, 4 vols., vol. IV, ed. Pamela Clemit and A. A. Markley (London: Pickering and Chatto, 2002), 118, 124.

2

TIMOTHY MORTON

Receptions

My brother Shelley [*mein Bruder Shelley*]
(Bertolt Brecht, 'On Thinking about Hell', in *Hollywoodelegien*)[1]

Poetry only exists in readings. Poets are to some extent the first readers of their own works. Since mechanical reproduction – since, that is, the invention of the printing press – and especially since the advent of copyright laws, poetry has detached from its authors and wandered somewhat freely in public space. Romantic poets were acutely aware of their afterlives, and their works reflect this. Shelley talked about afterlife in many of his works, meditating upon the very process I am describing. In *Queen Mab*, death and sleep are 'wonderful' (1.1) because of their suspension of daily routines and habitual patterns; they allow the possibility for thinking about how things could be otherwise. Imagining your own death is necessarily about stepping outside the normal framework of life. In *Alastor*, we get to glimpse poetry going on after the death of the Poet protagonist, as great swathes of blank verse writhe around his corpse. The gigantic images in *Prometheus Unbound* and *The Triumph of Life*, too complex and sinuously vast to take in at once, appear to keep unfurling even while we are not reading them. This is not unrelated to Shelley the political disseminator, placer of messages into bottles and balloons, floater of propaganda across waters, maker of paper boats, the one who wrote about the 'Ashes and sparks' of his writing being swept along by the west wind of history to 'quicken a new birth' ('Ode to the West Wind', 67, 64). It is fitting that, almost two centuries after his death, the *Liberal* – the journal that he started with Leigh Hunt and Byron – has gained a new lease of life. Shelley made the idea of poetic afterlife the climax of his *Defence of Poetry*. Poets are 'the unacknowledged legislators of the world' (*Pr* 297). If 'unacknowledged' means 'unconscious', then even while their writers are alive poems are doing their work outside and beyond the scope of their authors.

Shelley was acutely aware of his audiences while alive, and carefully integrated this awareness into his writing. This was the man whose pamphlet *The Necessity of Atheism* attracted the attention of a passing clergyman in an Oxford street. Shelley could write ballads on bread in the tradition of the radical workers' underground, and texts that encouraged upper-class reformers. *Queen Mab* is an explicitly, gloriously didactic poem, of which Shelley remained fond, presenting it in 1817 to a Mr Waller with the remark that the sentiments of 'equality & liberty & disinerestedness, & entire unbelief in religion of any sort, to which this Poem is devoted, have gained rather than lost that beauty & that grandeur which first determined him to devote his life to the investigation & inculcation of them' (*L* II.567). The original text was printed to look like an innocuous fairy-tale, 'A small neat Quarto, on fine paper & so as to catch the aristocrats: They will not read it, but their sons & daughters may' (*L* I.361). And this was not enough. Shelley composed *The Daemon of the World*, a reduction of *Queen Mab* to a long but manageable poem that laid bare its scintillating imagery – the feel of the previous work without some of the content. In the same volume, *Alastor* takes us on an inward journey that charts what it might feel like to be a radical poet. Shelley wished to navigate both the ostensibly political and the private spheres, and to show how they were intertwined.

Moreover, Shelley wanted to reach an audience in ways far deeper than mere modulation of the rhetorical surface. Indeed, Shelley became more and more sensitive, as did his contemporaries, to the downgrading of explicitly didactic poetry in the hierarchy of genres. But this did not mean that poetry should shun its reader: quite the opposite, in fact. Numerous works actively compel the reader to adopt a position that Shelley favours. 'A Refutation of Deism' creates an atheist third position out of the Platonic dialogue that exposes the inadequacy of both the Christian and Deist interlocutors. In general, Shelley's work anticipates what would later be called constructivism. Constructivism is a poetics that builds a structure in which the reader's mind, their thoughts and ideas, become the raw materials. The goal of this poetics is to produce not a pretty, neat object – many of Shelley's works seem to sprawl out of control – but, on the contrary, to excite and puzzle us into a complex thinking process. In this respect Shelley is the exact opposite of Keats, whose equally radical strategy was a precursor of objectivism. Keats wanted to create objects that were so extraordinarily dense, sticky, and hard to extricate ourselves from that they reconfigure our very idea of what materials and matter could be. Between them, Shelley and Keats set the agenda for poetics up to the present day.

After his death, readers struggled over Shelley's poetic body. The struggle was divided between a tendency to contain his lyricism within an apolitical frame, and an urge to extend his political influence. It is too simplistic to say that these processes never combined. A careful reading of Mary Shelley's prefaces to the *Poems* of 1824 shows that she was interested in preserving the political Shelley, in however secretive a form. This was a time of political turmoil, and Shelley's very family were at times keen to disown him, or seriously rewrite him. 1824 was the same year in which William Hazlitt's *Select British Poets* dislocated the lyricism from the politics: 'The late Mr Shelley . . . was chiefly distinguished by a fervour of philosophic speculation, which he clad in the garb of fancy, and words of Tyrian dye. He had spirit and genius, but his eagerness to give effect and produce conviction often defeated his object, and bewildered himself and his readers' (*CH* 334). In the more extensive remarks in Hazlitt's review of the *Posthumous Poems*, 'Shelley's style is to poetry what astrology is to natural science – a passionate dream, a straining after impossibilities, a record of fond conjectures, a confused embodying of vague abstractions, – a fever of the soul' (*CH* 335). Charles Lamb, reacting more intensely against Shelley's politics, put it more succinctly: 'For his theories and nostrums they are oracular enough, but I either comprehend 'em not, or there is miching malice and mischief in 'em. But for the most part ringing with their own emptiness' (*CH* 346). This sort of judgement depended very much on where you stood with respect to his politics. In the opinion of Henry Crabb Robinson: 'even in his worst works, I have no doubt there is the enthusiasm of virtue and benevolence' (*CH* 347).

The culmination of this depoliticization of lyric was the way in which texts such as Palgrave's *Golden Treasury* (1861) kicked Shelley upstairs into a heaven of weightless beauty. The sanctification process is visible in the Shelley Memorial in University College Oxford, where in Henry Weekes's sculpture Mary supports the poet in the posture of the Christian *pietà*. Fear helped produce this Shelley. Edward Moxon, who published the *Collected Works* in 1841, was successfully prosecuted for blasphemous libel in the last case of its kind in England. William Clark's pirate edition of *Queen Mab* (1821) had already attracted the attention of the Society for the Suppression of Vice. A demonization and simultaneous beatification of Shelley took place in bowdlerized versions such as *The Beauties of Percy Bysshe Shelley* (1830). A second generation of criticism, produced in the main by William Michael Rossetti (in his 1870 and 1878 editions) and Algernon Swinburne, changed the picture handed down by Medwin and Hogg. Swinburne, more positive about Shelley's republicanism than some, tried to rescue the poet from Arnold's comment that Shelley tries but fails to 'render' nature: 'His aim is . . . to render the effect of a thing rather than the thing itself; the soul and spirit of life rather than the living form'.[2] Edward Dowden's biography of 1886 changed the picture again, by adding substantial amounts of evidence and a more careful discussion of those moments in Shelley's life which others, such as Hogg, had made much of. Frederick James Furnivall, who had been part of the Christian Socialist movement, founded the Shelley Society in 1886. The Society promptly staged *The Cenci*, a somewhat radical act even at the time, given the incestuous content.

Shelley's drowned body ascended easily into the Victorian cult of death. His lyrics streamed safely from heaven, even here, for the radical ear, suggesting that things could be otherwise, that other worlds are possible. When Lizzie Eustace declares her admiration for the line on Ianthe's soul, 'Immortal amid ruin' (*Queen Mab*, 1.137), the contrast between ruined earthly life and undying ideas was one that Shelley himself would have wanted to convey.[3] A fey, ghostly, Gothic Shelley enjoys an afterlife in popular music and cinema. He becomes an opium-crazed master of ceremonies in Ken Russell's film *Gothic*, a travesty that depicts the origins of *Frankenstein* as an opium-crazed romp. The pop group The Cure, leaders of goth style, released a version of *Adonais*.[4] Shelleyan Orphan released three albums of ethereal music in the 1980s and 90s.

Dead Shelley has been as popular as red Shelley, the one whom Engels and Marx venerated and who finds his biographer in Paul Foot. Dead Shelley became the effete poet of free association, the passive, suicidal bohemian pin-up. In his extraordinarily revisionist biography Thomas Jefferson Hogg declared that Shelley 'evaporated like ether, his nature being ethereal' (*Hogg* 1.301). At the behest of his daughter-in-law, Jane, Lady Shelley, who commissioned Hogg, Shelley turns into something like wisteria, 'an elegant, beautiful, odoriferous parasitical plant' (1.301). Lady Shelley created a shrine to him at Boscombe Manor, and Charles Kingsley lamented people's interest in mesmerism, mysticism, and '[reading] Shelley in secret'.[5]

Literary history slid from dead Shelley to adolescent Shelley, from a fantasy object to a fantasist. Humphry House and T. S. Eliot made him out to be an adolescent, and Eliot went further by declaring 'enthusiasm' for Shelley 'to be an affair of adolescence'.[6] 'Repellent' is Eliot's word for Shelley's ideas, which he reduces to vegetarianism (*ibid.*). *Enthusiasm* is code for what T. S. Eliot did not like about Puritanism, a politicized inner light – the word was already dangerous in Shelley's own day. Shelley was either too dead, or too alive. Indeed, the aliveness extended to Shelley's interest in putting sexuality, gay and straight, into his writing. Adolescent Shelley was a good way of dismissing the politics. In a further twist of the same infantilizing logic, one could always say that the politics was like lead that tied the angel to the ground, as W. S. Walker did in a review of the *Posthumous Poems*. The ethereal Shelley, 'Ariel' (one of his nicknames), was the one whom Matthew Arnold had pegged in 1881 as a 'beautiful and ineffectual angel, beating in the void his luminous wings in vain' (*Arnold* 1.237).

Two things fall out in Arnold's neutering assessment. First, and most obviously, there is no sense here that Shelley was a political writer, indeed a political poet. Secondly, and perhaps even more damagingly, lyric itself becomes vanity, ineffectual beauty. This is taken to an extreme in F. R. Leavis's association of *Shelleyan* and *lyrical*, a label that brings to mind the way punks used to intone the word 'hippy'.[7] (Ironically, since 'shell' is a metonymy for 'lyre' in classical poetry, Leavis's usage is not far off the mark.) Leavis kicks an emasculated, demonized figure when he's already down. It takes a lot of work to repoliticize the lyrics *as* lyrics, to find a politics in their very lyricism. But this is just what German Marxist readings, the next significant moment of Shelley's reception, tried to do.

The reception of Shelley in socialist poetics in Germany in the first half of the twentieth century is particularly striking. Bertolt Brecht, Walter Benjamin, and Theodor Adorno were all fascinated by what they saw as a radical use of lyric. Brecht translated *The Mask of Anarchy* in 1938. In the *Arcades Project*, Benjamin quoted and cited a translation of nine stanzas from the third part of *Peter Bell the Third*. But, significantly, it was also the aesthetic, lyrical Shelley that magnetized their extraordinary readings, although some of the work they were interested in, such as *The Devil's Walk*, did communicate explicitly political messages. Paul Cassirer's 1922 edition of Shelley's *Dichtungen* was a great inspiration. It contained excerpts from *Hellas*, *Prometheus Unbound*, and *Adonais*; Alfred Wolfensten's afterword quoted from *The Mask of Anarchy*. This edition worked its way into the pages of the anti-fascist journal *Das Wort*.

The very angel whom Arnold had scorned and Swinburne admired was the object of this re-evaluation. This was very high-stakes stuff for supporters of Communism who were taking a stand for art against the crassly utilitarian reductionism of Stalinist poetics. Robert Kaufman has given decisive accounts of this moment in Shelley's afterlife, in a number of essays that examine why Shelley on, say, the power of the imagination in *The Defence of Poetry* should have become so appealing to the three writers. The radical Shelley that they uncovered formulated a poetics that tampered with modern life's drastic limitations and monstrous distortions of social potential. Rather than stipulating one course of action or another, this poetics provided a space for radical practice. The gesture of refreshment was in itself a political act, a suspension of habitual and normative ways of carrying on. This was the Shelley of the sword of lightning that consumes its own sheath (*Pr* 285). It is as if, in the face of their own modernist concepts about the death of the aura of lyrical charm, Shelley's lyricism is able to do the most fundamental political work of all, holding open the possibility of an as yet unfulfilled sensuous existence.

The Left-wing, Kantian reading of Shelley has only recently been fully acknowledged in Anglo-American scholarship. It remains, in a strange sense, in the future of Shelley criticism, an unexplored possibility. The needle of Anglo-American criticism jumped over this German groove and New Criticism picked up on the ethereal, depoliticized lyricist, sometimes with an ear more attuned to Shelley's gifts and less quick to dismiss him than Arnold, Eliot, and Leavis in their different ways. Frederick Pottle, Carlos Baker, Harold Bloom, and Earl Wasserman all developed extensive and positive readings of Shelley. In America in particular, Shelley came a long way from the moment immediately after his death, when, according to the *Philadelphia Monthly Magazine*, he was 'here considered as a dark, selfish unbeliever' (*CH* 350; see 380–1). A Rhode Island reviewer, like Coleridge, speculated that all Shelley would really have needed was a helping Christian hand that could tolerate his scepticism (*CH* 357). The *American Quarterly Review* (1836) ranked Shelley with Byron and Wordsworth and praised his 'enquiring and doubting' spirit.[8] Ralph Waldo Emerson seemed not to get it: 'this *Defence of Poetry* looks stiff and academical' (*CH* 373; see 422). Only Margaret Fuller dared to say that 'many, even of devoutest Christians, would not refuse the book which contains *Queen Mab* as a Christmas gift' (*CH* 414). Nathaniel Hawthorne imagined him living two decades longer and becoming 'reconciled to the Church of England', publishing 'a volume of discourses treating of the poetico-philosophical proofs of Christianity on the basis of the Thirty-Nine Articles' (*CH* 418).

Shelley has enjoyed an afterlife in numerous popular forms. One poem got up and walked on its own while he was still alive. *Queen Mab* and its astonishingly detailed and extensive notes were pirated and circulated by the radical underground by such publishers as Carlile and Benbow, and later by the Chartists. The pirating that went on during Shelley's lifetime was against his stated wishes, though perhaps he wanted to avoid for himself the still pressing legal ramifications of his atheism and hostility to the crown, especially in the wake of his disastrous custody trial. *The Mask of Anarchy*, in particular its rousing conclusion ('Rise like lions after slumber' (368–72)), has been used in numerous occasions of political protest.[9] Leigh Hunt published it in 1832 in the white heat of the struggle for Parliamentary reform, having suppressed it when Shelley submitted it to the *Examiner*. The poem inspired the nonviolent direct action advocated by Mohandas K. Gandhi, who quoted it during his work in South Africa. Gandhi's idea of nonviolence influenced Martin Luther King. The students in Tiananmen Square, Beijing, scene of a massacre in 1989, chanted *The Mask of Anarchy*. Stephen Ellis's 1999 book on Liberia is entitled *The Mask of Anarchy*.[10] Arundhati Roy quoted it in an essay in her *War Talk*.[11] The pop group Scritti Politti gave the poem a postmodern run for its money in the 1980s.[12] Most recently John Vanderslice's song *Pale Horse* cites *The Mask of Anarchy*.[13]

Thabo Mbeki, the President of South Africa, quoted it in an official address in 2003.[14]

It is ironic that one of the often overlooked aspects of Shelley's life may prove among his most lasting legacies. Vegetarianism was emerging as a modern way of eating in Shelley's time, and was widely seen as cranky. In 1890, Gandhi became a member of the London Vegetarian Society, partly due to his reading of Henry Salt's *A Plea for Vegetarianism*, which cited Shelley, as had many of his other publications in the same vein. Shelley's vegetarianism also inspired George Bernard Shaw, who quoted the vegetarian section from part 5 of *Laon and Cythna* in justifying the diet. There are at least eleven known posthumous editions of *A Vindication of Natural Diet*, and three of the essay 'On the Vegetable System of Diet', which was unpublished in Shelley's lifetime. Very many vegetarian writers have discussed Shelley's adherence to the diet. Nowadays, Shelley is seen as prescient about health, nutrition, and the future of the planet.

NOTES

1. Bertolt Brecht, *Poems 1913–1956*, ed. John Willett and Ralph Manheim (London and New York: Methuen, 1987).
2. Algernon Charles Swinburne, *Essays and Studies*, 5th edn (London: Chatto and Windus, 1901), 219.
3. Anthony Trollope, *The Eustace Diamonds*, 2 vols. (New York: Dodd, Mead, 1928), I.258–9.
4. The Cure, *Adonais*, on *Join the Dots: B-Sides and Rarities, 1978–2001* (Rhino/Elektra, 2005). The song was originally the B-side to the single *The 13th*.
5. Timothy Webb, *Shelley: A Voice Not Understood* (Manchester: Manchester University Press, 1977), 15.
6. T. S. Eliot, 'Shelley and Keats', in *The Use of Poetry and the Use of Criticism*, 2nd edn (London: Faber and Faber, 1964 (1933)), 89.
7. F. R. Leavis, *New Bearings in English Poetry* (London: Chatto and Windus, 1950), 89.
8. Clement Dunbar, *A Bibliography of Shelley Studies: 1823–1950* (New York and London: Garland, 1976), xxii.
9. Paul Foot, 'Poetry of Protest', *Socialist Review* 155 (July–August 1992), 18–20.
10. Stephen Ellis, *The Mask of Anarchy: The Destruction of Liberia and the Religious Dimension of an African Civil War* (New York: New York University Press, 1999).
11. Arundhati Roy, 'Confronting Empire', in *War Talk* (Cambridge, Mass.: South End Press, 2003), 112.
12. Scritti Politti, *Lions after Slumber*, on *Songs to Remember* (Rough Trade Records, 1982).
13. John Vanderslice, *Pale Horse*, on *Cellar Door* (Barsuk Records, 2004).
14. Thabo Mbeki, 'President's Official Opening Address: Indaba 2003', paragraph 42, http://www.anc.org.za/ancdocs/history/mbeki/2003/tmo504.html.

PART II

Works

3

KAREN WEISMAN

The lyricist

In a compelling and enduringly fascinating article of 1954, Frederick Pottle issued a polemic entitled 'The Case of Shelley'.[1] Situating himself against the prevailing – and very modernist – New Critical dogma that Percy Shelley exhibits dissociation of sensibility, incoherent image patterns, and sundry other offences against early 'formalist' creeds, Pottle insisted that Shelley is (as he unabashedly put it) 'a great poet'. He sought to augment his claim by insisting that, contrary to the charges of effeminacy rampant among anti-Shelleyans, he found Shelley to be indeed 'manly'. But he also offered a strange prediction, and we had best check our smugness before simply dismissing it, for the quixotic reputation of Shelley is one of the more eccentric phenomena of literary history: he goes on in the essay to lament that 'It is clear to me that within fifty years practically everybody will be saying about Shelley what the New Critics are saying now. The disesteem of Shelley is going to become general, and it may continue for a century or more' (374).

Pottle's poignancy provides a good index of the histrionics that have accompanied the reputation of Shelley, a histrionics that seems in fact to rely on a reading specifically of Shelleyan *lyric* for its force. Those critics complaining about Shelley's effeminacy, or immaturity, or political naivety, seem to be reacting to an alluring and virtuosic lyric fluency that is socially motivated even as it is self-effacing, politically charged even as it is directed to cognoscenti, and deeply expressive even as it is insistently aware of its linguistic inefficacies. It has been a good deal less than a century since Pottle first offered his sad prognosis, and the esteem of Shelley, and especially of Shelleyan lyric, has already climbed to (and again somewhat receded from) staggering heights of approbation. When post-structuralism took the paradigm-baton from New Criticism, the effacements and self-subversions inherent in Shelleyan lyric became signatures of sophistication, not, as T. S. Eliot derisively labelled them in 1933, the signs 'of adolescence'.[2] In 1936, F. R. Leavis notoriously complained that Shelley has a 'weak grasp upon the actual', and in fact Pottle believed that the judgement of Leavis, or someone like him, would probably define the century's general evaluation of Shelley.[3]

Much later in the century, however, one of the seminal essays of North American deconstruction – Paul de Man's 'Shelley Disfigured' – took one of Shelley's more difficult poetic images and labelled it, triumphantly and now famously, as 'the figure for the figurality of all signification'.[4] Though it would have been news to de Man that he was responding to Leavis or, better yet, to Victorian angst, his analysis may also serve as something of a gloss to one of the Victorian age's salient assessments of Shelley: Matthew Arnold, seduced by Shelley's lyricism but disillusioned by its putative empirical detachments, by what de Man might call its self-conscious figurality, charged in 1881 that Shelley was 'a beautiful and ineffectual angel, beating in the void his luminous wings in vain' (*Arnold* 1.237). And yet, between Arnold and the New Critics, as Pottle points out, roughly between 1895 and 1920, Shelley was regarded as 'England's greatest lyric poet' (371). It is not just that Shelley inspires diametrically opposed aesthetic assessments, though he does that too; rather, it is that he inspires diametrically opposed definitions of his very aims and procedures. Plainly, Shelleyan lyric touches nerves, always has and, it is fair to conjecture, always will.

Lyric itself is a very complicated term, one whose meaning or description enjoy little scholarly consensus. Though it is generally understood that lyrics tend to be short non-narrative poems that are expressive of intense feeling or thought, in fact many long poems contain, or are even defined by, important lyric parts: Wordsworth's long epic, *The Prelude*, is a lyrical epic, and Shelley's *Prometheus Unbound* is a lyrical drama. The lyric has a long and complicated history, with classical, biblical, and post-biblical roots that cross many national cultures, languages, and expressive types. Shelley was a voracious reader and deeply learned in various literary traditions; he was also a deft experimenter with inherited forms and genres, and his lyricism often bears the mark of the polyglot's eclecticism. For the purposes of this chapter I will try to narrow the scope and concentrate on lyric forms that would have been readily identified by Shelley's contemporaries. I will seek not to survey all of Shelley's lyrics, but rather to give a sense of the range and common tendencies of select representative examples. In so doing, perhaps we might loosen some of the knots that bind Shelley to so many contradictory judgements.

The ode is a good place to begin because it provides such fecund ground for scholarly debate. The Romantics are often credited with having perfected the ode of passionate meditation that seeks to resolve a personal or more generally human problem. In the seventeenth century Abraham Cowley adapted Pindar's Grecian odes, and his so-called irregular Pindaric stanzas evolved into the Romantics' most recognizable forum for celebration of the sublime. Shelley in turn adapted Cowley's forms, and the models of Wordsworth and Coleridge, to produce odes which at once affirm and deny the very efficacy of odic form to celebrate or to clarify human desire. The 'Hymn to Intellectual Beauty' and 'Mont Blanc', written as companion poems in 1816, provide fine examples of this learned tension. 'Intellectual Beauty', which is in fact an ode, is addressed to a spiritual entity whose real presence cannot be affirmed and whose manifest evidence relies on insubstantial, fleeting, or invisible images.

> The awful shadow of some unseen Power
> Floats though unseen amongst us,—visiting
> This various world with as inconstant wing
> As summer winds that creep from flower to flower,—
> Like moonbeams that behind some piny mountain shower,
> It visits with inconstant glance
> Each human heart and countenance;
> Like hues and harmonies of evening,—
>   Like clouds in starlight widely spread,—
>   Like memory of music fled,—
>   Like aught that for its grace may be
> Dear, and yet dearer for its mystery.   (1–12)

In this poem, as in most of Shelley's lyrics, he takes exceptional care with the pattern of end-rhyming, a technique consistent throughout his career. Here the rhyme scheme manages to unite the formidable 'unseen Power' with the vulnerable 'flower' and transient 'mountain shower', even while the Power's 'inconstant glance' is immediately joined, in the intimacy of an end-stopped couplet, with the human 'countenance' that incessantly longs for it. This is the Shelley whose etherealized lyricism led to charges of confusion and immaturity in the earlier part of the twentieth century, and whose commitment to the actual was held under suspicion. But it is also the Shelley whose manipulation of inherited lyric forms was to transform him into the master of received formalist conventions.

'Mont Blanc' takes as its point of reference the highest peak in Europe to begin its meditation on the 'awful power' that comes down 'in likeness of the Arve' river, only to conclude with an apostrophe not to the spiritual Power, nor even to the maker of symbols of the Power (the poet), but to the mountain itself:

> The secret strength of things
> Which governs thought, and to the infinite dome
> Of heaven is as a law, inhabits thee!

And what were thou, and earth, and stars, and sea,
If to the human mind's imaginings
Silence and solitude were vacancy?   (139–44)

In both of the above-quoted instances (from 'Intellectual Beauty' and 'Mont Blanc'), the poet displays the characteristic stylistic moves that have by turns enraged and enthralled his readers. The ode traditionally trades on the reading audience's consensus about its object of address, certainly about the existence of that object. It is also a dialectical form, one that looks to resolution of contraries, or at least some sort of confident closure, in its 'epode', or synthesizing stanzas. In 'Intellectual Beauty' and 'Mont Blanc', Shelley undermines the ode's consensual expectations by figuring first the process by which the sceptical mind establishes emblems of its desired other. It is for this reason that 'Intellectual Beauty' begins with a series of obtrusive similes, all of which dignify things absent, shadows of the world that itself is posited as the insubstantial image of a power greater than it. The anaphoric repetition of the word 'like' ('*Like* hues and harmonies of evening,—/ *Like* clouds in starlight widely spread,—/ *Like* memory of music fled,—/ *Like* aught that for its grace may be . . .') serves as an obtrusive reminder of Shelley's aesthetic control. For such use of simile calls insistent attention to the lyrical process: in rejecting the absolute equivalents of metaphor in favour of the obtrusiveness of the mere *likeness* proposed by simile, Shelley refuses the presumption of surely locating his spiritual anchor even while he advertises the frenetic quality of his urge to do so.

For all of its uneasy praise of a metaphysical absolute, 'Intellectual Beauty' is a lyric with one eye to the ground and the other to the heavens: the poet is poised between praise of an extra-textual presence on the one hand, and, on the other, the self-reflection that is driven to conceptualize the very foundations of poetic praise. This is a dynamic characteristic of Shelley's lyrics generally. For his radical scepticism, by which he is unable simply to affirm the simple existence of the entity he praises, still does not seek to undermine belief in its being. What it does accomplish, however, is a radical insistence on the world in which he is situated – a world which may well provide him with the impulse to transcend it, but a world all the same that even his most impassioned transcendental longings still lay bare. After asking vain questions about the origins of evil and pain, he notes:

No voice from some sublimer world hath ever
To sage or poet these responses given—
Therefore the name of God, and ghosts, and Heaven,
Remain the records of their vain endeavour [.]   (25–8)

Shelley names names too, but he is aware of the conditions of ineffability to which his lyricism must be committed. This is the poet who would have been very much at home with Arnold's description of him as 'ineffectual angel', though here the lyric inefficacy is flagrantly staged.

'Mont Blanc''s concluding question boldly requires that the reader take notice of the human mind refracting it, of the poetic principle that would transform its obtrusive actuality into a potent symbol that, nonetheless, forecasts first and foremost the symbol-making capacities of the human mind. Indeed, earlier in the poem Shelley apostrophizes the mountain:

> Dizzy Ravine! and when I gaze on thee
> I seem as in a trance sublime and strange
> To muse on my own separate fantasy,
> My own, my human mind, which passively
> Now renders and receives fast influencings,
> Holding an unremitting interchange
> With the clear universe of things around. (34–40)

'Mont Blanc' is one of the notable exceptions to Shelley's usual habit of establishing regular end-rhymes in his lyrics. As William Keach has observed, this poem exhibits a highly irregular rhyme scheme, one further distorted by the many instances of enjambment and slant (or imperfect) rhyming.[5] In the above-quoted lines, for example, 'thee' pairs easily with 'fantasy', but three lines pass before 'interchange' recalls the 'strange' trance that marks a self-musing, though one that still encompasses the 'clear universe of things around'. The confluence of self-regard and the self's immersion in the empirical world is herein suggested, but not before the reader is made to question her bearings: the poem struggles with the dizzying limitations of, and thrilling possibilities for, lyric assertion of the mind's encounter with the world as well as with the language that seeks to meet it. Indeed, it is important to observe that, although he seems to be contemplating his own human mind, that mind renders and receives the lessons of the great object confronting it. From the separate fantasy of his own human mind, from teetering on the tightrope of solipsism towards the *terra firma* of the clear universe of things around, the poem seamlessly moves towards unabashed political undertones:

> Thou hast a voice, great Mountain, to repeal
> Large codes of fraud and woe; not understood
> By all, but which the wise, and great, and good
> Interpret, or make felt, or deeply feel. (80–3)

The mountain has a voice, and the mountain further figures a transcendental Power ('Mont Blanc yet gleams on high:—the power is there' (127)), yes, but as the final stanza reminds us, the mountain would be just a mountain if not for the fiction-making predilections of the human mind. The ode form may well establish expectations of confident praise, but Shelley's deft handling of it calls attention to the very formalist conventions he appropriates and subverts.

Partly because of the necessary compressions of lyric form, but principally because of his own resistance to dialectical closure, Shelley's self-ironic gestures have sometimes been read as extreme assertions of belief, though his belief claims as many manifestations as there are readers of his poetry; that is, he has been taken both as doctrinaire Platonist, firmly committed to the tenets of a dualistic universe, and as radical atheist, unswerving in his devotion to a humanism entirely stripped bare of transcendental longings. He has also been taken as a radical solipsist, whose wanderings in the world are closed to any speculations but those which reflect his own mind. But the space that Shelley occupies in his lyric poetry in particular is essentially a space between contraries. More important, perhaps, it is also a space between self-reflection and the outward gaze. And that space is so compressed, so resistant to definition, that it becomes vulnerable to misconstrual as ideological bad faith, that is, as constituting an empty gesture that clarifies little and that gives up nothing to the 'clear universe of things around'. Not only does the inward-looking stance of Shelley's lyric positioning not undermine the worldliness of his concerns, it in fact reinforces it: his self-reflexiveness is constantly questioning, constantly checking, the efficacy of his utterances. It is for this reason that the more overtly political odes, such as 'Ode to Naples' and 'Ode to Liberty', exhibit such careful handling of odic form and structure. They are directly responsive to the events of the day even as they draw on ancient poetic forms to express a lyric tension between desire and fulfilment. Indeed, if the dialectic is for Shelley a habit of mind as much as a foundation of his writing life, then the political lyrics are equally responsive to the rhythms of dialectical movement. 'Ode to Liberty', written in 1820 in response to the Spanish revolution and its establishment of constitutional government, traces specific political events and specific political aspirations, even as it insistently reminds of the poem's prominent artistry. More important, it lays bare one of the more subtle elements of Shelleyan lyricism, which may be defined as the peculiar compatibility of metaphysical abstraction with political and social preoccupation.

For those readers conceiving of Romantic lyric as the expression of the merely solipsistic gaze, Shelley's investment of the lyric with a particularizing worldliness, a worldliness that can equally digest the lyric's etherealized abstractions, this is indeed a challenging form. Framed by a dream vision in which a 'voice out of the deep' (15) narrates the history of the aspirations of political liberty, the poem provides an echoing counterpoint to Thomas Gray's eighteenth-century poem, 'The Progress of Poesy', which records the march of poetry and its forms through the ages. This point of departure is indicative of the main dialectical thrust of the 'Ode to Liberty' itself. For the 'Ode to Liberty', though tracking a movement in political expression, is equally a poem that asserts the primacy of the poetic voice in establishing the fundaments of liberty. Still, the essential inefficacy of poetry and its fictions, its naked inability to effect real change in the empirical world of political disquiet, is nowhere more evident than in the midst of substantial political upheaval. The noise of battle, the stomping of armies, the roar of protest: these are the cacophonous sounds of actuality that would efface the careful whisper of the poet's voice, no matter how urgent his message, no matter how meaningful his prophetic call for freedom. And yet it is the poet who gives voice to the subtler language of the soul's fundamental desires, and it is the poet who is invested with the power to strip away the blindfold of ideology that encumbers subjects and citizens as they struggle to recognize the conditions of their self-enslavement. 'Ode to Liberty', in this respect, is really a poem about the relationship between liberty and poetry, though it clearly struggles against the oversimplified equation of poetry with progress.

In the mythological/allegorical history of the world that Shelley relates, chaos rules where Liberty, addressed as 'thou' throughout the poem, is not:

> Art's deathless dreams lay veiled by many a vein
> Of Parian stone; and, yet a speechless child,
>   Verse murmured, and Philosophy did strain
> Her lidless eyes for thee.   (57–60)

Finally 'Athens arose' (61), and so begins the history lesson within the dream vision. But freedom comes and freedom goes, and tyrants triumph again after liberty is allowed to run a short course. One dialectical movement of 'Ode to Liberty' traces precisely the coming and going of liberty in various social contexts even as it traces the progress in the sophistication of poetry's exertions on its behalf. But what of the deathless dreams of Art? If art redeems, indeed if lyric redeems, it also fails to sustain the moment of redemptive power, for this poem is above all a reminder of the chaos that displaces liberty, of the ideology that hoodwinks us into unclear perception of the murmurings of Verse. Mark Kipperman has noted that the poem's ambiguities 'reveal most clearly Shelley's awareness of the strange ideological power of language, which both necessitates poetic revision and leadership and always renders that authority problematic'.[6] Indeed, the stanza which indicts 'the pale name of PRIEST' goes to the heart of the matter, for here Shelley acknowledges the inherent inefficacy of language and poetry as well as the urgency of our need of it:

> O, that the words which make the thoughts obscure
>   From which they spring, as clouds of glimmering dew
> From a white lake blot heaven's blue portraiture,
>   Were stript of their thin masks and various hue
> And frowns and smiles and splendours not their own,
>   Till in the nakedness of false and true
>   They stand before their Lord, each to receive its due!
>
> (234–40)

Words, especially the poet's words, are never simply, or merely, indicative of the nakedness of false and true. Indeed, the embellishments of poetry precisely constitute the thin masks and various hues and frowns and smiles and splendours that Shelley insists are 'not their own'. The immediate referent, to be sure, is ideology, but surely such adornments also describe the conditions of verse, the very conditions in which Shelley's lyricism is constituted. By this stanza of the poem we have already witnessed so many descriptions of liberty's dissolution, that calling on poetry's redemptive power to unmask the disguises of oppression possesses now a diluted appeal. If poetry and liberty are inextricably intertwined, and if poetry shares with ideology the key ingredients of 'various hue' and 'splendours not their own', then in fact the foundations of liberty contain the seeds of their own destruction. The cycle endlessly repeats, and verse repeatedly asserts its claim to the liberation of the soul; however, the tensions between liberty and the art that would hasten and then sustain it cannot be resolved.

In the penultimate stanza, the poet asks, 'Have not the wise and free / Wept tears, and blood like tears?' (269–70). At this point the narrative breaks off, and 'the solemn harmony' of 'the spirit of that mighty singing / To its abyss was suddenly withdrawn' (270–2). As a result,

> My song, its pinions disarrayed of might,
>   Drooped; o'er it clouded the echoes far away
> Of the great voice which did its flight sustain,
>   As waves which lately paved his watery way
> Hiss round a drowner's head in their tempestuous play.
>
> (281–5)

The poet's song loses its might and becomes silent, and we are left with an image of chaos, of waves hissing 'round a drowner's head in their tempestuous play'. The ambivalence of the close speaks to the ambivalence with which poetry is implicitly treated throughout the poem. The waves may be hissing, and hissing may well suggest the serpent re-entering paradise, just as the serpent of oppression re-enters the domains of liberty at various points in the cycle of liberty and oppression endlessly repeating throughout history. But those hissing waves are engaged in tempestuous play, which is as much flirtatious as it is dangerous.

The play is no fun, of course, for 'the drowner' around whose head the play is hissing, but that is precisely the point: liberty as an abstraction is impersonal, and the effort to actualize it in real situations in the world is the work of an endless flowing following an endless ebbing which itself follows a song that beckons always. Shelley knows that poetry and the actual are reciprocally related to one another. If poetry conditions the yearning for liberty and strips bare the ideological encrustations that enslave us, then poetry also obfuscates and tantalizes where it cannot deliver. Here, Shelley the ethereal poet whose lyrics flap in the void in vain is at one with the Shelley whose politics are the primary commitment of his life. The lyric abstracts the world even as it recognizes that abstracting the actual and rendering it in verse is what feeds the actual; that is, the articulation of hope, and of the cultural bases of identity, partly constitutes the world of action, even though that very articulation also pales in force beside the onrush of oppression. In acknowledging the limits of the lyric in the world of political action, Shelley acknowledges what the ode insistently prescribes: the give and take, the push and pull, of the world and the word.

If the ode affords Shelley an opportunity to highlight the dialectical nature of his imagination and intellect, then the sonnet brings to the fore his facility with compression and concision even while sustaining the dialectical tensions evident in his longer lyrics. Newly re-emerged in England as a vital form in the late eighteenth century, the sonnet comes to Romanticism freighted with a history of the recording of disappointment and unease. Other uses of its expressive possibilities have been deployed, to be sure, but Shelley frequently gestures in the direction of its various Petrarchan associations, which is to say that he exploits the sonnet form's singular suitability for negotiating both the conditions of defeat and the parodying of its rhetorical procedures. Typically, such gesturing serves both to affirm and ironize the tradition he chooses to inherit. This is most evident in his sonnet 'To Wordsworth', which laments the transformation of Wordsworth's early revolutionary and left-leaning fervour into a sterile conservatism that infected, in Shelley's view, not only his politics but also his poetry.

> Poet of Nature, thou hast wept to know
> That things depart which never may return:
> Childhood and youth, friendship and love's first glow,

Have fled like sweet dreams, leaving thee to mourn.
These common woes I feel. One loss is mine
Which thou too feel'st, yet I alone deplore.
Thou wert as a lone star, whose light did shine
On some frail bark in winter's midnight roar:
Thou hast like to a rock-built refuge stood
Above the blind and battling multitude:
In honoured poverty thy voice did weave
Songs consecrate to truth and liberty,—
Deserting these, thou leavest me to grieve,
Thus having been, that thou shouldst cease to be.[7]

Shelley here offers a variant on the so-called Shakespearean sonnet, but after two quatrains he inserts a couplet that all the same exhibits a mere slant rhyme ('stood' / 'multitude'). The rest of the poem then concludes with a quatrain. As such, there is no concluding couplet, but the last four lines of the sonnet (with their alternating end-rhymes) are in fact all joined together in assonance. Though the ostensible couplings are 'weave' / 'grieve' and 'liberty' / 'to be', the final lines conclude with the odd and unnerving pairing of 'to grieve' / 'to be'. Something is not quite right in the world of poetry; something just will not come together as it should, leaving Shelley to deplore the dissonance that accompanies the breaking down of rock-solid structures. Lines 9–10, the oddly placed couplet in which Shelley pays homage to the 'rock-built refuge' once preserved by Wordsworth, themselves form the most solidly packed structure in this short piece. They rhyme, but only imperfectly. It is as if he is asserting that the fault lines of the lithic (stone) monument of Wordsworth's commitment must always have been lurking, perhaps even in his youth. And yet even this tightly packed solid surprise of confluence, as it were, is out of place. For rather than supporting the structure of the sonnet from within, it forces a heavy weight of collapse on the rest of the poem: as I noted above, Shelley refuses to end the poem with the conventional couplet, choosing instead the assonance of coupling 'to grieve' with 'to be'. That final 'to be' is paired, of course, with 'liberty' – a condition that Shelley charges Wordsworth with forgetting: though his voice did 'weave' poems consecrated to truth and liberty, 'thou leavest me to grieve'.

The final line, in which Shelley sees Wordsworth's defection as a form of death, brings us back to the beginning of the poem, in a cyclical pattern that belies the sonnet form's conventional efforts at resolution, or at least conclusion. The Wordsworth who has ceased to be what he once was is the very 'Poet of Nature' of the first line who has also wept to know 'That things depart which never may return'. If Wordsworth taught him how to mourn the loss of treasured states of being, then he taught him so in the guise of a Poet of Nature, whose recognition of the repeating pattern of loss and rebirth in the world is paramount. The end of the poem brings us back to the beginning, but it is a beginning about endings that ought to – but cannot – cycle back to regeneration. This 'Poet of Nature' mourns the loss of childhood and youth, friendship and love's first glow. Shelley reads Wordsworth as essentially elegiac, and refuses to find strength in what remains behind, as Wordsworth famously does in his 'Immortality Ode', because Wordsworth has all but brought cyclical continuity to a close. If his light once shone on a boat navigating 'in winter's midnight roar', then his desertion of his poet drowns Shelley as well as Wordsworth. The return to the beginning, then, becomes not an opportunity for renewal but rather an endlessly repeated death.

Shelley exploits further the sonnet's elegiac associations in his most remarkable short poem, 'England in 1819'. Here he makes use of the sonnet's necessary brevity precisely to signal the infinite range of his hopes and the long extension of his disappointments about his country's political ills.

> An old, mad, blind, despised, and dying King;
> Princes, the dregs of their dull race, who flow
> Through public scorn,—mud from a muddy spring;
> Rulers who neither see nor feel nor know,
> But leechlike to their fainting country cling
> Till they drop, blind in blood, without a blow.
> A people starved and stabbed in th' untilled field;
> An army, whom liberticide and prey
> Makes as a two-edged sword to all who wield;
> Golden and sanguine laws which tempt and slay;
> Religion Christless, Godless—a book sealed;
> A senate, Time's worst statute, unrepealed—
> Are graves from which a glorious Phantom may
> Burst, to illumine our tempestuous day.   (1839)

The disjunction of the formal concision and the roll call of fiascos produce an effect of agitation: this is a condition of political adversity poised to burst its chains, and yet it is the very chain of the sonnet's structure which enables any kind of defining coherence to be articulated in this morass of national calamity. Shelley offers a catalogue of the sorry state of his country, a technique that recalls an epic cataloguing, or a taxonomical categorization of sickness. Like the earlier sonnet 'To Wordsworth', this poem too sees its objects of lament as 'graves'. Unlike the earlier poem, however, it concludes with a triumphant couplet that transforms death into birth. The apocalyptic subjunctive ('a glorious Phantom may / Burst') does not exactly come out of nowhere; it is already intimated in the remarkable control by which an entire epic tragedy is implied in its first twelve lines.

Historical epics tend to end with one side of the conflict finally triumphing after much defeat and death. In the extraordinary lyric concision of 'England in 1819', triumph is marked as an effort of the imagination to grasp wholly the monumental defeats and insults of the age and to give them a defined and limiting order. The clarity of that realization is what prepares for the concluding couplet's apocalypse of hope. The reality being well defined, the remedy surely cannot be beyond conception. The day is already 'tempestuous': why not dream the dream of its illumination, why not assert the boldness of an imaginative vision? We have but fourteen lines to encapsulate the record of our losses and the urgent ecstatic hope for redemption; but then, our very existence is circumscribed, and Shelley reminds us of our mortality by imaging the catalogue of horrors as 'graves'. Rebirth is thus given as enlightenment, as clarity, for the glorious Phantom may well 'illumine our day'. The lyric realizes the work of concise clarity, which is the work, after all, of forward-looking hope, for that is what establishes a defined forum for hope for the future. If Shelley is the beautiful angel flapping his luminous wings in the void, then we must re-examine our understanding of the void: surely the linguistic universe here is what lifts the empirical world into view. As in the poem 'To Wordsworth', Shelley's masterful use of the sonnet form transforms brevity into the long reach of lyric assertion. It also turns the moment of loss into the endless catalogue by which it is known. The dialectic, then, is not merely of thought: it is integrally absorbed into the fabric of his formalism.

Nowhere is the obtrusiveness of Shelley's self-conscious fictionalizing more prominent than in his elegiac lyrics, and no poem better characterizes the breadth of Shelley's lyric fluency than *Adonais*. Written in response to the death of John Keats, the poem recognizes the long and venerable tradition of pastoral elegy, one whose ritualized lamentation captures precisely the paradoxes that are so ingrained in Shelley's lyric writings. The pastoral elegy is both highly formalized and deeply personal: it is the lone cry of an individual in anguish even as it is the marking of social bonds and historical affiliations; it is the recognition of mortality even as it affirms the principles of permanence to which human life aspires. If scholarly debate has found no resting place of consensus in which to evaluate, or even to read, the poetry of Shelley, then *Adonais* must represent the extreme end of consensus breaking. For the poem has been accused of promoting both a facile Platonism and an aggressive and unyielding philosophical scepticism; it has been labelled both as a self-pitying indulgence and as an assertion of social and intellectual connectedness. One aspect of the poem, at least, that has not been under question is its high degree of artifice. Shelley himself referred to it as 'a highly wrought piece of art', and no one has really ever disagreed with him. As such, it has much to tell us about Shelley's sense of lyricism and of the possibilities for lyric assertion.

The pastoral elegy is a lyric form that calls upon a venerable tradition, one moving from Theocritus' First Idyll and Virgil's Tenth Eclogue and finding its way, in the English tradition, through to Spenser's *Astrophel*, the elegy for Sidney, and on to Milton's *Lycidas*, the latter serving as the most famous pastoral elegy in the English language. Writing late in the tradition, then, Shelley appropriates the conventions of pastoral machinery, and even pastoral consolation, and turns them on their heads. For if the pastoral elegy typically finds consolation in the contemplation of cyclical renewal and of a higher order, then *Adonais* charges the cycle of renewal with standing as a monument to death itself. The turn to consolation in Shelley's poem is highly qualified, for in fact it converts life into death:

> *We* decay
> Like corpses in a charnel; fear and grief
> Convulse us and consume us day by day,
> And cold hopes swarm like worms within our living clay. (348–51)

Milton's *Lycidas* famously concludes with its speaker acknowledging the dawning of a new day, which represents the dawning recognition of the continuity to which we are all bound: 'Tomorrow to fresh woods and pastures new'. Shelley's rendering of the tomorrow of freshness, however, is actually a fantasy about metaphysical otherness that still leaves the empirical world in the dust. It is for this reason that the poem has been labelled as both a Platonic assertion and a suicidal drive. As stanza 52 bears out in particular, Shelley imagines a principle of permanence that utterly transcends the temporal world:

> The One remains, the many change and pass;
> Heaven's light forever shines, Earth's shadows fly;
> Life, like a dome of many-coloured glass,
> Stains the white radiance of Eternity,
> Until Death tramples it to fragments.—Die,
> If thou wouldst be with that which thou dost seek!
> Follow where all is fled!—Rome's azure sky,
> Flowers, ruins, statues, music, words, are weak
> The glory they transfuse with fitting truth to speak.   (460–8)

Shelley appropriates the pastoral form, but the pastoral consolations become for him the signs of insufficiency, the recognition that the monuments of art in which he would locate his own poem are themselves unanswerable to the great task of explicating or assuaging the pains and shocks of mortality. The sheer speed of the verse, one of the signatures of Shelley's lyricism, practically tumbles the reader into the inexorability of death, into the prospect of disappointment in the changing and passing of the many, which is in apposition to the flying of Earth's shadows. And though the medial pause is a natural feature of the English pentameter line, no such small relief is realized in the line announcing that one must die 'If thou wouldst be with that which thou dost seek'. This is the Shelley whose lyricism, like Keats's nightingale in the ode that Shelley's poem consistently echoes, is one that sings above the world, as it were, one that knows that any real actualization of an ideal must risk losing it. Still, the move to fresh woods and pastures new remains the beckoning call of the tradition that Shelley has chosen to subvert; it is the desire that he cannot fulfil in whole, but which the lovely flowers, ruins, statues, music, and words still aspire to. And yet there is no assurance here of the integrity of his fantasy of a dualistic universe which can resolve the puzzle of our suffering in a world of mutability. The 'One' which is stained by the life which is 'like a dome of many-coloured glass' seems to be offered as a fiction within fiction, that is, as an obtrusive fantasy of fulfilment so remote from the quotidian world of pain that it is no matter, finally, that it cannot be rightly captured in lyric. In secularizing the English tradition, Shelley still bows in the direction of the Christian eschatology of Spenser and Milton, but his refusal to be cheered up by it stands as a potent insistence upon the remnants of what does remain. And what remains is art, and its continuity, and its traditions that can be incorporated, digested, and reconstituted. Indeed, this is the very point of the poem's recognition of the elegiac tradition from which it all the same swerves sharply. Thus, at the beginning of the poem, before the stanzas of pseudo-consolation, Shelley calls repeatedly for the 'most musical of mourners' to 'weep anew'. He addresses Urania, mother of the muses, at one point:

> Most musical of mourners, weep again!
> Lament anew, Urania!—He died,
> Who was the Sire of an immortal strain,
> Blind, old, and lonely, when his country's pride,
> The priest, the slave, and the liberticide,
> Trampled and mocked with many a loathed rite
> Of lust and blood; he went, unterrified,
> Into the gulph of death; but his clear Sprite
> Yet reigns o'er earth; the third among the sons of light.   (28–36)

The strain may well possess a brutal logic, but it is an immortal strain that Milton sired, and Shelley situates himself as inheritor of the music. This is a world in which those who would sing are trampled and mocked, and yet still the poet calls for the most musical of mourners to weep anew. It is a world in which we decay, and in which our songs are utterly insufficient to the task of comprehending that decay. Shelley stares right into the heart of the charge against lyric ideology, which is a charge against the poets for aestheticizing and displacing the empirical world of suffering.

For Shelley, lyric is neither escape nor panacea. But it is what rises to the challenge of our human affiliation with each other and with our respective pasts. Even in the final lines of the poem, which have sometimes been regarded as Shelley's prescient forecast of his own death by drowning, the redemptive moment is one which connects the song of the burdened poet with the tradition he has swallowed:

> The breath whose might I have invoked in song
> Descends on me; my spirit's bark is driven,
> Far from the shore, far from the trembling throng
> Whose sails were never to the tempest given;
> The massy earth and sphered skies are riven!
> I am borne darkly, fearfully, afar;
> Whilst burning through the inmost veil of Heaven,
> The soul of Adonais, like a star,
> Beacons from the abode where the Eternal are.   (487–95)

The breath whose might he has invoked in song is a reference to Shelley's own remarkable poem 'Ode to the West Wind', and it is the only time in Shelley's oeuvre at which he cites his own poetry. The One remains, and that gave scant reassurance. But here, the poem remains too: the integrity of the utterance is what converts the pastoral ideal into an internalized state. Milton's fresh woods and pastures new become the poet's call for the most musical of mourners to weep anew, for art to be created in the very conditions of astonished deprivation. This is not a lyricism that turns from the world, then, so much as it is a lyricism that looks hard at it even through the lens of art's limiting mediations. The artifice that Shelley handles so masterfully in *Adonais* becomes a device that imposes defining strictures and form on what would otherwise be the morass of his dismay in the world. It is not simply that art is redemptive; rather, it is within the forum of artifice that Shelley can take up the conventions in which life's cruellest but most obtrusive fact – mortality – can be negotiated. The artifice by which we confront death becomes the art that speaks for life.

Such an art can only lead to precarious triumphs, however. If Shelley's lyrics have been oft noted for their self-reflexive inflections, then his so-called 'Jane' poems, written towards the end of his short life in 1822, take self-regard to a level of aesthetic extremity that in fact clarifies the relation-ship between the external world and the self that suffers in its self-knowing. The poems were written on the occasion of Shelley's friendship with Jane Williams, one of the friends who had gathered in Pisa during the poet's self-exile in Italy. Like many of Shelley's lyrics, their incorporation of personal elements becomes part of the self-mythologizing of their author, in which he transforms himself and his surroundings into a text, as it were, one that can in turn be read back into the texture of his life. Two poems in particular, 'To Jane. The Invitation' and 'To Jane. The Recollection', provide a particularly apt entry point into this issue of lyrical self-dramatization. The poems had initially been conceived by Shelley as a single unit, and only at a later point did he split them into two distinct pieces, the first anticipating, and the second remembering, a cherished walk with a good friend during a particu-larly warm late winter day. It has often been noted by critics that the poet's wife, Mary Shelley, also attended the commemorated walk, but that only Jane seems to have made it into the textualization. This very omission becomes a fact in the poems' interpretive structure, as the incipient spring promises a fulfilment known primarily for its transience, its inability to satisfy in perpetuity. The muted sexuality teams with the poet's apprehen-sive scepticism to produce a set of poems that cry *carpe diem* even as they cancel the force of the poet's calling. The 'invitation' section is a remarkably fast-paced poem, its tetrameter lines beckoning the 'best and brightest' – the poem's addressee – to 'this halcyon morn / To hoar February born' (9–10). There is a sense of real running towards this ideal escape; the poem exhibits a high degree of enjambment, as lines spill over into their successors and the poet breathlessly spills forth an array of reasons for leaving the world of 'long pain' (45). But the poems invite and recall a day of intensity whose real moment does more to mark the essential alienation of the poet than to alleviate real distress. The poems appropriate a pastoral tradition, as many of Shelley's poems do, but this is a pastoral that turns against itself, that transforms pastoral ease into an anti-pastoral stance, or at least into a reflection on such a stance. As such, they lay bare the fundamental tensions of Shelley's lyricism, the chameleon turns of his lyric eclecticism that defies facile synthesis.

Percy Shelley never published these poems himself; they had been intended exclusively for Jane, and Jane knew full well that she had not accompanied Shelley alone. Whether as private document or public artefact, the means by which Shelley sutures the wounds of his domestic dissatis-faction provide textual markers of his surgical work. Excising Mary from this day of natural quirks is only one comment on perpetual unease, strife, and disaffection. The halcyon morn, after all, is born to February; the seasons are out of sync, providing a ray of sun that promises much but which must all the same be forestalled. And the beauty of this 'fair day' (2) is notably less beautiful than the poem's object of address, since Jane is 'Fairer far than this fair day'. Like all *carpe diem* poems, it is acutely aware of youth that must grow old, seasons that must cyclically change, and beauty that must die. Like many pastoral poems, it contains the seeds of its own self-subversion, since the moment of anticipated bliss is stolen from a world of care to which the poet must return. The poet leaves a notice on his door:

> 'I am gone into the fields
> To take what this sweet hour yields.
> Reflexion, you may come tomorrow,
> Sit by the fireside with Sorrow—
> You, with the unpaid bill, Despair,
> You, tiresome verse-reciter Care,
> I will pay you in the grave,
> Death will listen to your stave—
> Expectation too, be off!
> To-day is for itself enough—
> Hope, in pity mock not woe
> With smiles, nor follow where I go;
> Long having lived on thy sweet food,
> At length I find one moment's good
> After long pain—with all your love
> This you never told me of.'
>
> (31–46)

Reflection, of course, is precisely what a fast-moving lyric pace would seek to circumvent; however, it is reflection itself that haunts this poem, and that anticipates the moment when anticipation will give way to recollection – that is, when what remains of the grand day of escape is the obtrusive fact of its existence in the text only. The invitation sprints hastily, but the form of its compressed hurry undercuts the moment of stasis, of suspended ease, for which it longs. Today may well be for itself enough, but the Hope that Shelley personifies and chastises is precisely what animates this fine February day, this spring moment that is neither spring nor rightly belonging to winter. Here we have a quirk of nature whose splendour by definition must die, but whose reinstatement – when spring really does arrive and the season presents its rightful blooms – will be the scene of sorrow, despair, and care all the same. The poet beckons Jane to the scene

> Where the melting hoar-frost wets
> The daisy-star that never sets,
> And wind-flowers, and violets

Which yet join not scent to hue
Crown the pale year weak and new,
When the night is left behind
In the deep east dun and blind
And the blue noon is over us,
And the multitudinous
Billows murmur at our feet
Where the earth and ocean meet,
And all things seem only one
In the universal Sun.— (57–69)

If all things seem only one in the universal sun, then the text has brought seasonal variation too to a stasis, and the wonder of the anomalously spring-like day loses its fantastic nature. Like many of Shelley's lyrics, and especially like many of his pastoral lyrics, the Jane poems invite expectation of pastoral ease only to convert the prospects of happiness to a fiction that must be revealed as such, that is, as effusive lyric fiction: the stasis that Shelley longs for – a daisy-star that never sets, flowers that yet join not scent to hue – is the cold pastoral that cannot be fully actualized. Though the day celebrated is a real day in the calendar of Percy Bysshe Shelley's life, its real existence *to him* is a matter of fiction, of the textualizing and hence monumentalizing of a serenity which is first and foremost an escape from quotidian distress. And that quotidian despair is the place from which the invitation is issued, and it is the place to which he returns once the walk is finished. If 'all things seem only one in the universal sun', then the fractured state of his unease is the spectre that haunts this poem.

The recollection twin of this invitation is written in a modified ballad stanza, rather than the swiftly flowing tetrameter couplets of its companion piece, and its metre is considerably slower. The heavy-footed pace of the later poem suits the elegiac grief it trumpets. 'For now the Earth has changed its face, / A frown is on the Heaven's brow', laments the poet, for the season has resumed its familiar wintry scene. But what is right in the seasons translates, for the poet, into all that is wrong in the world. The final stanza picks up the imagery of the reflecting pools that lie 'under the forest bough' (54):

Sweet views, which in our world above
Can never well be seen,
Were imaged in the water's love
Of that fair forest green;
And all was interfused beneath
With an Elysian glow,
An atmosphere without a breath,
A softer day below—

Like one beloved, the scene had lent
To the dark water's breast,
Its every leaf and lineament
With more than truth exprest;
Until an envious wind crept by
Like an unwelcome thought
Which from the mind's too faithful eye
Blots one dear image out.—
Though thou art ever fair and kind
And forests ever green,
Less oft is peace in S[helley]'s mind
Than calm in water seen.   (69–88)

It is not that the mind cannot see aright; the poet despairs because the mind's eye is too faithful. Similarly, the soft day presents to the scene with 'more than truth exprest'. Is more than truth a greater truth? Or is it untruth? The reality of the spring scene is that it had been winter, and it had not been just with Jane, but with the poet's wife, from whom he had been feeling emotionally, and probably sexually, estranged. In the interplay of Shelley's life and Shelley's poetry, there exists a space in which he figures himself as a product of his own textualizing, his own fictionalizing impulses. In this, he is a lyric poet whose lyricism does not efface the world so much as it make it. Shelley lives a fluid realm of hope and despair, joy and its cruel dissolution, that is monumentalized in a poetry whose creative impulses stand at the centre of his life. Shelley's lyric, then, like the spring day which is not really spring, like the private walk with Jane which in fact had included Mary, like the bright day that in fact reverts to the dank scene which properly defines its season, is both a reflection of a life and that life's constitutive centre.

The lyrics of Shelley are reciprocally involved in their author's existence, who inhabits a writing life whose fictionalizing is his real life impulse. This is not self-indulgence so much as it is self-creation, a creation that achieves a stasis, paradoxically, that is only fleeting, and that must be given over to reflection and interpretation for basic sustenance. Shelley's lyrics take hold of the actual precisely by widening the lyric's grasp; that is, they open to include the dialectical negotiations by which poetry comprehends the world.

NOTES

1. Frederick Pottle, 'The Case of Shelley', repr. in *English Romantic Poets: Modern Essays in Criticism*, ed. M. H. Abrams (Oxford: Oxford University Press, 1975), 366–83. Subsequent references are given parenthetically in the text.
2. T. S. Eliot, 'Shelley and Keats', in *The Use of Poetry and the Use of Criticism* (Cambridge, Mass.: Harvard University Press, 1933), 87.

3. F. R. Leavis, *Revaluation: Tradition and Development in English Poetry* (Harmondsworth: Peregrine-Penguin, 1983 (1936)), 172.

4. Paul de Man, 'Shelley Disfigured', in *The Rhetoric of Romanticism* (New York: Columbia University Press, 1984), 116.

5. William Keach, *Shelley's Style* (New York and London: Methuen, 1984), 195.

6. Mark Kipperman, 'Shelley and the Ideology of the Nation: The Authority of the Poet', in *Shelley: Poet and Legislator of the World*, ed. Betty Bennett and Stuart Curran (Baltimore: Johns Hopkins University Press, 1996), 58.

7. Percy Bysshe Shelley, 'To Wordsworth', in *Alastor; or, the Spirit of Solitude: And Other Poems* (London: Baldwin, Cradock and Joy, Carpenter and Son, 1816).

4

JEFFREY N. COX

The dramatist

Shelley and the theatre

Like Wordsworth or Keats, Shelley has been thought of primarily as a lyric poet rather than as a dramatist. But he was in fact a powerful dramatist who worked with the theatrical conventions of his day in order to remake the stage for the future. We need to pay closer attention to Shelley's attention to drama and theatre. Shelley's engagement with drama was a life-long affair, from a childhood interest in acting to a planned performance of *Othello* with Shelley as director undertaken by his final circle of friends at Pisa that included Byron and Trelawny, from a play he may have written with his sister Elizabeth at the age of eighteen to the 'Fragment of an Indian Drama', left unfinished at his death, that owed something to the Sanskrit drama *Sakuntala*.[1] He read widely in the dramatic tradition, familiarizing himself with Athenian drama in the original, translating the Spanish baroque dramatist Calderón, and admiring the Italian pastoral playwright Guarini; he was immersed in the English dramatic tradition, from Sir Walter Scott's three-volume *Ancient English Drama* (1810) and Charles Lamb's *Specimens of English Dramatic Poetry* (1808) through Shakespeare, Ben Jonson, and Beaumont and Fletcher, and on to Thomas Otway, John Gay, and William Congreve.

While it has often been asserted that he was ignorant of the contemporary stage, Shelley, having as friends in Leigh Hunt and William Hazlitt two of the greatest theatrical reviewers of the time, saw a fair number of plays during stays in London. These included works by Shakespeare (catching Edmund Kean as Hamlet and Shylock); Richard Brinsley Sheridan, the great comic writer of the late eighteenth century and manager of one of London's two major theatres; George Colman the Younger, manager of the summer theatre in the Haymarket and one of the most influential dramatists of the turn of the century; Henry Hart Milman, whose *Fazio* starred Eliza O'Neill and was in Shelley's mind as he wrote *The Cenci*; and the key melodramatist William Dimond who among many other works dramatized Byron's *Bride of Abydos* (which again starred Kean).² Shelley was particularly taken with the new acting style embodied in the powerful Edmund Kean and in the startling Eliza O'Neill, who during her brief period on the stage was seen as the worthy successor to Mrs Siddons. These actors intrigued him enough to shape his conception of the main characters in *The Cenci*. Introduced to Mozart's *Don Giovanni* by Thomas Love Peacock, Shelley became an opera fan, seeing at least five operas in the two months before his final departure from England and continuing to enjoy the opera and especially its ballets once he arrived in Italy. His interest in the opera influenced the form of *Prometheus Unbound*.³

Shelley's awareness of the contemporary theatre led him to keep abreast of key contemporary British and European playwrights. He read and considered a range of Romantic attempts to remake British tragedy, including Joanna Baillie's *Plays on the Passions*; Coleridge's *Remorse* (Drury Lane, 1813), the most successful tragedy of the early nineteenth century; and the enormously popular Gothic tragic drama *Bertram; or, The Castle of St Aldobrand* (Drury Lane, 1816), by Charles Robert Maturin, which appalled Coleridge even as it thrilled audiences. In his *Shelley and Byron* (1976), Charles Robinson has tracked the ongoing process of debate and cross-inspiration that marked Byron's and Shelley's differing work in the drama. Shelley was keenly aware of experiments in the masque and the pastoral drama by his friends Leigh Hunt and Horace Smith. His readings of the European drama of the day brought him into contact with the Romantic classicism of Alfieri, the history plays of Schiller, and Goethe's *Faust*, with its encyclopaedic reworking of Western drama.

If the age, and particularly Byron, pitted a classicizing drama against that of the Elizabethan and Jacobean periods, Shelley finds inspiration in both. He takes up the form of Greek tragedy through an imitation of Aeschylus' *Persians* in his 'Lyrical Drama' *Hellas* and more complexly through a revision of Aeschylus' *Prometheus Bound* in *Prometheus Unbound*. He not only translated Euripides' *Cyclops*, the one complete surviving satyr play, but also showed a knowledge of the comedies of Aristophanes in his satirical *Swellfoot the Tyrant*, a punning reference to Sophocles' *Oedipus Tyrannus*. In *The Cenci* (finally performed by the Shelley Society in 1886) and the unfinished *Charles the First* (and perhaps in an abandoned play on Tasso), he draws on the tradition of the history play, with its roots in Shakespeare and with major efforts in the period by Schiller and Goethe and, on the London stage, by Coleridge in *Remorse*. Beyond his turn to Greek or Shakespearean tragedy, Shelley's engagement with Calderón, Tasso, and Goethe and his reading of A. W. Schlegel's *Lectures in Dramatic Art and Literature* indicate his involvement with what was known as

'Romantic' as opposed to ancient drama. He also turns in *Charles the First* (and in a different way in *Prometheus Unbound*) to the masque, a courtly form recently revived and revised by Leigh Hunt in his *Descent of Liberty*; draws on the four-act melodrama for the structure of his four-act *Prometheus Unbound*; and even dabbles in the popular harlequinade in *Swellfoot* and *Prometheus*. Shelley's dramatic work virtually reworks the history of the drama, from high tragedy to popular theatrical forms.

Stuart Curran has described *Prometheus Unbound* as adopting a 'transcendental form' or a 'composite' mode that moves beyond all generic limits.[4] We should extend his insight to all of Shelley's plays that continually experiment with both traditional forms and contemporary theatrical practice. Noting Shelley's tendency to create hybridized dramas that mix immediate issues with traditional forms, high art and low theatre, we might suggest that Shelley's work in drama – both one of the most prestigious of literary forms, at least in its tragic aspect, and one of the most popular of genres – represents the two-sided cultural project in which he, along with his friends in the circle around Leigh Hunt, engaged: remaking the cultural tradition and reconnecting with popular culture.

In the drama, Shelley sought cultural power – the ability to make new cultural objects and through them to renew the society that makes use of them – by restaging the past and by taking the stage in the present in order to shape the future. Shelley's goal is to liberate drama from what he sees as false models in order to remake tragedy and then to liberate us from tragedy itself in order to remake the world. Offering a tragedy of the entrapped self that is also a tragedy of closed form, he then draws on a wide range of theatrical forms in an attempt to imagine our liberation from the tyranny of the self and from the tyranny that the selfish exert over the world.

The tragedy of the self

Drama, and in particular tragedy, occupies a central place in Shelley's *Defence of Poetry*. Shelley sees contemporary tragedy as split between a moribund neoclassical drama and the moralistic melodrama:

> Tragedy becomes a cold imitation of the form of the great masterpieces of antiquity . . . or a weak attempt to teach certain doctrines, which the writer considers as moral truths; and which are usually no more than specious flatteries of some gross vice or weakness, with which the author, in common with his auditors, are infected. Hence what has been called the classical and domestic drama. Addison's 'Cato' is a specimen of the one; and would it were not superfluous to cite examples of the other! (Pr 285)

Believing that drama declines in periods of oppression, Shelley sees the drama of the *ancien régime* and of the post-Napoleonic restoration collapsing into formal imitation on the one hand and moral assertion on the other. Neoclassical tragedy strives continuously to reanimate the dead body of traditional dramatic form while the domestic drama or melodrama claims to offer a new tragic vision while merely staging clichéd morality. Both the form and the vision of the drama need to be reimagined. Thus, while Shelley draws upon the dramatic tradition, he does so not to recreate slavishly past forms but to experiment, claiming the 'license' of innovation he locates in the Greek tragic writers (Preface to *Prometheus Unbound*, P II.472). He also works 'to avoid the error of making them [his characters] actuated by my own conceptions of right or wrong, true or false'; 'There must be nothing attempted to make the exhibition subservient to what is vulgarly termed a moral purpose' (Preface to *The Cenci*, P II.731, 730).

Shelley believes that the power of the drama lies in its ability to impart 'self-knowledge':

> The tragedies of the Athenian poets are as mirrors in which the spectator beholds himself, under a thin disguise of circumstance, stript of all but that ideal perfection and energy which every one feels to be the internal type of all that he loves, admires, and would become . . . In a drama of the highest order there is little food for censure or hatred; it teaches rather self-knowledge and self-respect. Neither the eye nor the mind can see itself, unless reflected upon that which it resembles.
>
> (*Defence*, Pr 285)

While we may believe that the path to understanding the self lies in isolated contemplation or quiet communion with nature, Shelley insists it takes place within the noisy, fully social confines of the theatre, itself a microcosm of the larger social order. A turn inward – what Shelley in *The Cenci* calls 'self-anatomy' – can only reveal to us what the self is today, in all its limitations and failings. Only through the other, paradoxically, do we see ourselves as we should become, as the quotation above suggests: 'Neither the eye nor the mind can see itself, unless reflected upon that which it resembles.' In watching drama, we behold titanic heroes and villains, images of what we might become and what we should shun that evoke sympathy or antipathy from us ('The imagination is enlarged by a sympathy with pains and passions so mighty, that they distend in their conception the capacity of that by which they are conceived'; *Defence*, Pr 285). Experiencing such unknown modes of being, the spectator beholds in another 'the internal type of all that he loves, admires, and would become', that is a paradoxical ideal self that exists in the other and that includes everything the current self lacks. Thus, tragedy teaches 'self-knowledge and self-respect'. As Shelley puts it in the Preface to *The Cenci*, 'The highest moral purpose aimed at in the highest species of the drama, is the teaching the human heart, through its sympathies and antipathies, the knowledge of itself' (*P* II.730).

Such self-knowledge, however, exists for the spectators and not necessarily for the characters. The characters in *The Cenci*, Mahmud in *Hellas*, Charles I, and even initially Prometheus are all trapped in false conceptions of themselves. This entrapment in 'self-anatomy' is clearest in *The Cenci*, and Count Cenci most fully embraces what Shelley terms in the *Defence* the 'principle of Self', which Shelley will explore as the ground not only of a self-destructive mode of consciousness but also of tyrannical social and political structures. Orsino, a priest who is a kind of Cenci-in-training, reveals that Cenci's entire family revels in 'self-anatomy':

> 'tis a trick of this same family
> To analyse their own and other minds.
> Such self-anatomy shall teach the will
> Dangerous secrets: for it tempts our powers,
> Knowing what must be thought, and may be done,
> Into the depth of darkest purposes.   (2.2.108–13)

Shelley links the turn to the self with a loss of true self-knowledge and self-control. The disinterested intellect would seem to offer through an anatomy of one's interior life the best path to a total comprehension and control of human nature, but this very 'freedom' from interest is won through a severing of ties with the surrounding world. Orsino suggests that this isolated intellect, murdering its links to others in order to dissect the self, ends up under the power of our deepest fears and desires, the 'dangerous secrets' within. In the end, the intellect is not free but compelled, 'Knowing what must be thought, and may be done'. As Orsino says of himself after Beatrice's penetrating gaze has revealed to him his own dangerous secrets, she 'made me shrink from what I cannot shun' (2.2.116); so Cenci and Orsino 'fell into the pit' (2.2.114). To combat this fall into a hellish monologue with one's own internal devils, one must turn to dialogue, to dramatic exchange. As Beatrice says after one of her father's assaults threatens to hurl her into the pit of a self-consuming insanity, 'You see I am not mad; I speak to you' (2.1.34).

Vicious oppression marks the world created out of such 'self-anatomy', and Shelley's plays explore societies in which the masters and commanders of the anatomizing intellect wield tyrannical political and social power. *Charles the First* treats one of the more disastrous instances of governmental oppression in English history, when the king sought an absolute and even divine authority in opposition to Parliament while Archbishop Laud and the Church aimed to stamp out religious freedom. *Hellas* depicts the Turkish suppression of Greek liberty. Shelley's *Oedipus Tyrannus* is named for its tyrant, Swellfoot, his portrait of George IV. Jupiter in *Prometheus Unbound* is a summary mythological figure of all historical tyranny.

The Cenci, fully involved with self-anatomy, displays historical tyranny in all its oppressive force. The world of the play, drawn not only from historical sources but from the rich history of representing 'Machiavellian' Italy on the British stage, is tightly ruled by the patriarchal triumvirate of Count Cenci as father and lord, the Pope as the holy father of the Church intent upon repressing all personal and public revolt, and the Blakean Nobodaddy they worship as God the Father. Shelley reveals interlocking sets of oppression, as the personal and familial tyranny of Cenci is supported by the social tyranny of a hierarchical social and religious system and has as its ideological mask a religion waged against the downtrodden and particularly against women in the name of the Father.

The play pivots on its most horrible act of oppression: Cenci's incestuous rape of Beatrice through which he hopes to subjugate the one person capable of opposing him, to subdue Beatrice's will to his own (4.1.6–12), finally to make her into a replica of his own self (4.1.85–8). Most commentators have found Count Cenci victorious as Beatrice falls into violence and her father's mode of religious self-justification. However, Cenci himself has to admit that 'I must give up the greater point, which was / To poison and corrupt her soul' (4.1.44–5). Shortly after a nightmare vision of an eternity ruled by an evil patriarch, where 'all things then should be—my father's spirit' (5.4.60), Beatrice proclaims, ''Tis past! / Whatever comes, my heart shall sink no more' (5.4.77–8). She then pits against a masculinist eternity a maternal realm of peaceful death, 'Like a fond mother' (5.4.117). As she exits to be executed, she and her mother bind up each other's hair in a final act of female bonding set against the masculine bondage of her father's world.

In her final moments of life, Beatrice gestures towards a feminine response to patriarchal violence, to a human community set against the hierarchical universe offered by traditional church and state, but it is only a gesture: there is no way within her world for her to act in concert with her ideals. Finally, she is caught in her historical moment, one defined by patriarchal power and the rhetoric and ideology of Catholicism; she does not live in the time of Mary Wollstonecraft or Mary Wollstonecraft Godwin Shelley. For Percy Shelley, the past is the arena of destiny, of fixity, of entrapment: history 'must be' what it has been. Thus, history is for him the proper realm of the tragic in a secularized world that can no longer draw upon collective myths: Beatrice Cenci, as a historical figure, must make the mistakes she makes, so that her history can carry the force of mythological fate. As Shelley says of her in the Preface to his play, 'Beatrice Cenci appears to have been one of those rare persons in whom energy and gentleness dwell together without destroying one another'; however, 'The crimes and miseries in which she was an actor and a sufferer are as the mask and the mantle in which circumstances clothed her for her impersonation on the scene of the world' (P II.735). Beatrice's entrapment within the ideology of her time and place is made clearer by a parallel passage in the *Defence of Poetry* where Shelley writes of a poet's commitment to the false doctrines of the day: 'The distorted notions of invisible things which Dante and his rival Milton have idealized are the mask and the mantle in which these great poets walk through eternity enveloped and disguised' (Pr 289–90). Beatrice's tragedy is exactly historical in that it occurs because she has a historically limited view of her world; she remains enclosed within the Catholic world vision she shares with her father and thus cannot become a true force for liberation, though she does try to become an emblem for possible liberation in her final moments with her family and particularly in asking Bernardo to keep alive her version of history, a myth of her innocence. Still, if we were left with the world of *The Cenci*, we would be presented with a tragic vision in which we are all trapped by the limits of our own ideology, our own historical horizon. The present, and the future, would forever be limited by the past.

Staging the past, imagining the future

One way of understanding Shelley's staging of the struggle between past and future, between tyranny and liberation, is to see him working out of the tradition of tyrant and martyr plays that Walter Benjamin has identified as comprising the distinctively early modern form of tragic drama – *Trauerspiel* or 'sorrow play' as distinct from Greek tragedy.[5] Benjamin works with seventeenth-century plays but keeps an eye on Romantic drama. He argues, not unlike Romantic commentators such as A. W. Schlegel, that there is a break between classical tragedy and modern 'sorrow plays'. Greek tragedy dramatizes the struggle between a great hero who expands our sense of human power and an external force located in the gods or fate which indicates that there is an extra-human order that extends beyond and limits man's power. Oedipus, the man who solved the riddle of the Sphinx, steps forth at the beginning of Sophocles' play as a self-made man who has risen to power not through hereditary succession but through the force of his intellect. While he has lived as if to prove that man could escape fate – the prophecy that he would kill his father and marry his mother – and defeat the monstrous realm that lies beyond the human, the play demonstrates that the gods finally order the world, even if that order makes no sense from a human perspective and thus might seem monstrous. Both the power of Oedipus' heroism and the inscrutable will of the gods point to a world ordered beyond our comprehension, the transcendent realm that Benjamin sees as the goal of Greek tragedy. And in *Oedipus at Colonus*, with the deification of Oedipus, we are provided with a glimpse of a unification of the heroically human and the divine order in a transcendent realm beyond the world of the stage.

For Benjamin, the *Trauerspiel* depicts not a superhuman hero but the all-too-human tyrant/martyr, and this monarch figure does not battle the gods but the chaos of history; the goal of the monarch is not a transcendent realm beyond the world of the play but instead a perfected rule that would structure the historical moment of the play as a 'golden age of peace and culture, free of any apocalyptic features' (80). Where the Oedipus trilogy or the *Oresteia* end with the discovery of an order that transcends that found at the beginning of the tragic cycle, Benjamin's 'sorrow plays' close upon a stark contrast between the fallen and fully material (and filled with things) world of history in which we are trapped and a perfected because perfectly empty eternal realm that does not fulfil our world but finally indicts it. Life is merely a dream, as we learn in Calderón's play. There is a gap between the eternal order glimpsed by Hamlet at the end of his play, where 'There's special providence in the fall of a sparrow' (5.2.219–20), and the earthly world, filled with dead bodies, where the fall of the king ushers in not providential order but the limited, fallen rule of Fortinbras. Greek tragedy celebrates the greater world to be discovered in the struggle between the human and the divine; sorrow plays mourn our immanent world that can never attain to the glories of the eternal.

In seeking to revisit the entire tragic tradition from tragedy to *Trauerspiel* and in trying to move beyond it, Shelley draws upon tyrant and martyr plays to place them within a composite or hybridized form that ultimately suggests the limits to the vision of these precursors. He sees the 'sorrow play' as the distinctively early modern form of tragic drama, so that his two plays set in this period – *The Cenci* and *Charles the First* – draw directly upon the patterns of the *Trauerspiel*. He historicizes this mode of history play by suggesting that it is a uniquely appropriate form through which to represent the particular historical moment that saw its birth. Herbert Lindenberger establishes how much such tyrant and martyr plays owed to the world view of the seventeenth century: tyrant plays 'flourished in periods such as the

Renaissance and the seventeenth century, in which a providential view of history could be taken seriously and the imagination could easily conceive that the awesome power in the newly centralized state might be exercised illegitimately'.[6] Shelley sought to expose this stark absolutism in government and religion, and the immanent, trapped world of the *Trauerspiel* provided the perfect form in which to set forth his account of the rise and fall of the tyrant in *Charles the First* and of Beatrice's martyrdom to historical limits.

As Shelley moves out from this period to tackle his own moment in *Hellas* or the visionary moment of *Prometheus Unbound*, he returns to Greek tragedy as a model to open up the sorrow play's formal limits and to move beyond its vision. This turn to a classical model enables him to break out of the sorrow play's vision of entrapment in history, invoked so vividly in *The Cenci*, to stage a kind of secular apocalypse in which we neither transcend human material life, as Benjamin argues occurs in Greek tragedy, nor confront an absolute gap between immanent historical fact and eternal ideal, as in the *Trauerspiel*, but instead discover the ideal in history, find the order we long for not in a realm after or beyond human life but in its historical fulfilment. What Shelley does is to combine mythic tragedy and historical sorrow play to create a myth of history in which time's unfolding will enable us to create a heaven on earth. While this full vision is offered only in *Prometheus Unbound*, even his most time-trapped play, *The Cenci*, offers a glimpse of imaginative freedom, as we have seen.

Liberatory drama

Shelley creates a range of dramas that imagine a movement out of a closed past, which at first seems to hold the present in the grasp of its dead hand, towards a liberated future. He stages tyranny in all its oppressive power yet enacts possible stands against it. In *Hellas*, he explores the ways in which tyranny is self-defeating, as if *The Cenci* resolved not through Beatrice's act of parricide but instead through Cenci's overreaching that, ironically, does finally bring an order for his arrest through the papal legate Savella at the very moment of his murder. The unfinished *Charles the First* might also have depicted the tyrant's self-destruction, or it might have focused on those standing against Charles, as *Swellfoot the Tyrant* depicts those who rise up against George IV. It is as if Beatrice organized a revolt rather than enacted private revenge. Finally, *Prometheus Unbound* offers a myth of a visionary breakthrough from the past. This play reworks the brief glimpses of the ideal afforded Beatrice in the final act of *The Cenci*, such that they appear prior to the traumatic encounter with the tyrant-father, and have the power to transform self and world. In order to envision this bridge to the future, Shelley will also need to offer a dramatic form capable of providing a vision wider than tragedy itself.

In *Hellas*, Shelley portrays the tyrant Mahmud's own tortured recognition that he must fall. Troubled by portentous dreams that signal his status as a Benjaminian tyrant/martyr, Mahmud provides an image of the miseries and splendours of being a monarch: 'Kings are like stars—they rise and set, they have / The worship of the world but no repose' (195–6; N). Mahmud begins to see that the efforts the Turks must expend to defeat the forces of liberation, even a victory such as the Battle of Bucharest (361–452), will lead to their own destruction: 'What were Defeat when Victory must appal? / Or Danger when Security looks pale?' (359–60). As Shelley displays what he calls his 'newspaper erudition', Mahmud hears of the defeat of his fleet and of a gathering number of rebel victories, including one led by a servant of Lord Byron, 'a western poet chief' (363). Facing a difficult present, Mahmud remains so trapped in the past that when Ahasuerus calls upon him to look to the future, Mahmud instead asks to revisit history, in particular to see the Phantom of his great ancestor, Mahomet the Second. As the Phantom appears to announce that all empires must fall and to predict the hour of Mahmud's defeat, a voice without proclaims that the Turks have reversed their losses to claim victory over the Greeks. Mahmud, now a martyr to historical change, can take no comfort in this victory, for he recognizes that he rules not over a timeless empire but for a historical moment:

> Come what may,
> The Future must become the Past, and I
> As they were to whom once this present hour,
> This gloomy crag of Time to which I cling,
> Seemed an Elysian isle of peace and joy.   (923–7)

He exits to quell the victory celebration.

A seemingly anomalous figure who in fact carries much of the play's message, Ahasuerus the Wandering Jew introduces an almost Gothic element into this classicizing play. Unlike the Phantom of Mahomet who has a prototype in the Ghost of Darius in *The Persians* (and who also recalls the Phantom of Jupiter in Shelley's *Prometheus Unbound*), Ahasuerus has no parallel in Aeschylus' play, his presence indicating the hybrid nature of Shelley's dramatic work. The play's experimental dramaturgy – along with its eclectic evocation of religion (shared with Byron's *Manfred*) in which a Jewish figure from Christian legend enters a classicizing play about Islamic Turkey – would have been clearer had Shelley not discarded the play's

Prologue, which echoes the 'Prologue in Heaven' of Goethe's *Faust* (translated by Shelley for the *Liberal*) with its debate between the Lord and Mephisto. At an ambiguously monotheistic gathering of 'the sons of God' or 'The senate of the Gods' (1, 73; *H*), Christ, proclaiming himself a follower of Plato, speaks for Greek liberty against Satan who claims power over the earth and calls upon Famine, Pestilence, Superstition, War, Anarchy, and Tyranny to help thwart freedom (133–60). Christ rebukes him, noting that 'Thou seest but the Past in the To-Come' (162). Satan, like Mahmud, cannot imagine a future that breaks free of historical tyranny. As the prophet Mahomet draws attention to the current struggle between Islamic Turk and Christian Greek, we might have witnessed a Goethean wager between Christ and Satan about the ultimate success of freedom's eternal striving had Shelley completed the Prologue.

Shelley returns to this syncretistic evocation of religion at the play's close. With the victory of freedom, 'Saturn and Love', the deities of the classical golden age, 'their long repose / Shall burst, more bright and good / Than all who fell, than One who rose, / Than many unsubdued' (1090–3). In a note, Shelley identifies these various religions as the paganism that fell with the rise of Christianity, Christianity itself, and the continuing religions of China, India, and native America. Seeming to recall both Milton's 'Nativity Ode' and Keats's 'Ode to Psyche', Shelley here historicizes religion, the search for transcendence, itself. This sceptical, even secularizing, use of religion is an important context for the appearance of Ahasuerus.

With his talk of 'the One, / The unborn and the undying' (768–9) and his claim that all that 'have been, are, or cease to be, / Is but a vision' (778–9), Ahasuerus has been read as directing us towards an ideal, transcendent world; Shelley has been seen as embracing an idealized Hellas that exists somewhere beyond this world of the oppressor and the oppressed. This transcendental turn would seem odd enough in a play based on 'newspaper erudition', but it also misreads what Ahasuerus has to say. Ahasuerus contrasts the One with material reality, prompting Mahmud to complain that his words 'cast on all things, surest, brightest, best, / Doubt, insecurity, astonishment' (790–1), which brings forth a rebuke from Ahasuerus:

> Mistake me not! All is contained in each.
> Dodona's forest to an acorn's cup
> Is that which has been, or will be, to that
> Which is—the absent to the present. Thought
> Alone, and its quick elements, Will, Passion,
> Reason, Imagination, cannot die;
> They are, what that which they regard, appears,
> The stuff whence mutability can weave

All that it hath dominion o'er, worlds, worms,
Empires and superstitions—what has thought
To do with time or place or circumstance?
Would'st thou behold the future?—ask and have!   (792–803)

Ahasuerus argues that the world of material things – both natural ('worlds, worms') and man-made ('Empires and superstitions', that is states and churches) – come and go, rise and fall. From the perspective of the One, from the position of an ideal observer able to see all of human history, these things are ephemeral – not dematerialized, not unimportant (Ahasuerus claims that he cares for even 'the worm beneath thy feet' (762)), but passing parts of a larger whole. Just as Dodona's forest arises in a way that fulfils rather than destroys the acorn cup, so is each historical moment both vital in itself and yet only a moment in the long dialectical process of history, with each new moment containing while surpassing the past. What remains constantly available as history unfolds is thought, the ideas, the ideals, the words that humanity creates in its attempt to understand the flow of history. While specific human institutions must pass, just as individual beings are born and die, the ideals that inspire free men and women – in this work, specifically the ideals created by ancient Greece – remain:

But Greece and her foundations are
Built below the tide of war,
Based on the chrystalline sea
Of thought and its eternity.   (696–9)

The mistake humanity always makes is to assume that the specific order of things that is now in power must always be. When we assume that we have found the final embodiment of the ideal, when we become convinced that we have the truth ('One God, one King, one hope, one law', as Hassan puts it (333)) and that we therefore have the right and even the duty to impose that truth on everyone else, as the followers of Islam in this play believe they must, then we fall prey to tyranny. While the forces of oppression have won for the moment at the play's close, Shelley, calling upon the precedents of Isaiah and Virgil, uses the final chorus to predict freedom's triumph in the future: as 'The world's great age begins anew', a new historical cycle will commence in which 'A brighter Hellas rears its mountains / From waves serener far' (1060, 1066–7):

Another Athens shall arise,
And to remoter time
Bequeath, like sunset to the skies,
The splendour of its prime.   (1084–7)

While Shelley is making a practical plea – that England and the rest of Christian Europe aid the Greeks to overthrow the Turks – he does so not in the name of Greek nationalism, or Christianity, or even some particular model of democratic government but in the cause of a probably unending historical struggle of constant reform in which we repeatedly find our actual institutions wanting in the face of the ideals of freedom set forth by philosophers and poets. A free Greece will be a wonderful thing; it will not be the millennium. Nor, as Demogorgon reminds us at the end of *Prometheus Unbound*, is there any millennium, if by that we mean an end of history; there is instead the possibility of constantly creating a more perfect social union that will fall into imperfection, even into tyranny, the moment we believe we have found an ideal state rather than perpetual reform.

If *Hellas* stages the momentary victory of tyranny even as it imagines a liberated future, *Charles the First* engages the moment when tyranny crosses the line from self-defence to self-destruction. Charles was for many a martyr. Gryphius wrote a Benjaminian martyr play entitled *Carolus Stuardus*. Salmasius's *Royal Defence for Charles I* carries the legend 'Carolus Martyr' on its frontispiece. Shelley works to replace Charles as martyr with those martyred by him in the inexorable march towards the Civil War. Charles is backed by the 'apostate Strafford', who follows 'aphorisms / From Machiavel' (1.1.54–6; *H*), and Laud, the archbishop of Canterbury – 'Rather say the Pope', exclaims the disgusted Second Citizen: 'he walks / As if he trod upon the heads of men' (1.1.58–60). Faced with a Parliament that contests his absolutist rule, a Scottish rejection of the Anglicanism promulgated by Laud, and a general resistance to taxes, Charles, a self-conscious absolutist who believes that 'a king bears the office of a God' (1.2.10), finds himself compelled to pursue policies that will only promote further discontent, as he is forced to call into session the very Parliament that has threatened his control. When a group of dissidents – Cromwell, Pym, Hampden, and Vane – seek to emigrate to North America, Charles has them stopped simply to demonstrate his power over them. His own actions are leading inevitably to his defeat by these very dissidents.

Had he finished the play, Shelley might have moved beyond Charles's downfall and execution as a tyrant to depict the resistance offered by such figures as Hampden, a hero for reformers in Shelley's time, who is often cited in Hunt's *Examiner* and for whom Major Cartwright named his reformist Hampden Clubs. Hampden expresses the desire to leave 'this wide prison, England' in order to explore the 'floating Edens' of the new world, 'Where Power's poor dupes and victims yet have never / Propitiated the savage fear of kings' (1.4.49, 23, 26–7). The fool Archy jokes that Hampden and his fellows seek 'to found / A commonwealth like Gonzalo's in the play, / Gynaecocoenic and pantisocratic' (1.2.362–4). While Archy refers to Shakespeare's *Tempest*, Shelley includes an anachronistic reference to utopian dreams in his day, both his own interest in the female-dominated society of the Nairs and Coleridge's and Southey's vision of creating an ideal pantisocratic community on the banks of the Susquehanna.[7] With his notes on the play indicating that he intended to set forth the 'Reasons of Hampden & his colleag[u]es for resistance', Shelley might have found within the opposition to Charles the adumbrations of movements to reform politics, society, and culture in his own day. These hints of revolt were given fuller exposition in the popular resistance found in *Swellfoot the Tyrant*.

To depict in *Oedipus Tyrannus; or, Swellfoot the Tyrant* a more recent despot, the ruling monarch George IV, Shelley turns away from early modern *Trauerspiel* both to ancient tragedy via a burlesque of Sophocles' *Oedipus* and to the contemporary stage, particularly the pantomime. Shelley again displays his 'newspaper erudition', not only drawing upon a long tradition within the radical press of transvaluing Burke's characterization of the people as the 'swinish multitude' but also evoking the political battle that emerged over George's attempt to divorce his long-estranged wife, Caroline, even though Shelley had his doubts about the political circus that was played out around Caroline: those who opposed the government rallied round her despite the fact that she was a dubious figurehead for reform.[8]

George IV, here Swellfoot the Tyrant, rules over Thebes/England, a land marked in the present by poverty and oppression but that in the past, as 'old annals tell' (1.1.42; *H*), was a prosperous, peaceful land where the people lived in harmony with their rulers. As in all his plays, Shelley's tyrant figure is given a clear ideology, with Swellfoot espousing in his worship of Famine a Malthusian vision in which 'Starvation, typhus-fever, war, [and] prison' are all welcome checks on population growth (1.1.76). In Swellfoot's Thebes, any demand that traditional rights be respected is considered 'sedition, and rank blasphemy!' (1.1.67). Despite high taxes, revenues have fallen, so Swellfoot's government introduces paper money, an adulteration of the currency that Shelley protested against in his unpublished *Philosophical View of Reform*. With unrest growing, the general Laoctonos, usually identified with Wellington, victorious at Waterloo, describes an attack upon the populace that might recall the charge on a peaceful reform meeting known as the Peterloo Massacre. Tyranny seems all-powerful; it appears to have an answer to every move against it, as Mammon proclaims, 'Do the troops mutiny? decimate some regiments; / Does money fail?—come to my mint—coin paper' (1.1.103–4).

However, the homecoming of Iona Taurina, Swellfoot's queen, threatens this oppressive rule in appearing to fulfil a prophecy that her return will bring either reform or civil war (1.1.113–16). To protect themselves from this threat, Mammon and his fellow ministers have sought to keep Iona away from Thebes through the offices of the Leech, the Gadfly, and the Rat, apparently representing various attempts to sully Queen Caroline's name. Iona can appear as a martyr here, particularly when she is linked to the wandering Io (1.1.153) from *Prometheus Bound*.[9] When the ministers' strategy fails, they agree to stage a show trial, supposedly to allow the Queen to demonstrate her innocence but actually to expose her to the poisonous contents of the Green Bag (a lawyer's bag in which the government claimed to keep its secret evidence against Caroline) which they believe will scar her and thus prove to the people that she is marked with sin.

However, even this subtler form of tyranny through the massaging of public opinion is doomed. Iona, preparing for her trial, proclaims, 'I, most content of all, / Know that my foes even thus prepare their fall!' (2.1.190–1). The government's monetary practices have undermined its economic power. Its use of the military against its own people has turned the army to the popular side (1.1.324–40). Famine, a key tool of Swellfoot's oppression, provides a ground for revolt. The trial miscarries, as the poisonous Green Bag is seized by Iona and emptied on Swellfoot and his ministers who are transformed into 'filthy and ugly animals' (2.2 stage direction). The altar of famine is transformed as Famine is replaced by the Minotaur and the swine eating loaves on the altar become bulls. The play celebrates a carnivalesque world in which the 'swinish multitude' is transformed into an active populace of John Bulls ready to overthrow tyranny. Where in *Hellas* it is the tyrant who changes, as he comes to understand himself as a martyr to history, in *Swellfoot* it is the people who are transformed into an active force for liberty. The one concern, expressed by the figure of Liberty before the play's denouement, is how much violence will be necessary to overcome the powerful forces of wrong.

While the threat of new violence does appear real at the drama's close, with Iona mounting the Minotaur to hunt down Swellfoot and his ministers, Shelley works a more playful overthrow by transforming the story of Swellfoot from Greek tragedy to more popular theatrical forms. The title page already suggests Shelley's mischievous attitude towards formal distinctions, as he calls his play a tragedy 'In Two Acts', a generic oxymoron on the British stage where a tragedy always had five acts, unless it was a piece such as Fielding's earlier burlesque of the tragic tradition, *The Tragedy of Tragedies; Or The Life and Death of Tom Thumb the Great* (Haymarket, 1731). The advertisement maintains the joke of the play's connection with Greek prototypes: it contends that Shelley's play is a direct translation (with the exception of a dropped 'seditious and blasphemous Chorus of the Pigs and Bulls') of its Greek original; we also hear of the other plays in the supposed Swellfoot trilogy and learn that 'Swellfoot' is the correct translation of Oedipus. Shelley's play does open as does Sophocles': the people of Thebes are gathered as supplicants because the city suffers disaster – the plague in Sophocles' play, famine here – and Oedipus/Swellfoot steps forth to speak to them. We leave the world of great tragedy rapidly behind, however, to enter a hybridized textual space where Jewish figures mix with Greek, where there is an Arch-Priest and a Council of Wizards, where allusions to Greek tragedy and to the Bible are mixed with characters such as the Gadfly and the Leech who seem to come from the political satires of William Hone. Shelley burlesques his precursor play, in the Chorus of the Swinish Multitude, for example, and while critics have noted the learned humour he deploys, the burlesque was a popular stage form, with audiences able to hear line-by-line parodies of *Hamlet*. *Swellfoot* at its close also echoes the Christmas harlequinade, the most popular stage form of the day, known for its unmaskings (here the transformation of the ministers into beasts and the swinish multitude into forceful John Bulls) and for the spectacular transformations of objects when struck by Harlequin's bat or sword (here the transmutation of bones into bread as Famine's temple becomes the Minotaur's throne). While this may all seem unsuitable for the stage, Shelley could have found models for such theatrical moments in a play such as Colman the Younger's wildly successful *Blue-Beard* (Drury Lane, 1798), with its transformation of the Blue Chamber into a chamber of blood, complete with enthroned skeleton. Just as the play uncovers the popular power necessary to overthrow tyranny, so it unleashes the energies of popular theatrical culture from the confines of the high cultural form of five-act tragedy, a project Shelley would continue in his four-act reworking of Aeschylus' *Prometheus Bound*.

Prometheus Unbound and Shelleyan theatre

Prometheus Unbound, Shelley's most audacious dramatic experiment, offers a carnival of theatrical forms as he imagines universal liberation. Offering a summary vision of Shelley's drama of tyranny and liberation, it can also help us begin to understand what a Shelleyan theatre might look like.

Shelley stages another struggle between tyrant and martyr, with Jupiter offering a mythic image of all the historical oppression suffered by humanity (3.4.164–7, 180–3). Embracing as his ideology a demonic parody of the Christian virtues of faith, hope, and charity, Jupiter rules through 'fear and self-contempt and barren hope' (1.8). Uniting the patriarchal cruelty of a Cenci with the punishing policies of a Swellfoot and the opposition to all innovation that marks Charles I, he lacks Mahmud's sense of insight or inner growth. Standing against him is Prometheus, who in the first act undergoes a martyr's spiritual growth through which he comes to understand that his past violent opposition to Jupiter has only strengthened his oppressor. Jupiter, a projection of man's fears and crimes, rules because humanity either cowers before him or adopts his own brand of violence as the only form of resistance. When the Phantasm of Jupiter appears to repeat the curse Prometheus has laid upon Jupiter, Prometheus, unlike Mahmud, turns from the violent past to embrace a future founded upon forgiveness and passive resistance. Prometheus' beloved, Asia, also undergoes a process of growth in the second act, where she learns lessons similar to those offered by Ahasuerus in *Hellas*; she comes to understand that 'the deep truth is imageless' (2.4.116), that the ideal order of things exists outside human expression and that all claims, particularly those made by religions, to have the final truth are false because partial.

As in a Benjaminian tyrant/martyr play, at the moment of apparent triumph, Jupiter falls. Shelley offers an almost comic image of the oppressor who crumples the minute people cease to fear him. Confronted by Demogorgon, Jupiter blusters, then collapses: 'Detested prodigy! / Even thus beneath the deep Titanian prisons / I trample thee! thou lingerest? Mercy, mercy!' (3.1.61–3). The rest of the play works out the consequences of this universal moment of liberation, with Demogorgon reminding us at the play's close that even such a moment is not the end of history but a temporary victory in man's struggle to make a heaven on earth (4.562–78).

Shelley's Preface to the play indicates how he saw his drama as re-envisioning Aeschylus' *Prometheus Bound*, and *Prometheus Unbound* reworks not only that play but the tragic tradition as a whole. The first act of Shelley's play does resemble Aeschylus', with the bound Prometheus engaging in a dialogue with various characters, including Oceanus in Aeschylus and Earth in Shelley, who offer timid council, and Zeus's messenger (Hermes in Aeschylus; Mercury in Shelley), and with speeches mixing with choral passages, the Oceanides being present in both plays; the wandering Asia, only invoked in this act, might recall the roving Io of Aeschylus' tragedy. Shelley's play rapidly leaves this tragic form behind, however, as the second act offers Asia's quest, as the third act moves from Jupiter's court to the pastoral retreat of Prometheus and Asia, and as the fourth act stages a cosmic dance of celebration. The closed form of tragedy gives way to the open structure of the quest romance, man's entrapment in the destructive repetitions of tragedy is superseded by the peaceful eroticism of pastoral drama, and from the perspective of the fourth act the tragic world of Jupiter's rule appears as an antimasque to the masque-like dance of the play's conclusion. Five-act tragedy, usually conceived of as the highest form of drama, is contained within Shelley's medley of forms in which the liberatory rhythms of the masque and even the harlequinade finally structure this four-act play. Tragedy does not offer, nor does any other single form, the 'deep truth'; just as in his lyrics Shelley offers image after image, each partial fragments of an impossible artistic whole capable of bodying forth eternity, so does he deploy a full range of dramatic forms.

This playful, revisionary stance towards the tragic tradition is finally the hallmark of Shelley's drama and of a dramaturgy capable of staging his plays. The stage of Shelley's day – with its cavernous theatres, its star actors, and its dependence upon music, sets, and special effects – has usually been dismissed as catering to low popular tastes, but it was an extremely exciting cultural site, marked by innovations in acting, lighting, and staging. This was the era of great actors such as Sarah Siddons and Edmund Kean, of brilliant stage designers such as Loutherbourg and Capon, of the introduction of gas lighting and the vampire trap, which allowed for sudden appearances and disappearances on stage. The multiple bill offered at London theatres enabled patrons to see more than one play a night, as tragedies were followed by comedies, farces, and harlequinades, and five-act comedies by melodramas and operatic romances; these theatres offered the same encyclopaedic array of theatrical types as Shelley's dramatic corpus.

Shelley knew a great deal about this theatre and about dramatic tradition, but he draws upon the conventional to experiment, to play, to make it new. Shelley's subversion of theatrical conventions is perhaps clearest in *Swellfoot*, a rollicking burlesque that begins as learned parody of Sophocles and ends as pantomimic call to popular resistance. We can see it as well when Ahasuerus walks from some Gothic novel into the middle of the classicizing *Hellas*. Shelley uses theatrical conventions only to break free from them, and he works to liberate his plays with their 'composite forms' from any single dramatic structure, finally to suggest that 'life' escapes the confines of any particular form of drama. Shelley admired the Greeks' ability to combine poetry, music, dance, and stagecraft. He found Shakespeare's combination of tragedy and comedy even more powerful (*Defence*, Pr 284). His plays are also combinatory, offering less an 'organic' whole than a series of dramatic moments that suggest the limitations of any one form to contain the complexity of life – and such fragmentation of dramatic form is exactly what one found in the theatre of the day, as the public demanded that favourite speeches and songs be repeated, as actors emphasized key passages and points, as the audience interrupted what was happening on stage. When we hear of songs and even characters and scenes being moved from one play to another, when we realize that some people entered the theatre late, after having dined, with their servants holding their places, and that others came only after the third act of the first play so that they could pay half price, we begin to get a sense of how this was a theatre of moments, of parts not wholes. Shelley's *Prometheus Unbound* takes full advantage of this theatre of moments to move through various dramatic forms without insisting they all be subordinated to a single formal movement.

The kind of dramaturgy needed for Shelley's plays was revealed in the wonderfully inventive production of *Prometheus Unbound* by the Rude Mechanicals, with Madge Darlington as director, in Austin, Texas in April of 1998. In keeping with the play's grounding in Aeschylus, the first act was staged using the conventions associated with modern productions of Greek tragedy – a stark set, robes for costumes, a strong choral element. However, the production went on to adopt a different style for each subsequent scene. For example, Act 3 scene 4, in which we receive reports about the trans-formations following upon the fall of Jupiter, was staged as if the characters were actors in a radio show, reporting news 'from the front'; at scene's end, the Spirit of the Hour runs onstage, just in with breaking news, and delivers the speech in an almost mocking way until he is overcome by the glory of the moment (and of the language). Stretched out over the three days of the Easter weekend, the production 'sampled' contemporary stage tactics (including the use of video and film) much as Shelley drew upon the entire range of dramatic forms known to him.

Shelley sought through his plays to stage tyranny and to imagine the ways of liberating ourselves from oppression. His liberatory vision must finally also liberate art itself, to suggest a form of drama that lies beyond any particular genre, perhaps any particular theatre. A truly Shelleyan stage would reveal that any political, social, cultural, or artistic form can be tyrannical, that only a constant process of re-forming – or making, break-ing, and making again – can protect both society and art from those 'foul shapes . . . Which, under many a name and many a form . . . Were Jupiter' (*Prometheus Unbound* 3.4.180–3).[10]

NOTES

1. Shelley and his sister Elizabeth may have written a play that they sent to Charles Mathews; see *Hogg* I.14.
2. Shelley's theatregoing can be deduced from Mary Shelley's journals, as Curran has done; see Stuart Curran, *Shelley's 'Cenci': Scorpions Ringed with Fire* (Princeton: Princeton University Press, 1970), 158n.

3. Ronald Tetreault, 'Shelley at the Opera', *ELH* 48 (Spring 1981), 144–71, and Curran, *Shelley's 'Cenci'*, 178–80.

4. Stuart Curran, *Poetic Form and British Romanticism* (New York: Oxford University Press, 1986), 180–203.

5. Walter Benjamin, *The Origin of German Tragic Drama*, tr. John Osborne (London: NLB, 1977). Subsequent references are given parenthetically in the text.

6. Herbert Lindenberger, *Historical Drama: The Relation of Literature and Reality* (Chicago: University of Chicago Press, 1975), 41.

7. Hazlitt criticized Shelley's interest in the Nairs and his sexual politics in general in 'On Paradox and Common-Place', in *Table-Talk* (1821), in *The Complete Works of William Hazlitt*, ed. P. P. Howe, 21 vols. (London: J. M. Dent and Sons, 1931), VIII.148–50. See also Shelley's letter to Hunt, 25 January 1822, *L* II.382 and n.

8. Michael Scrivener, *Radical Shelley: The Philosophical Anarchism and Utopian Thought of Percy Bysshe Shelley* (Princeton: Princeton University Press, 1982), 262–3. Shelley may have drawn directly upon a piece in Hunt's *Examiner*, 'A New Catechism for the Use of the Natives of Hampshire: Necessary to be Had in All Sties', *Examiner*, 30 August 1818, 548–50; see the note in *IP* II.426–7.

9. Curran has suggested Io as a model for Beatrice Cenci as well; Stuart Curran, *Shelley's Annus Mirabilis* (San Marino, Calif.: Huntington Library, 1975), 130–4.

10. I have made some similar observations to those in the essay in a different context; see 'Romantic Tragic Drama and its Eighteenth-Century Precursors: Remaking British Tragedy', in Rebecca Bushnell, ed., *Companion to Tragedy* (Oxford: Blackwell, 2005), 411–34.

5

JACK DONOVAN

The storyteller

Narrative experimentation

How, my dear Mary, are you critic-bitten
   (For vipers kill, though dead) by some review,
That you condemn these verses I have written
   Because they tell no story, false or true?
                      (*The Witch of Atlas*, 1–4; N)

When he addressed these lines to his wife Mary in August 1820 in the dedication to *The Witch of Atlas*, Shelley's tongue was firmly in his cheek. Not only does the poem tell a story, it transforms a range of mythic motifs into a brilliantly playful fantasy on creative power and the life of the imagination so as to reflect on the art of storytelling itself. But the *Witch* is addressed to a cultivated literary intelligence, and Shelley knew that the close and informed attention it calls for not all readers would be willing or able to give. So his lines aim to disarm in advance the disappointment of those in search of what in the subtitle he calls 'human interest', embodied in a tale that plainly declares itself as either fiction or fact; such, he archly suggests, are the critics of the reviewing periodicals who up till then had mostly delivered disapproving or outraged opinions on his verse – when they had bothered to notice it at all.

Despite the gentle teasing and the mock-serious tone, Shelley is here touching on an important feature of his own work: the narrative experimentation that marks every phase of his career. If we set aside for the moment his prose fiction and drama, and fix a lower limit – inevitably somewhat arbitrary – of about sixty lines, we can calculate that in a writing life of barely fourteen years he produced some forty poems in which developed narrative is the dominant organizing principle. These range from the 4,818 lines of the epic-romance *Laon and Cythna* (1817; revised as *The Revolt of Islam*, 1818) to the four rapidly moving fifteen-line stanzas of 'The Fugitives' (1821). His verse narratives make up a representative sample of the styles that defined the literary character of the age: from the humanitarian realism of 'A Tale of Society as It Is: From Facts' (1811) through the feminine–sentimental domestic tale of *Rosalind and Helen* (1819) to the variations on the ballad form in *The Devil's Walk* (1812) or *The Mask of Anarchy* (1819); from the symbolic fables 'Athanase' (1817) and 'The Sensitive-Plant' (1819) to the mythic rewriting that he undertook in 'Arethusa' (1820), for example, or *The Witch of Atlas* itself. *Peter Bell the Third* (1819) constructs a farcical version of a Romantic poet's career bristling with particularized contemporary satire. 'Ghasta; or the Avenging Demon' (1810) adopts the Gothic and 'Zeinab and Kathema' (1811) the oriental among fictional modes in current fashion; while 'The Retrospect: Cwm Elan, 1812' and *Epipsychidion* (1821) are early and late attempts to give narrative shape to his affective and artistic autobiography.

Shelley criticism has typically adopted the lyrical and the ethical–political as primary categories of critical investigation, thereby, however unintentionally, diminishing an important feature of his art – that he was 'impelled throughout his career to the poetry of story'.[1] The present chapter aims to set 'the poetry of story', verse narrative, in the foreground while extending this principal area of interest in two respects. It crosses the traditional generic boundaries that distinguish the narrative, dramatic, and lyric modes in order to consider the specific working of narrative in any one of them or across them all, and it develops an enlarged idea of its topic on an analogy with the notion that Shelley himself came to entertain of poetry as original imaginative composition whether in verse or in prose (*Pr* 280–1, 292–3). Accordingly, while principally concerned with narrative poems and with narrative in poetry, this overview also brings Shelley's prose fiction and prefaces, his letters, and his literary, political, and philosophical essays within its scope. The terms of this broader approach help to focus attention on what is distinctive in his narrative practice in relation to that of his contemporaries.

The work of those contemporaries defines an especially important context for Shelley's in this regard because his career as an author falls within a golden age of verse narrative in English. By the time Shelley began to write steadily towards the beginning of the second decade of the nineteenth century, Walter Scott had published three of his series of hugely successful verse romances – *The Lay of the Last Minstrel* (1805), *Marmion* (1808), and *The Lady of the Lake* (1810) – based in the military conflicts, customs, and manners of medieval and Renaissance Scotland and England. Thomas Campbell's immensely popular *Gertrude of Wyoming* (1809) had fictionalized a historical incident in which the treachery of war turns a domestic idyll to tragedy in a pastoral fantasy of America in the revolutionary period.

Romances of exotic and marvellous adventure, Robert Southey's *Thalaba the Destroyer* (1801) and *The Curse of Kehama* (1810) had elaborately worked the fields of Islamic and Hindu mythology. Shortly thereafter, the intriguing blend of travel, confession, and politics in Byron's 'romaunt' *Childe Harold's Pilgrimage I and II* (1812), followed by *The Giaour* and *The Bride of Abydos* (1813), and *The Corsair* (1814) – the so-called 'Turkish Tales' – would make him the successor to Scott as a prodigy of contemporary publishing, and establish the eastern Mediterranean as the fictional location par excellence of violent adventure and demonic introspection. Shelley was closely acquainted with these poems, which develop complex narratives through multiple episodes as well as providing quantities of information in footnotes and/or appendices to explain and illustrate the unfamiliar history, customs, and religions from which their stories were invented. Byron's and Scott's earned huge returns; Campbell's sold extremely well, Southey's less so. All were widely and seriously discussed – not always favourably – in the major critical periodicals. Some of the most astute and influential reviewers of the time recognized in the subjects of these tales – variously remote in time, place, or culture – in the literary innovations they introduced, and (for Scott and Byron especially) in the unparalleled success they obtained with readers a new dimension in modern literature, which they deemed, for better or worse, to be one of the defining features of the imagination and taste of the age.[2]

Romantic verse narrative on this scale – as a rule these poems were designed to fill a single volume – thus possessed great popular appeal and could earn both financial reward and critical esteem. They held up seductive examples to a young writer; and when in 1809 the eighteen-year-old Shelley first turned his hand to a narrative poem of length and ambition sufficient to occupy a slim volume on its own, he adopted as model Walter Scott, who was just then approaching the height of his extraordinary success. Scott's influence is evident right through the four cantos and 1,456 lines of Shelley's *The Wandering Jew*, in its easy octosyllabic metre and interpolated lyrics as well as in individual incidents, while the character types, Italian setting, and supernatural terrors of the poem conspicuously display their debt to recent Gothic fiction, a mode in which Shelley proved himself an adept in the two prose novellas or romances (as he called them) *Zastrozzi* and *St Irvyne*, which were published in the same year (1810).[3] In common with contemporary writers throughout Europe, Shelley was intrigued by the legendary figure of the Wandering Jew, doomed to remain alive in torment of soul until Judgement Day for having mocked Christ on the way to Calvary. As he inherited it, the tradition of the Wandering Jew combines two types of narrative having radically different cultural status: the Gospel account of

Christ's passion, held to be divinely revealed and so to convey sacred truth, and a body of stories about an afflicted vagabond deriving from folk-tale and popular literature. The heterogeneous union that results from mixing the two produces a series of dissonances and ambiguities – is the sinner a saint? the villain a hero? – which in Shelley's version serve a distinctly polemical end. He plainly intends his title-character's tortured history as a revision, its impact to be felt and its implications grasped only in relation to the sanctioned narrative of the incarnation of Christ in which the crucifixion stands as the supreme act of love that redeems humankind from the burden of original sin. Over against this central narrative of the Christian religion, which Shelley regarded in its institutional forms as a collusive support of political power in modern states, is to be set another that emphasizes the relentlessly inventive cruelty with which God punishes the Wandering Jew: he is, as the subtitle of the poem styles him, 'the Victim of the Eternal Avenger'.[4]

The Jew's story occupies the third of the poem's four cantos. The first two relate how, under the assumed identity of a young Italian, Paulo, he rescues the terrified Rosa from being forced to enter a religious order; the fourth how the young nobleman Victorio, sexually obsessed with Rosa, is duped by a witch into accepting from Satan what he believes is a love-philtre, which he administers to her with fatal consequences. The revelation of Paulo's identity and the account of his sin and punishment are elaborately prefaced by a scene that begins in the castle to which he has carried Rosa –

> Absorbed awhile in grief he stood;
> At length he seemed as one inspired,
> His burning fillet blazed with blood—
> A lambent flame his features fired.
> 'The hour is come, the fated hour;
> Whence is this new, this unfelt power?—
> Yes, I've a secret to unfold,
> And such a tale as ne'er was told,
> A dreadful, dreadful mystery!   (543–51)

The narrative then continues on the shore where the storm-lashed ocean rages in concert with his agitated soul and with the harrowing life-story he is about to relate.

The intensely dramatic nature of this scene of narration qualifies in important respects the fable that it introduces. The Jew cannot explain or control the agonizing compulsion to recount his life, nor can he divulge more than a small part of all that he knows (1007–11); the first condition

signals his affinity with the inspired prophets and sibyls of classical literature, the second his affinity with them as well as with such figures as
Shakespeare's ghost of Old Hamlet and the author of St John's Gospel,
whose authority is mysteriously enhanced by knowledge they cannot disclose.[5] Like the sin of Coleridge's Ancient Mariner, a character that deeply
impressed Shelley's imagination, the Jew's sacrilege and the unparalleled
punishment it attracts have endowed him with a unique insight (800–15)
from which proceed both the strangeness and the authenticity of what he
tells. Prodigious length of life and ceaseless wandering have made him a
repository of stories that can disconcert but also liberate the listener. His
dark narrative thread runs through history carrying the occult knowledge
that political power and religious orthodoxy need to suppress to ensure
their own survival. Hence his continuing attraction for Shelley who reintro-
duces the figure of the Wandering Jew, now given one of his traditional
names, Ahasuerus, in *Queen Mab* (1813), where he retells the biblical story
of creation–fall–redemption as the record of divine malice and crime rather
than divine love; and again in *Hellas* (1822) where, reflective and philosophical, he pronounces with the solemnity of an oracle on the folly of the
ruler's self-interest in seeking to know the future.

This first fully developed scene of narration in Shelley's verse offers a
natural point of departure for examining what will become important
features of his narrative practice. It functions as a prelude to a communication of hidden knowledge, which is explicitly recognized as being only
part of a larger whole that remains unexpressed, by a supernatural being
possessed of peculiar authority to listeners whose state of mind and
personal situation fit them peculiarly to hear it. Even so, there is resistance
to be overcome: such a revelation, having the power to alter fundamentally how the listeners understand their relation to the world, is painful
both to tell and to hear, the more so as it contradicts the familiar narratives that underpin their culture. A distinct erotic interest and the force of
natural sublimity in the physical environment joined to a strong but
ineffable compulsion to tell contribute further to a fascination designed
to bear down any reluctance to entertain what is alien and troubling. The
care with which Shelley puts in place these circumstances stresses the
importance he attaches to them as conditioning what is told as well as
endowing it with the energy and strangeness that enthral listeners. Apprehension, danger, resistance, struggle, sexual tension, and intense awareness
of surroundings are also the stock in trade of the Gothic fiction in which
Shelley was well read. The sublime landscapes, sexual obsession, implac-
able vengeance, and challenge to religious orthodoxy disposed in a narrative whose hidden logic is brought to light only as the true identity of an

ambiguously diabolical transgressor is disclosed – these are defining features of *The Wandering Jew* and of Shelley's prose romance *Zastrozzi* alike. In them, as well as in *St Irvyne*, he exploits these elements to work variations on the theme of revenge that he will re-explore in a varied succession of narratives in his major poetry – *Laon and Cythna, Rosalind and Helen, Prometheus Unbound,* and *The Cenci* are familiar examples, as is Mary Shelley's novel *Frankenstein*. Shelley first elaborated such narratives in the Gothic idiom, and their constituent characters and motifs, though often modified and recombined, nonetheless retain something of their original intensity when they reappear in his later verse.[6] The circumstances are typically those arresting ones that accompany our most decisive disclosures and discoveries; Shelley deploys them from *The Wandering Jew* forward in order to invest a critical challenge to authority with the shock and thrill of a secret discovered to those fictional characters, and the readers for whom they stand in place, who urgently require to hear it.

Radical history

'Who has known me of old', replied Earth,
'Or who has my story told?'

Shelley has Mother Earth ask this question, issue this challenge, in his elegiac ode 'Lines Written on Hearing the News of the Death of Napoleon' (1821; *H*), a small instance of a larger impulse in his work to tell the world's story as a response to contemporary history (17–18). Or retell it: the narrative impulse appears characteristically in his major poems as an urge to challenge and correct, to devise counter-narratives meant to be read against those accredited ones that serve to legitimize existing structures of power and privilege. *Queen Mab* (1813) and *Laon and Cythna* (1817), his two most substantial verse narratives, are of this kind. Both incorporate an overview of history from earliest times reaching to an imagined future, related by a supernatural being to a specially chosen individual. A scene presenting the occasion of narration and laying down its conditions introduces the vision. In each poem this is a recognizable variation on the paradigm established in *The Wandering Jew*, but altered to accommodate the greatly lengthened temporal perspectives and explicit political content of these more ambitious works.

Shelley wrote of *Queen Mab*: 'The Past, the Present, & the Future are the grand & comprehensive topics of this Poem' (*L* 1.324). The conspectus is elaborated in the text so as to enforce the perception that history and prophecy are equally generated by an urgent necessity to understand a present that is judged to be in crisis. In order to set our own epoch in a true narrative sequence, we learn, the longest perspectives on past and future need to be opened. Well and good. But given the difficulty of achieving consensus on what is happening now, how can one agree on what has happened or will happen in time remote from the present? What confidence, in other words, can we place in the scheme of history that the poem's narrator, queen of the fairies, announces as the true one? As if aware of this implicit challenge, Mab locates the source of her authority squarely in the human sphere:

> to me 'tis given
> The wonders of the human world to keep:
> The secrets of the immeasurable past,
> In the unfailing consciences of men,
> Those stern, unflattering chroniclers, I find:
> The future, from the causes which arise
> In each event, I gather.   (1.167–73)

So as accurately to comprehend the past, that field of scanty records and conflicting conjecture, the illumination of an upright conscience is called for; to imagine the future aright one must grasp the causes that link one event to another in an unbreakable chain. Mab communicates these assurances to the soul of the sleeping Ianthe who has been selected to receive the revelation because she possesses goodness, sincerity, and virtue to a degree unexampled in her age. Morality is thus joined to science and philosophy to track the chronicle of the world far enough backward, and project it far enough forward, to establish a sequence adequate to show the present as it is. In one sense, these extended vistas simply translate into imaginative vision the new time-perspectives opened up by the study of archaeology, geology, astronomy, comparative mythology, and comparative religion, which were central developments of the European Enlightenment of the seventeenth and eighteenth centuries. In another, such a greatly expanded theatre of history is necessary to gauge the profound import of the cataclysmic events in Europe since the beginning of the French Revolution, which mounted a practical challenge to the fundamental certainties and air of permanence that upheld existing political systems. The traditional civic and religious narratives that served as their support were, in consequence, forced to compete with others, like Mab's better adapted to current secular and libertarian ideals.

Mab's revelations are of this order and anything but the fairy-lore that might have been expected of a poem bearing her name as title. She gives voice to an enlightened contemporary intelligence in the service of radical political ends and directed at the sincere and principled conscience. The overall narrative movement of the poem, historical survey and frame considered together, enacts a process of education in which virtue is completed by reason and science. Shelley succinctly formulates its political object in *Proposals for an Association of Philanthropists*, the prose pamphlet he completed a few months earlier: 'knowledge is incompatible with slavery' (*Pr* 67). The emancipating instruction that is imparted in the poem takes two forms, an epitome of universal history and a dense apparatus of footnotes citing critical thinkers from the ancient Roman poet Lucretius through the French *philosophes* Holbach and Condorcet to Hume, Paine, and Godwin. The grand narrative of history that these authorities are called to witness and underwrite imagines a succession of civilizations over aeons of time, which are plotted on a geological scale. Their inevitable extinction and passage to oblivion, figured in their ruined monuments, are those of all political regimes in which despots seconded by parasites and priests have oppressed their subjects – an exemplum condensed to the length of a sonnet in Shelley's 'Ozymandias'. By contrast, the memory of virtuous action will never pass away because it is essentially aligned with the 'silent eloquence' of Nature, which speaks to those with ears to hear of 'Peace, harmony, and love' (*Queen Mab* 3. 196–7). The eventual triumph of virtue is also settled on a more reasoned foundation, the principle of perfectibility, according to which any improvement that can be imagined can eventually be achieved because of the innate human faculty for approaching ever closer to perfection. An image of such a future state is sketched in which humanity's capacity for conforming to the ideals inherent in Nature is realized, though without specifying the means for attaining this end. In the process religion is rendered obsolete, its promise of a transcendent reward for the righteous individual being replaced with the collective fulfilment and social wellbeing of the developing race: 'O happy Earth! reality of Heaven!' (9.1).

The wasting away of religious tyranny as nature evolves through time towards perfection offers a secular alternative to the biblical version of cosmic history from Creation, through the Fall and Redemption to the Second Coming, which religious orthodoxy held to be definitively revealed in Scripture.[7] Mab's story of human progress towards self-realization directed by virtue and free intellectual enquiry will become one of Shelley's master narratives, recognizable in a series of long poems from *Laon and Cythna* to *Prometheus Unbound*, *The Mask of Anarchy*, and *Hellas* as well as in the prose essays *A Philosophical View of Reform* and *A Defence of Poetry*. Recognizable, but not identical; Shelley's work never again exhibits Mab's assurance of inevitable advance towards a state of existence unequivocally good. The modifications that he introduces to accommodate generic, thematic, and stylistic differences over a career marked in an exceptional degree by self-conscious innovation and experiment, as well as by continued intellectual reappraisal, have the effect of relocating emphases, striking dissonant and ironic chords, raising new questions – all of which modify the capacity of the liberation-narrative to create significant order in the material offered by contemporary experience. To these examples should be added the various miniaturized, curtailed, or attenuated narratives of deliverance that Shelley embeds in lyrics such as 'Feelings of a Republican on the Fall of Bonaparte', *Lines Written among the Euganean Hills*, or 'Sonnet: To the Republic of Benevento'. These are instances not of simple repetition but of determined refashioning of the original story in continually altering textual conditions, a sustained attempt to realize its potential, question its validity, test its possibilities.

A stringent and comprehensive test of those possibilities is carried out in *Laon and Cythna* (1817). The representation of history in *Queen Mab* owes a debt to Enlightenment philosophical historians who plotted the course of human development over long ages and in broad cultural categories with the object of illustrating its fundamental laws. Such a bird's eye view, while it can construct a total narrative of great explanatory power, must also be able to incorporate particular recent events and characters into its general scheme if it is to have contemporary relevance. *Laon and Cythna*, Shelley's longest poem and his most ambitious effort in the narrative mode, boldly engages with the defining occurrence of recent history, the French Revolution, which he considered 'the master theme of the epoch in which we live', as well as with those characters best qualified to embody it. Not those who actually did so; refusing to bind itself to historical incidents and individuals, the poem adopts the visionary's licence to represent an ideal version of them – what might have happened as model for what ought to happen if the Revolution were ever to be re-enacted with permanent success. To this end Shelley shifts the scene of the action to modern Greece and Constantinople where a struggle for liberty is played out between the Greeks and their Ottoman rulers. The relocation to the birthplace of western democracy on the unstable fringe of a decidedly old-fashioned empire emphasizes the poem's exemplary status as an image of 'such a Revolution as might be supposed to take place in an European nation', as he wrote to a prospective publisher (*L* 1.504, 563). The full title introduces a dual point of view in which imaginative fiction builds a prophetic bridge between the past and the future: *Laon and Cythna; or, the Revolution of the Golden City: A Vision of the Nineteenth Century*. Readers are thus apprised that history will here be regarded as proleptic; the poem will look backwards as the necessary condition of looking forwards.

By the time the fictional revolutionary struggle begins, both the French Revolution and its hypothetical Greek reconstruction have already been recounted in brief and eminently partisan narratives in the Preface and Canto 1. These define the sympathetic perspectives, essentially those of Tom Paine and Mary Wollstonecraft, within which Shelley intends it to be received. A mythical perspective is then added. The point of departure of the disclosures to the narrator by a supernatural female messenger in Canto 1 is not the situation of contemporary Europe but the simultaneous birth of cosmic and human time.

> 'from the depth of ages old,
> Two Powers o'er mortal things dominion hold
> Ruling the world with a divided lot,
> Immortal, all-pervading, manifold,
> Twin Genii, equal Gods—when life and thought
> Sprang forth, they burst the womb of inessential Nought.

> 'The earliest dweller of the world alone,
> Stood on the verge of chaos: Lo! afar
> O'er the wide wild abyss two meteors shone,
> Sprung from the depth of its tempestuous jar:
> A blood-red Comet and the Morning Star
> Mingling their beams in combat—as he stood,
> All thoughts within his mind waged mutual war,
> In dreadful sympathy—when to the flood
> That fair Star fell, he turned and shed his brother's blood.' (346–60)

With this primal image of birth, struggle, and death commences what narrative theorists term the *fabula* (or story) of the poem: that is, the first of its events considered in their absolute chronological sequence as opposed to the first event to occur in the textual order (or narrative discourse), which is the narrator's moment of post-revolutionary despair with which the poem opens. Providing a tantalizing glimpse (and no more) of cosmic origins, the scene introduces a number of elemental relations – division, opposition, correspondence, repetition – which in effect comprise the basic narrative vocabulary of this poem and many later ones alike. They also establish a causal link between the cosmic and human spheres. Metaphysical dualism such as is here dramatically displayed is neither a philosophic principle nor a religious conviction for Shelley; but, as one of his primary intuitions, it has great imaginative significance for his writing. He elaborates narrative figures on its foundation in *Prometheus Unbound* and *The Cenci*; gives it enigmatic lyric voice in 'The Two Spirits: An Allegory'; divides the two husbands in *Rosalind and Helen* and the two female lovers he planned to include in the fragment 'Athanase' (*P* II.312–3) according to its logic of polarity; and works an intriguing variation on the theme in the pairing of the 'Song of Apollo' and the 'Song of Pan'.[8]

Several other scenes of cosmic origin in his poems (for instance, *Prometheus Unbound* 2.4.32–97, *Hellas* 46–53, 'Ode to Liberty' stanzas 2 and 3, *The Witch of Atlas* stanzas 32–3) share features with the primal scene in *Laon and Cythna* and among themselves, though none is identical to any other. All are manifestly framed not to conform to any authoritative mythical source, but rather to provide an appropriate starting point for a narrative whose course is already and otherwise determined. So each is rather a beginning regulated by its end than vice versa, and as such aims to alter fundamentally our understanding of how the world came to be what it is by bringing into play the shaping force and affective power of our curiosity to know the origin of things. In particular, such scenes seem always to be intended as alternatives to the sanctioned account of creation from nothing in Genesis. Shelley offers a type for their reception by the enquiring and adventurous mind in the discovery by the Poet of *Alastor* in the sculptures of ruined Ethiopian temples of 'The thrilling secrets of the birth of time' (128).

In the 'dawn of things' (370) sketched in *Laon and Cythna* a variant on the murder of Abel by Cain occupies the position of the biblical Fall, violence replacing disobedience as the Original Sin. Since that initial human transgression, the supremacy of the evil deity has continued unchecked, only relieved by periodic reassertions of the Spirit of Good, notably in the flowering of ancient Greek civilization and in the French Revolution. The time scheme thus compresses events in the textual order so as to proceed directly from the foundation of the cosmos to ancient Greece to contemporary France without any specified intervening incidents, in this way yoking a myth of archaic times to definitive moments of first ancient and then contemporary history in a brief narrative that illustrates how the Revolution ought to be understood: as the latest episode in a perpetual cosmic struggle. This secret logic of world history, like the grand biblical narrative encompassing the world's creation, corruption, destruction, and regeneration, is composed of a small number of decisive and divinely ordered interventions in the human sphere which will eventually issue in the apocalyptic defeat of evil and establishment of good (429–32). The characters of the romance narrative in Cantos 2 to 12 act out a revolutionary plot that acquires a particular moral value in the light of this scheme of history, though they themselves never receive the revelation as such. The exclusivity of this supernaturally revealed narrative marks it as the preserve of an intellectual elite, for which the narrator stands as representative; and indeed it has much in common with the views and interests current in the circle of writers, including Peacock and Leigh Hunt, which formed round Shelley in Marlow in 1817.[9]

When the boat in which this revelation is communicated has conducted the narrator to the temple of the Spirit of Good, Laon, himself newly arrived together with Cythna after their execution in the Golden City, takes up the narrative retrospectively and by the end of the poem has brought it up to the present of narration, which is the post-revolutionary moment where it began. His fictional autobiography, the medium within which the revolutionary romance unfolds, is structured by major turns back upon itself, each introduced by a scene of narration modelled upon the historical and personal crisis of the first canto. These are resolved by the intervention of a character who brings special knowledge of past events outside Laon's experience; the ensuing narrative attaches the (till then) missing past to the present moment, enabling it to go forward on a new basis until another crisis is reached, which is similarly negotiated. The Hermit's disclosures to Laon (4.11–28), Cythna's to Laon (7.3–9.36), and their child's to them both (12.24–31) operate in this way. Exercises in political and moral education as well as occasions for reassembling a fractured family group, these embedded reports are placed at critical moments in the poem's narrative economy precisely in order to repair failures of connection. They are the mechanism for establishing a mental continuum that binds the present to past and future, thus providing the individual with a rationale for action in time as well as restoring the intimate personal relations that sustain it. The family is thereby recommended as domestic and sentimental ideal in direct contrast to the treacherous and violent public domain of politics.[10] Similarly, as the Preface makes clear, Shelley wishes *Laon and Cythna* to remedy a generalized failure of confidence in post-revolutionary Europe by providing an exemplary narrative of the crucial episode of modern history, foregrounding its retelling from remote beginnings in myth by fictional narrators whose personal and public characters authenticate its claims to truth.

The kind of truth aimed at is obviously not a matter of simple historical accuracy. Nor did Shelley intend what he calls the poem's 'moving and romantic adventures' to embody any authentic record of events. In this respect, *Laon and Cythna* emerges recognizably from contemporary interest in historical romance and concern for the special sort of truth for which it could function as vehicle.[11] Godwin, for example, had challenged the existence of any firm distinction between history and romance, reaffirming the Aristotelian view that the value of fiction lies in its reshaping of the past into an intelligible pattern in which we may perceive its essential nature.[12] Further, both Godwin and Walter Scott had recognized the capacity of a narrative of individual lives developed with large freedom from the constraint of historical verisimilitude to move readers and influence their conduct.[13] Scott's *Waverley* (1814) and Wordsworth's *The White Doe of Rylstone* (1815) were notable recent endeavours to graft romantic plots to revolutionary episodes in history so as to increase their affective power. The historical substratum of *Laon and Cythna* has profounder contemporary resonance than either the Jacobite rising of 1745 in *Waverley* or the sixteenth-century rebellion of northern barons in Wordsworth's poem. But in all three texts it is the inventive potential of the romance plot, its fictionality, which allows history to serve the ends of prophecy. It was only by implicating historical narrative with the individual lives of its actors, Godwin had claimed, 'that we shall be enabled to add, to the knowledge of the past, a sagacity that can penetrate into the depths of futurity' (292). His remark aptly glosses Shelley's intention to provide in his poem *A Vision of the Nineteenth Century*.

In order for that vision to counterbalance the despair of sympathizers after the defeated revolutionary experiment in France, it was necessary for the poem to end with a victory of sorts. This Shelley contrives by evoking the example to future ages that Laon and Cythna will become, then by transporting them and their child to the temple of the Spirit of Good where their posthumous existence will consist in perpetually contemplating the re-enactment in art of the Spirit's history, of which the story of their own struggle for liberty constitutes the most recent chapter. The boat journey that carries them there is one of Shelley's most recurrent and characteristic narrative motifs. As an instrument of closure it typically conducts either to a posthumous transcendent region (as here and in *Adonais*) or to an imminent material one (as in *Lines Written among the Euganean Hills* or *Epipsychidion*) – either, that is, to a version of Heaven, remote from, and so of dubious relation to, the human world; or to an intimate society of the like-minded who are bound by affectionate ties, a kind of earthly paradise that is subject, as it were by definition, to inevitable loss. In poems that end on a death – *Alastor* is another example, though the destination of its voyage is an image of isolated solipsism – it is the journey itself, strange, fearful yet irresistibly enlivening, which engages the poet and arrests the reader; while those that issue in some haven of this world advertise its fragility even as they celebrate the gratification promised by its sensuous details. Neither type of ending is allowed to function as a resolution. In this each is typical, for at their close Shelley's major narratives habitually insist on their own uncertainty and incompleteness. The 'I cannot say . . . I dare not guess' in the Conclusion to 'The Sensitive-Plant', 'the cold world shall not know' that shuts down the story in the final line of *Julian and Maddalo*, the narrator's promise that what remains to say 'I will declare another time' in the last stanza of *The Witch of Atlas*, the 'if' of indemonstrable supposition in the final passages of both *Rosalind and Helen* and *Prometheus Unbound* – all expose to view the artifice of the conclusion's traditional privilege of defining the meaning of a narrative by limitation.

That characteristic indeterminacy is implicated both with contemporary event and with mythical–historical overview at the end of *Hellas*. The Greek struggle for independence had begun but was still of uncertain issue when Shelley finished the drama in autumn 1821; lacking the narrative coherence conferred by closure the subject could not be 'treated otherwise than lyrically', he claimed in the Preface. The celebrated refusal to look into the future in the final choral ode is therefore in the first place no more than common prudence. But by having the chorus evoke alternately the myth of the Golden Age of peace and plenty and later Greek myths of tragic outcome Shelley makes of the current conflict a synecdoche for the total past and future course of history, poised uncertainly between idyll and catastrophe.

> O cease! must hate and death return?
> Cease! must men kill and die?
> Cease! drain not to its dregs the urn
> Of bitter prophecy.
> The world is weary of the past,
> O might it die or rest at last!   (1096–1101; *N*)

All that can call a term to the hopeful or gloomy attempt to read the future in the past is the textual closure that conspicuously denies resolution as it finishes the poem on a note of exasperation and exhaustion. The drama that could only be a lyric has not resolved but extrapolated from the undetermined story it began with, thereby implicitly challenging the rationale of earlier narratives like *Queen Mab*, *Prometheus Unbound*, and *Laon and Cythna*, which elicit the reader's hope on the premise that the past may be morally redeemed in time to come provided we first understand it aright. The drama offers its own inability to make a satisfactory end as a figure for those competing dynamics of history, narrative, genre, and text which baffle and exhaust the chorus, leading it to the silence of death or repose in a creative impasse of brilliant concentration and focus.

Other poems of 1819–22, narrower in scope and more explicitly experimental, are also designed so as to foreground the nature and possibilities of narrative. The pranks of the Witch of Atlas, for example, proclaim the bliss of the inventive storyteller intoxicated by a love of mischief, mocking literary custom, authority, and decorum, and in this way taking the possibilities of story to surprising new limits. Freed from the constraints of tradition while displaying ample traces of its origins in myth, the plot of *The Witch of Atlas* invites the reader to measure and savour the originality of its departures from what is expected and legitimated by established narrative modes. The unfinished *The Triumph of Life* might be thought of as the *Witch*'s opposite, or dark double, its great images of enchainment, blindness, concealment, and amnesia standing, among other things, for our imperfect faculty for discovering in experience that unambiguous narrative intelligibility which the poem consistently denies. Being able neither to conclude nor to connect with one another, its stories together generate only enigma; and the questions the narrator asks are left not unanswered but responded to by further story that itself eludes secure interpretation. Shelley here sets in a strained and incongruous relation the grand narrative of events and the biography of the prophetic individual artist, which about a year previously he had integrated into a progressive model of the history of creative art in *A Defence of Poetry*. If *The Witch* conveys the confident exhilaration of a narrative conducted with the maximum of liberty, *The Triumph* illustrates the perilous fascination that results when narrative both intrigues us and eludes our need for meaning.

The fictional self

'What is thy tale?'   (*Rosalind and Helen* 593)

On 3 January 1812 the nineteen-year-old Shelley, expelled from Oxford the previous March and having eloped and married against his family's wishes in August, initiated one of the important connections of his life when he wrote from Keswick to the novelist and political philosopher William Godwin. Shelley was about to enter active politics – the following month he sailed to Ireland to disseminate propaganda for political reform – and he addressed the 57-year-old Godwin as a figure of intellectual and moral eminence, the author of the aspiring reformer's political convictions and his attachment to progressive causes, an alternative to the father from whom his expulsion and marriage had estranged him. The ensuing exchange of letters with a man he had never met furnished the occasion to sketch a self-portrait that integrated the personal upheavals of the previous year into a structured autobiographical sequence. Over the next six months Shelley represents himself to his ruminative and sceptical correspondent as having undergone a decisive personal crisis at about the age of seventeen when he resolved to abandon the privileged life he had been born to for one governed by impartial enquiry and principles of justice and benevolence – a decision which has called down the wrath of established authority upon his head. Before the conversion for which his reading of Godwin's works was chiefly responsible, he writes, the need to escape from a loveless family life had sent him to books of magic, alchemy, and romance, an addiction that ceased when his newly acquired sense of mission redirected his energies to the world as it is. His recovery from generalized debility of mind and will has been completed by the love he has found in marriage. Repudiating as juvenile freaks his own Gothic romances *Zastrozzi* and *St Irvyne*, he has decided to devote himself to discursive prose that aims to promote virtue and improve the lot of the oppressed. Yet, he claims, even these extravagant fictions, born of his early distemper of spirit, retain a particular value in view of an idea he has formed of a writing career:

> If any man would determine sincerely and cautiously at *every* period of his life to publish books which should contain the real state of his feelings and opinions, I am willing to suppose that this portraiture of his mind would be worth many metaphysical disquisitions [i.e. systematic studies of mental phenomena].
>
> (*L* 1.242)

Such a developing record of intellectual and sentimental life, which would constitute a unique case study in psychology, needs to be set against some later remarks on life-writing as retrospective self-representation and self-analysis:

> If it were possible that a person should give a faithful history of his being from the earliest epochs of his recollection, a picture would be presented such as the world has never contemplated before. A mirror would be held up to all men in which they might behold their own recollections and, in dim perspective, their shadowy hopes and fears . . . But thought can with difficulty visit the intricate and winding chambers which it inhabits. (*Pr* 185–6)

This project for a comprehensive reconstitution of the self, closer to the usual understanding of autobiography, obviously overlaps with the other, mental record set down over time. Shelley was keenly aware of the factors that impeded each. In other prose fragments he returned to the difficulty of accurate recollection and the elusive nature of one's own mental phenomena; he also recognizes the obstacles to communicating one's inward life to another and the inaptness of philosophy to define or words to express our nature.[14] His sceptical estimate, entirely characteristic, of the possibility of any authentic self-portraiture might seem good grounds for not writing in the autobiographical mode at all. And indeed Shelley did not produce a major study of himself as artist in the manner of Wordsworth's *Prelude* or Coleridge's *Biographia Literaria*, nor did he develop a public persona such as Byron's Childe Harold or the couple formed by Don Juan and his knowing narrator. Nonetheless, throughout his career he represents himself both directly and in various fictional guises, including the first person of his lyrics; and his leading themes are those that he fashioned in the correspondence with Godwin in early 1812: intellectual and moral self-determination, the search for love, the public purpose and personal stresses of the writer's life.

In assessing this strain in Shelley's poetry and prose one needs to remain aware of the role of decorum, the topics and language proper to a given kind of writing, in shaping his various fictional selves. Thus the public character of the poet in the prefaces to *Laon and Cythna* and *Prometheus Unbound* excludes the affective and confessional revelations of the Dedication to *Laon and Cythna* and *Epipsychidion*, just as the poet-figures Laon, Lionel (in *Rosalind and Helen*) and the maniac in *Julian and Maddalo* resemble their author in intimate ways not possible in either a preface or an inner course of experience recounted in the first person. These characters are three in a succession of such figures beginning with the Poet of *Alastor* and continuing to Rousseau in *The Triumph of Life*, and including Athanase, the narrators of 'Hymn to Intellectual Beauty' and *Lines Written among the Euganean Hills*, and the 'frail Form' of *Adonais* (stanzas 31–4). Interesting attempts have been made to read these poems as forming a connected portrait of the artist which, although perfectly embodied in no single work, can yet be pieced together from elements dispersed through them all.[15] While far from transparently autobiographical, this story exhibits multiple relations with Shelley's public and private, intellectual and emotional life, and is as much a means for him to explore and create his idea of himself as to express a sense of self he has already developed. The revolutionary role of the poet-figure in his work, in consequence of his unusual sensibility and visionary power, is to bring the consciousness of his time into being, a function that Shelley conceives in its broadest terms through the progressive history of imaginative creation in *A Defence of Poetry*. In his fictional narratives of the poet it is the exercise of this function that first mines and then destroys its subject. Hence the ravaged and morbid youth grown old before his time, a principal actor in the Shelleyan cast of characters, and the various narratives of decline and death in which he is involved.

The essential outlines of his story appear in miniature in the 'Ode to Liberty'. Its nineteen stanzas trace the manifestations of Liberty from ancient Athens to contemporary Europe and speculate on its future prospects. In the manner of an eighteenth-century progress poem like Gray's 'The Progress of Poesy' (1757) this meta-history of civilization links the development of the arts and sciences to the irregular appearances of political freedom through time. The frame formed by the first and last stanzas follows the course of the inspiration that generates the poem's historical narrative from its irresistible inception to its sudden and unaccountable arrest and the emphatically repeated destruction of the voice which has articulated it in poetry. But such a morbid conception of the destiny of the poet who assumes the prophetic mantle needs to be set against the experience of the non-human or superhuman figures in, for example, 'To a Sky-Lark', *The Witch of Atlas*, 'Song of Apollo', and Shelley's exuberant translation of the Homeric 'Hymn to Mercury', poems which together contain a treasury of stories that sing the confident, daring, mischievous, uninhibited, and spontaneous joy of poetic creation.

The romance genre, with which so many of Shelley's major poems have affinities, has memorably been characterized as 'the epic of the creature, man's vision of his own life as a quest'.[16] The creature and the quest are apt co-ordinates for an appreciation of the whole of his narratives. The unreconciled opposition between a liberation plot that is only intelligible in historical form and the story of personal decline that is the necessary vehicle for the creative endeavour to bring it about, variously combined with the wanderings and failures of desire – such is the territory that his narratives make peculiarly their own. Shelley's exceptional sensitivity to the limitations of the poet's vision and to the shortcomings of the instrument of language itself clearly extends to the limited capacity of narrative to represent and explain. Stories may demand to be told or retold because oppressive circumstances have silenced or distorted them, but from *The Wandering Jew* forward his texts regularly show that the act of telling can never be complete, the story told never definitive; nor can the narrative discourse master its material or resolve the problems that narrative itself brings to view. Shelley's habit of returning to important elements of a finished narrative in order to rework them in a new combination or with discordant additions derives from this awareness. The domestic tales in *Rosalind and Helen* replay elements of the epic romance of *Laon and Cythna* from a feminine perspective so as to throw an oblique and ironic light back upon it, while the domestic tragedy of *The Cenci* systematically subverts the order and values of *Prometheus Unbound*, which defines the road from endurance to freedom as passing through the construction of a regenerated self. In the experimental poems that he wrote between 1819 and 1822, especially, Shelley exposes the narrative mode itself to a searching critical reappraisal. On a global view of them, his narratives represent a sustained attempt to offer their just due to both the creature and the quest, while rendering their uneasy relation in the imperfect human medium of story.

NOTES

1. C. H. Herford, *Shelley's Narrative Poems*, 2 vols. (London: Chatto and Windus, 1918), I.45.
2. For example: Francis Jeffrey on Southey's *Thalaba* (*Edinburgh Review* 1, October 1802), on Byron's *The Corsair* and *The Bride of Abydos* (*Edinburgh Review* 23,

April 1814), and on Scott's *Marmion* (*Edinburgh Review* 12, April 1808); George
Ellis on Byron's *Childe Harold's Pilgrimage* 1–2 (*Quarterly Review* 7,
March 1812), and on Scott's *The Bridal of Triermain* (*Quarterly Review* 9,
July 1813).

3. See the detailed commentary in *CP* 1.189–234.
4. The gaps in the textual history of the poem leave open the possibility that 'the
Victim of the Eternal Avenger' may be an unadopted alternative title.
5. Virgil, *Aeneid* 6.625–7; Lucan, *Pharsalia* 5.174–89; *Hamlet* 1.5.13–20; The
Gospel according to John 21:25.
6. See further: Tillotama Rajan, 'Promethean Narrative: Overdetermined Form in
Shelley's Gothic Fiction', in *Shelley: Poet and Legislator of the World*, ed. Betty
T. Bennett and Stuart Curran (Baltimore: Johns Hopkins University Press,
1996), 240–52; Peter Finch, 'Monstrous Inheritance: The Sexual Politics of
Genre in Shelley's *St Irvyne*', *Keats-Shelley Journal* 48 (1999), 35–68; Introduction to *Zastrozzi* and *St Irvyne*, ed. Stephen C. Behrendt (Peterborough, Ont.:
Broadview Press, 2002).
7. M. H. Abrams, *Natural Supernaturalism: Tradition and Revolution in Romantic Literature* (New York: Norton, 1971), 32–7.
8. Shelley expands upon his interest in Manichean dualism in 'On the Devil and
Devils' (*Pr* 264–75).
9. Marilyn Butler, *Romantics, Rebels and Reactionaries: English Literature and its
Background 1760–1830* (Oxford: Oxford University Press, 1981), 113–37.
10. Gary Kelley, 'From Avant-Garde to Vanguardism: The Shelleys' Romantic
Feminism in *Laon and Cythna* and *Frankenstein*', in *Shelley: Poet and Legislator of the World*, ed. Bennett and Curran, 73–87 (79).
11. Stuart Curran, *Poetic Form and British Romanticism* (Oxford and New York:
Oxford University Press, 1986), 128–57; David Duff, *Romance and Revolution*
(Cambridge and New York: Cambridge University Press, 1994), 154–216.
12. Aristotle, *On the Art of Poetry*, in *Aristotle Horace Longinus: Classical Literary
Criticism*, tr. T. S. Dorsch (Harmondsworth: Penguin, 1965, 1984), 43–4.
13. William Godwin, 'Essay of History and Romance', in *Political and Philosophical Writings of William Godwin*, vol. v, *Educational and Literary Writings*, ed.
Pamela Clemit (London: Pickering, 1993), 291–301 (subsequent references
given parenthethically in the text); Walter Scott, Preface to *The Bridal of
Triermain*, in *The Bridal of Triermain, Harold the Dauntless . . . and Other
Poems* (Edinburgh: Robert Cadell, 1836), 4–5.
14. 'On Love', 'On Life', *Pr* 169–75.
15. Judith Chernaik, *The Lyrics of Shelley* (Cleveland, Ohio: Case Western Reserve
University, 1972), 8–31; Nora Crook and Derek Guiton, *Shelley's Venomed
Melody* (Cambridge: Cambridge University Press, 1986), 133–5; Timothy
Clark, *Embodying Revolution: The Figure of the Poet in Shelley* (Oxford and
New York: Oxford University Press, 1989).
16. Northrop Frye, *The Secular Scripture: A Study of the Structure of Romance*
(Cambridge, Mass.: Harvard University Press, 1976), 15.

6

JEFFREY C. ROBINSON

The translator

Introduction

Conventional wisdom presumes that translation would rank low in poetic intention among the Romantic poets, concerned with the seer's 'unmediated vision' of the cosmos and nature, the feeling-ful exploration of the terrains of past experience, dream-states, and shifts and quickenings of mood, and the passions evoked in indignation at the 'wrongs' meted out on the unfortunate and dispossessed members of society. All of these occasions for poetry indicate for Romanticism signs of poetic and human authenticity and of the resurgence of social and spiritual possibility originating in the individuated consciousness. Translation, fundamentally derivative and secondary, an act of mediation doomed to fail, and at the core inauthentic, at best would serve as an apprentice activity for the neophyte poet, a five-finger exercise the effects of which the true poet might absorb as a strengthening of the fabric of original work.

Indeed, little in the way of Romantic translations has the massive presence of the neoclassical monuments of translation such as Dryden's *Aeneid* or Pope's Homer. At the same time, a poem like Keats's 'Chapman's Homer' sonnet acknowledges famously that a great translation can profoundly illuminate an otherwise inaccessible work, and not any translation can enact such a transformation: the success of a translation in this regard can be as authentic as any success in poetry. After surveying the landscape of Romantic translations in poetry, this chapter will turn to Shelley's substantial output of translations, situating them in the framework of Shelley's poetics and Romantic poetic intentions.

Aside from Shelley's, Romanticism produced a number of locally influential literary translations, such as (to name a few) Helen Maria Williams's translation of Bernardin de St Pierre's immensely popular and influential sentimental novel *Paul et Virginie*, Coleridge's translations of Friedrich Schiller's plays which are quoted in literature throughout the Romantic period from Austen to Hemans, and H. F. Cary's highly influential translation of *The Divine Comedy* which became important for Keats's engagement with Dante. Helen Maria Williams also studded her translation of *Paul et Virginie* with sonnets of her own yet spoken by the novel's characters; these lyric outbursts or improvisations could be said to 'translate' the thoughts of the protagonists that, as we say, 'get lost in translation', becoming a kind of supplement or postponement of the inevitable vanishing of the high pitch of the passion-love that defines much of the novel's energy. The same could be said of Charlotte Smith's *Werther* sonnets which 'translate' the unspoken lyric turmoil of Goethe's hero.

Not influential but nonetheless monumental was Wordsworth's translation, in heroic couplets, of the first three books of Virgil's *Aeneid* in the early 1820s. Those scholars who find that among the several unpublished versions of *The Prelude* Wordsworth made substantial revisions during the same years as his work on the *Aeneid* note the presence of a greater than usual ornamentalism and baroque imagery and language attributable to his translation of the Roman poet. Wordsworth's Virgil is to a degree a throwback to Dryden's neoclassicism.

By contrast, Shelley's generation of poets considered translation as part of an effort to contact the poetries of other ages and other nations and cultures, countering the English tendencies towards parochial nationalism and localism. Two of the most prolific as well as the most popular poets in this vein were Tom Moore and Felicia Hemans who each attempted to recover, in translation and imitation, the poetry and poetic temperament of Ireland. Hemans, furthermore, popularized in English the lyric poetry of Germany, as did the somewhat younger Irish nationalist poet James Clarence Mangan (who also translated the Middle Eastern poets Saadi and Hafiz).

Also relevant to the ambiance that produced Shelley's translations are instances of Englishing work from mythologies and foreign literatures, instances of imitations and recoveries or revisionings such as Mary Tighe's recovery of the Psyche myth (*Psyche*), Leigh Hunt's *The Story of Rimini*, his recovery of the Paolo and Francesca episode in Dante's *Inferno*, Keats's 'Isabella' drawn from Boccaccio, and early Wordsworth's recovery of Burger's ballad 'Lenore' in his poem 'Strange Fits of Passion', Burger having been actually translated in a popular poetic version by William Taylor (1796). The range of translation to recovery emerges graphically in the case of the Paolo and Francesca story which, in addition to Hunt's poem, includes actual translations by Hunt and Byron and Keats's sonnet 'As Hermes once . . .'. This sonnet and Keats's own dream from which the poem emerged (see the letter to George and Georgiana Keats, March 1819)[1] suggests how present the episode must have been among Keats and his friends.

The poets in Leigh Hunt's circle, including Shelley, were very interested in translation as an element in their progressive poetic and political programme of cultural expansion. Hunt's book of poems *The Feast of the Poets* (1811, 1814, 1815) ends with a group of his translations from ancient Greek and Roman poets; similarly his next book *Foliage* (1818) concludes with a similar suite of translations. That the 'original' poetry in *Foliage* is paginated with prefatory Roman numerals and the translations in arabic numerals suggests that the book's primary poetic vision resides in a poetry of another time and place. Similarly, the poem 'Feast of the Poets' rejects the then current notion of a 'best', 'laureate' poet, obviously chosen by persons aligned with the ruling national government, proposing instead that all poets be crowned with laurel. In the poem this decision, coming from the master of ceremonies Apollo, who here is more of a drunken Dionysus than a serene and aloof Apollo, announces Hunt's clear preference for a promiscuous heterogeneous community of poetic voices. It is but a short step to a concluding display of poems in translation, as if the Feast of Poets now includes non-English temperaments and idioms speaking at the dinner table of poetry. Interestingly, Hunt constructs a 'parallel text' for his Latin poems: English translations at the top of the page, Latin at the bottom.

This dramatic exfoliation of poetic specimens is further expressed in the choice of poets for translation and poetic subjects. Hunt emphasized Greek (and some Latin) poetry because he saw it as 'breathing' the life of poetic authenticity and, by extension, the life of a vital community. Moreover, he selected less the 'monumental' poetry of the ancient world (although there are two beautiful passages from the *Iliad* and the *Odyssey*) and more poetry with a pastoral and lyric bent: the Homeric Hymn to Bacchus, Idylls of Theocritus, Greek lyric (Anacreon), and Latin lyric (Catullus and Horace), all more playful and at times erotic poetry. (Thomas Love Peacock's erotic *Rhododaphne* (1817) includes a free translation of the Homeric Hymn to Dionysus.) This reinforces the notion promulgated by Marilyn Butler and Jerome McGann that the progressive poetry of the Regency Decade sought to bring poetic playfulness and the erotic myths of classical mythology into the foreground as an anti-repressive gesture.[2]

Shelley, very simply, seems to have produced his translations in line with the poetic predispositions of Hunt and his contemporaries. Most of his poetic translations were written from 1818 until his death, that is, during the peak of his career. He did not, in other words, associate translation with poetic exercise and apprenticeship. The question then arises: why did he not attempt to publish more of them? Only three pieces (a fragment from

Moschus, a sonnet of Dante, and a scene from *Faust*) were published by Shelley. Why, if Leigh Hunt was publishing his own translations, was not Shelley publishing his, which, in fact, Hunt had praised and was to praise again? Although there are no firm answers to these questions, one can observe and speculate: Shelley, first of all, did not get any of his work published easily; it may be that, over time, he would have seen more translations into print. Or it may be that, coming from Eton where translations represented for the students a kind of linguistic callisthenics, Shelley did not immediately associate translation with published performance. It is worth noting that Mary Shelley, just two years after her husband's death, saw to it that translations appeared in her 1824 edition of his poetry, moreover, at the end of the volume in the manner of Hunt.

One of Shelley's most ambitious translations was that of Plato's *Symposium*, which Shelley called *The Banquet*; it will not be discussed here since the focus is on poetic translations with the intention of situating them within Shelley's poetry and the poetry of Regency Decade Romanticism. Let us enumerate Shelley's verse translations (the dates given as ascribed by his early twentieth-century editor Thomas Hutchinson; references to this edition are cited as *H*). All except 'From the Greek of Moschus' and a sonnet of Dante to Guido Cavalcanti (published in his volume *Alastor* in 1816) appeared after his death in 1822. Mary Shelley in her *Posthumous Poems of Percy Bysshe Shelley*, published by John and Leigh Hunt in 1824, collected for the first time a substantial number of translations: 'Hymn to Mercury, from Homer', 'The Cyclops, from Euripedes' composed in 1819, a 'translation from Moschus', 'Scenes from the "Magico Prodigioso" of Calderon' composed in 1822, and 'Scenes from the "Faust" of Goethe' being Act 1 scenes 1 and 2 with scene 2 having been previously published in Leigh Hunt's journal the *Liberal* in 1822.[3] Then in her 1839 edition of Shelley's poems, Mary Shelley included 'Homer's Hymn to the Moon' composed in 1818, 'Homer's Hymn to Castor and Pollux' composed in 1818, 'Homer's Hymn to the Sun' composed in 1818, 'Homer's Hymn to Minerva' composed in 1818, some 'Greek Epigrams' including 'To Stella', 'Kissing Helena', and 'Spirit of Plato' all from Plato, and 'Circumstance' (*1839*). Later in the nineteenth century were published Dante's First Canzone of the *Convito*, from Dante's *Purgatorio* (28.1–51) 'Matilda Gathering Flowers', 'Homer's Hymn to Venus' (composed in 1818);[4] lines 1–26 from Virgil's Tenth Eclogue;[5] a fragment of Bion's 'Elegy on the Death of Adonis', a sonnet by Cavalcanti to Dante (perhaps written in 1815);[6] and lines 360ff. from Virgil's Fourth Georgic.[7] Let us now turn to some of the individual translations both to describe them and to speculate on the particular use and intention he had for them.

Greek

It is perhaps too easy to take (as has Timothy Webb) Shelley's famous statement in the *Defence of Poetry* about the near-tragic impossibility of successful poetic translation – like putting a violet in a crucible (*Pr* 280) – as the poet's ruling assessment, one that conforms to the standard view: translation is loss – less than, destructive of, the original.[8] Yet his apparent assent to the principles in Hunt and his circle, both about the socioliterary value of poetic translation – it is a gain of other voices, other tales, other visions which enrich the present's connection to the great stream of world poetry – and about the importance of the erotic in poetry, would suggest the opposite. Moreover, the influence of his translations – in thematic, formal, and linguistic ways – on his own 'original' poems indicates that he found a source of vitality in translated works that belies Robert Frost's infamous remark that poetry is what gets lost in translation. A careful reading of Shelley's translations in relation to his own poems, in fact, may lead one to posit 'translation', for him, as the essential visionary act of poetry itself and perhaps a definition of Shelley's Romantic poetics.

All of this appears affirmed in Shelley's longest, and perhaps best, translation, that of, as he calls it, 'Homer's Hymn to Mercury', a joyous, playful version of one of the most joyful literary events of Greek literature. It recounts the story of the birth of Mercury, his startlingly precocious maturation, his construction of his lyre out of the shell of a tortoise, the manifold tricks he plays on gods and mortals, including Apollo to whom he eventually gives the lyre out of deference to the god's great musical and poetic power. Shelley chose to re-fashion the Greek epic metre into what at the end of the Regency Decade had been pegged as a playful stanza, the *ottava rima*. As his contemporary Barry Cornwall (Bryan Procter) wrote:

> The octave rhyme (Ital. Ottava rima)
> Is a delightful measure made of ease
> Turn'd up with epigrams, and tho' it seems a
> Verse that a man may scribble when he please,
> Is somewhat difficult. . .[9]

The opening line embodies a connection, in Barry Cornwall's mind and one might guess in Shelley's, between translation and this stanza form. It follows that translation is associated not with poetic labour but with ease, scribbling (as Byron often described his own writing), and pleasure, with, in other words, 'waste' and 'excess', poetic values that pointedly stand outside the realm of the market and exchange and belong to the political and poetic radicalism that characterizes Shelley's work. Nowhere do these poetic values reach greater realization than in the masterpiece of Shelley's friend Byron, *Don Juan*. Here the *ottava rima* stanza – six lines of alternating *ab* rhymes, followed by a concluding rhymed couplet *cc*–produces a poetry of playful, outrageous reversals, deconstructions, and juxtapositions perfect for comic but also for transformative poetry. For example,

> And Julia sate with Juan, half embraced
> And half retiring from the glowing arm,
> Which trembled like the bosom where 't was placed;
> Yet still she must have thought there was no harm,
> Or else 't were easy to withdraw her waist;
> But then the situation had its charm,
> And then—God knows what next—I can't go on;
> I'm almost sorry that I e'er begun.   (*Don Juan* 1.115)

Not surprisingly, then, Shelley uses the *ottava rima* stanza to expand or 'dilate' upon the original Homeric line. Compare, for example, a modern translation by Thelma Sargent ('I have taken very few liberties with the text') with Shelley's:

> So Hermes spoke and, picking up the creature [tortoise] with both hands,
> Went back into the house with his lovely new plaything.[10]

And Shelley:

> Thus having spoken, the quaint infant bore,
>   Lifting it from the grass on which it fed
> And grasping it in his delighted hold,
> His treasure prize into the cavern old.   (45–8; *H*)

Shelley splits the verb and the object with a two-line shift of attention away from the main point – taking the tortoise into his house in order to kill it – to the more peripheral drama of lifting and grasping the tortoise from the grass; the phrase 'his delighted hold' proposes a pleasure in Mercury's hands at the prospect of turning the animal into a musical instrument.

Shelley's *ottava rima* encourages a beautiful paradox in his interpretation of the Hymn: the relationship between poetic construction and a poetry of chance or spontaneous poetry, what Shelley calls 'the power of unpremeditated song' (590; *H*). The playfulness residing in the stanza itself nonetheless allows for its appearance as a highly artificial or constructed thing. At the same time the repeated dilations of the original increase the opportunities for play of sound patterns, in particular the rhymes and consonance. His own poetry mirrors, in this sense, the figure of Mercury himself, a maker, elaborately constructing the lyre out of a tortoise, and yet a kind of naif who sings spontaneously about the gods and goddesses.

It is Shelley who twice in the poem introduces the word 'unpremeditated' to describe Mercury's singing, anticipating the song of his Sky-Lark who 'pours forth profuse strains / Of unpremeditated art' (5). (Later in the nineteenth century the poet Swinburne, with the same emphasis on spontaneity, referred to the Homeric hymns as 'miraculous effusions of genius', a position that Shelley at once accepts and, in his own translations, complicates.)[11] The conjunction of construction (the elaborate, rule-bound stanza) with spontaneous unpredictability has become a poetic ideal in postmodern poetics.

This principle might accord with a challenge for translation as an act of visionary poetry: how do you 'carry-across' a poem from another language and yet allow it to breathe life (the unpredictable, the unpremeditated) in a new language? Hermes, or Mercury, seems the perfect god of translations, one who can play tricks of language and yet also is the god of crossroads – in this case, the intersection between one language and another. A commonplace of Romantic poetics is the attempt to call up the locus of unpremeditated song in the midst of the highly mediated or constructed art of the modern world. But Shelley wishes to infuse into his translations some of the unpremeditated, or 'naive', elements as a way of countering the assumption of the secondary status typically accorded translation: he would like to be a Mercury of translation. As a footnote to this observation, Shelley calls his hero by both his Greek and Roman names: Hermes and Mercury, as if to emphasize that the best poetic translation enacts a betweenness, a fundamental oscillation of two languages and visions. It is also possible that the oscillation between 'Greece' and 'Rome' in the naming of the god marks a deliberate refusal to settle either for the language of the empire (Rome) or for the language of the conquered but more 'authentic' source (Greece); perhaps Shelley posits a poetic translation as occupying a space between or beyond those of the source or target languages.

But poetically 'Homer's Hymn to Mercury' ends not so much with Mercury triumphant but with Apollo to whom Mercury gives his lyre:

> And then Apollo with the plectrum strook
> The chords, and from beneath his hands a crash
> Of mighty sounds rushed up, whose music shook
> The soul with sweetness, and like an adept
> His sweeter voice a just accordance kept.   (672–6)

Shelley extends the scope of musical effect in volume and speed and intensity. Sweetness, a notion not in the original, comes, for Shelley, from Dante's final canto of *Paradiso*, to connote the literally unutterable effect on the pilgrim of divine love. Only Apollo, not the trickster Hermes, can register such intense transformations. Apollo extends the range of Mercury's poetic antics, absorbs and transcends them.

Shelley's Mercury accords with the poetics at work in two other Romantic poems written in *ottava rima*. The first is Shelley's *The Witch of Atlas*, written a year or two after 'Homer's Hymn to Mercury' but featuring a figure not unrelated to Mercury, the Witch – a magical trickster in her own right, capable of playfully performing grotesqueries on unsuspecting humans that alter, usually for the better, their sense either of the tragic nature of their lives or their own self-importance. The second poem is, of course, Byron's *Don Juan* (and *Beppo* and *The Vision of Judgement*) which, although it has no trickster figure (other than perhaps the poet himself) pulling the poetic strings, exploits the stanza for its capacity for poetic 'waste' and 'excess' in the service of popping the bubbles of convention both in poetry and social pretension.

Aside from Euripides' *The Cyclops*, Shelley's other specimens of Greek poetry either are or have the feeling of the fragment or lyric. And like the lyric they project voices that seem to come from domains other than that of ordinary consciousness. The fragments of the Homeric Hymns evoke cosmogonies and theogonies, while the fragments from the elegies of Bion and Moschus call up classical pastoral poetic ritual. Together they compose not only a suite of translated poems but also translated voices pitched far from the social sounds of early nineteenth-century England. (One wishes that Shelley's 'suite' of translations would have been heard by his contemporaries more than they were.)

The effect of the Homeric Hymns upon Shelley's poetic vision is patent: they offer what might be called a cosmological (as well as mythic) idiom. To give some examples:

> the wind
> And the huge billow bursting close behind,
> Even then beneath the weltering waters bear
> The staggering ship—[Castor and Pollux] suddenly appear,
> On yellow wings rushing athwart the sky,
> And lull the blasts in mute tranquillity,
> And strew the waves on the white Ocean's bed[.]
>
> ('Hymn to Castor and Pollux', 13–19; *H*)

We recognize the anthropomorphic act of one part of nature (fuelled by mythic figures) upon another – strewing the waves on the Ocean's bed – as a Shelleyan vision of interanimation in the cosmos. Similarly, in 'Homer's Hymn to the Moon' the scattering of 'Far light' in the sky projects this non-human-centred involvement:

> Around the earth,
> From her immortal head in Heaven shot forth,
> Far light is scattered—boundless glory springs;
> Where'er she spreads her many-beaming wings
> The lampless air glows round her golden crown.   (3–7; *H*)

Enjambments within the heroic couplets contribute to the 'scattering' effect, as in:

> Then is made full the circle of her light,
> And as she grows, her beams more bright and bright
> Are poured from Heaven, where she is hovering then,
> A wonder and a sign to mortal men.   (16–19)

And from 'Homer's Hymn to the Sun' the scattering works as an erotic interpenetration of light rays and elements in a manner that anticipates the 'Ode to the West Wind':

> [The Sun's] countenance, with radiant glory bright,
> Beneath his graceful locks far shines around,
> And the light vest with which his limbs are bound,
> Of woof aethereal delicately twined,
> Glows in the stream of the uplifting wind.   (16–20; *H*)

(Contrast the Sargent version of the last lines: 'His splendid fine-woven garment shimmers about him / And flutters in the breath of the winds as he drives his stallions' (Sargent, *Homeric Hymns*, 80).)

Ultimately what we are calling Shelley's cosmological idiom, the interpenetration of elements from the cosmos (including earth), has an erotic manifestation, apparent in Shelley's relatively long fragment from the 'Homeric Hymn to Aphrodite' (Shelley titled this 'Homer's Hymn to Venus'). This Hymn recounts at length Aphrodite's love affair with the mortal Anchises (father of Aeneas), which, however, is described as an infusion of divine love from Zeus to Aphrodite. Contrasting Sargent with Shelley is again revealing:

> into the heart of Aphrodite herself
> Zeus cast sweet longing to lie in love with a man
> . . . .
> So for Anchises Zeus aroused in her heart sweet desire,
> A man godlike in form who was then tending cattle
> Among the high-ranging hills of Ida abounding in fountains.
> Aphrodite, lover of smiles, looked on him [Anchises] and loved him,
> And desire and desperate longing laid hold on her heart.
> (Sargent, *Homeric Hymns*, 47)

In Venus Jove did soft desire awaken,
That by her own enchantments overtaken,
She might, no more from human union free,
Burn for a nursling of mortality.
. . . .
Therefore [Jove] poured desire into her breast
Of young Anchises,
Feeding his herds among the mossy fountains
Of the wide Ida's many-folded mountains,—
Whom Venus saw, and loved, and the love clung
Like wasting fire her senses wild among.   (42–59; *H*)

This moment in the original Hymn sets in motion the long account of the
exchange between Aphrodite and Anchises, but Shelley's fragment ends
right here, shaping it as a climax of divine desire for a mortal. In Shelley's
version, moreover, desire turns back onto the goddess in a gesture of auto-
eroticism, so that, unlike the narrative of the Homeric Hymn, Shelley's
fragment has no implications of its use value for the course of human history
(Aphrodite to Anchises to Aeneas to . . . Rome) but more for eroticism (and by
association for the poetry which carries it) as waste and excess (wasting fire).

   One might consider as a late Romantic instance of poetry-as-waste the
following 'epigram' from the Greek, this lovely one 'from the Greek of Plato':

Kissing Helena, together
  With my kiss, my soul beside it
    Came to my lips, and there I kept it,—
For the poor thing had wandered thither,
  To follow where the kiss should guide it,
    Oh, cruel I, to intercept it!   (1–6; *H*)

So slight as to hardly merit notice, this poem in fact is an elegant study of
an 'epipsyche' – disembodied, yet playfully generating a logic or erotic
spirituality, into which, with delicate rhythm and rhyme, weaves a visionary
poetry. In a similar vein of expansiveness within the tight epigrammatic
form is the more famous dilation from Plato that becomes the epigraph for
Adonais:

Thou wert the morning star among the living,
  Ere thy fair light had fled;—
Now, having died, thou art as Hesperus, giving
  New splendour to the dead.   (1–4; *H*)

The pronounced asymmetry of odd vs. even line lengths, the hypertrophied
decasyllabics pitched against the short six-syllable lines, emphasizing respectively extension (living, giving) and truncation (fled, dead), proposes

that a visionary poetry of death must encounter the turbulence created in the imaginative juxtaposition of finalities and starry continuities.

For a poet of Shelley's restlessly visionary propensities, elegy becomes the great challenge and crisis (just as does political tyranny – compare *The Mask of Anarchy*). How does one 'begin again' in the face of the death of the beloved, as death constricts the imagination of the living to near vanishing point? One can look upon the fragment-translations of Bion's 'Elegy on the Death of Adonis', Moschus' 'Elegy on the Death of Bion', and Virgil's Tenth Eclogue as studies in the challenge of death to the poet and as an unanticipated preparation for the writing of *Adonais* on the death of Keats (1821), which Shelley considered his most finished poem.

In his translations from Bion and Moschus Shelley moves from the heroic couplet or other rhyming patterns to blank verse, as if to emphasize that elegy begins from a more or less normative consciousness (in the identification with the dead). With 'Fragment of the Elegy on the Death of Bion (From the Greek of Moschus)', only a thirteen-line opening section of the poem, Shelley appears to be practising the ritual element of the pastoral elegy, the weeping and mourning of nature; the lines are stately pentameters. At the same time the push towards a ritualized poetry must make way for a living buoyancy of Shelleyan language once nature begins its mourning:

> Ye Dorian woods and waves, lament aloud,—
> Augment your tide, O streams, with fruitless tears,
> For the beloved Bion is no more.
> Let every tender herb and plant and flower,
> From each dejected bud and drooping bloom,
> Shed dews of liquid sorrow, and with breath
> Of melancholy sweetness on the wind
> Diffuse its languid love [.]   (1–8; *H*)

By contrast, Shelley seems to have translated that portion of Bion's 'Elegy on the Death of Adonis' that highlights the sexual desire paramount in the Adonis/Aphrodite relationship; 'Sleep no more, Venus', cries the mourning speaker, attempting to wake the goddess into her pain:

> Sleep no more, Venus, wrapped in purple woof—
> Wake violet-stolèd queen, and weave the crown
> Of Death—'tis Misery calls,—for he is dead.   (3–5; *H*)

The quotation from *Macbeth* ('Sleep no more' (2.2.35)) suggests the goddess's implication in the death of her mortal beloved, but the sound echoes the triumph of imagination at the far end of Milton's *Lycidas*: 'Weep no more, woeful shepherds, weep no more, / For Lycidas your sorrow is not dead—' (165–6).[12] Shelley transforms the pastoral elegy's sequential release from grief into a palimpsest of 'misery' and the joy of its unburdening. Such a collapsing of the elegiac drama of transcendence into a complex moment of intensity leads to the highly sexual and bodily evocation of Adonis and the goddess's response, which seems to be Shelley's real fascination with Bion's poem:

> The lovely one lies wounded in the mountains,
> His white thigh struck with the white tooth [of the boar]; he scarce
> Yet breathes; and Venus hangs in agony there.
> The dark blood wanders o'er his snowy limbs,
> His eyes beneath their lids are lustreless,
> The rose has fled from his wan lips, and there
> That kiss is dead, which Venus gathers yet.   (6–12)

Shelley brilliantly engages the tragedy that is elegy's subject while attending to its release in imagination, elegy's irony and subsequent comedy: the 'kiss is dead', but his dark blood, a sign of death, through the personification by the poet, 'wanders', that is, lives. All pastoral elegists practise this drama, but in Shelley's case death (or tyranny) of imagination is the welcome challenge of his poetry as a (political) act of transformation of vision. In this instance transformation is located in the eros of the goddess's mourning, which ends the fragment:

> 'Stay, dearest one [says Venus], . . .
>   and mix my lips with thine—
> Wake yet awhile, Adonis—oh, but once,
> That I may kiss thee now for the last time—
> But for as long as one short kiss may live—
> Oh, let thy breath flow from thy dying soul
> Even to my mouth and heart, that I may suck
> That . . .'   (40–7)

Latin literature hardly occupies Shelley's translation interests at all. There is nothing from the major Latin poems – for example those of Lucretius, Virgil, and Ovid – nor from the lyric poets Catullus and Horace who engaged Hunt. He did, however, translate a fragment of Virgil's Tenth Eclogue, an elegiac poem, and a section from Virgil's Fourth Georgic where, in anticipation of his deep interest in Dante, as translator and formal imitator, he employs a *terza rima* rhyme scheme.

But before turning to Shelley's translations from the post-classical world, we need to consider his translation from a curious, little-known play by Euripides, *The Cyclops: A Satyric Drama*, composed in 1819 and published posthumously by Mary Shelley in 1824, a work considered by editors to

be a first draft. Aside from some good choral lyrics and very readable blank
verse, the primary value of the play for readers of Shelley lies in the plot
and thematic elements, because they celebrate the virtues of Dionysian
ecstasy and Odyssean trickery valued by Hunt and his circle. In keeping
with the preference for the Homeric Hymn over the Homeric epic, Shelley
recovers a play that relocates the epic hero Odysseus (here Ulysses) with
satyrs; wiliness does not rise out of a finely honed reasoning mind, but
rather its use facilitates the escape from the Cyclops and in the process
converts the chorus of satyrs to a new god:

> And we, the shipmates of Ulysses now,
> Will serve our Bacchus all our happy lives.   (717–18; *H*)

The political resonance of the play fits with the Cockney programme in
the poetics of political resistance where the mind-expanding possibilities of
wine along with its blurring of mind/body distinctions challenge the effect
of political repression on the mentality of subdued political subjects: Euripides' Cyclops is figured as a tyrant. The satyrs anticipate their freedom from
the one-eyed tyrant in lyric that looks forward to the poems of Thomas
Lovell Beddoes:

> Soon a crab the throat will seize
>   Of him who feeds upon his guest,
> Fire will burn his lamp-like eyes
>   In revenge of such a feast!
> A great oak stump now is lying
>   In the ashes yet undying.
>   Come, Maron, come!
> Raging let him fix the doom,
> Let him tear the eyelid up
> Of the Cyclops—that his cup
>   May be evil!
> Oh! I long to dance and revel
> With sweet Bromion [Bacchus], long desired,
> In loved ivy wreaths attired;
> Leaving this abandoned home—
> Will the moment ever come?   (613–28)

There is an allusion in the play to the Homeric Hymn about Bacchus and
the Pirates, just translated by Leigh Hunt – a poem also about the victory
that the wine god achieves over the tyrannical master of the ship. In both
poems, as well as in the Homeric Hymn to Mercury, the politics of resistance joins with a poetics that features a site of imaginative confusion and
trickery, pointing to techniques of bewildering the eye of tyrannical control.

Dante

Like the translations from the poetry of ancient Greece and Rome, those from Dante, though fewer in number, at once participate in the progressive poetics of Shelley's contemporaries and contribute to the character of his own work. The nature of the contribution is different from that of the earlier translations; if the latter demonstrate Shelley's poetics of transformation, the crisis for visionary poetics of the elegy, and the necessity for poetry to 'outwit' and confuse the ideology of a society in which, as Hazlitt says, 'the police spoils all', then the Dante translations attend to intellectual love, Shelley's version of the progressive vision of eighteenth- and nineteenth-century poetry that insists upon the union of eros, mind, and language – in Thomas Gray's phrase: 'thoughts that breathe, words that burn'. The final stanza of his translation of Dante's first canzone of *The Convito*, for example, becomes the epigraph for *Epipsychidion*, Shelley's great swollen lyric of intellectual passion-love.

His translation of Dante's sonnet to the poet Guido Cavalcanti (published first in the *Alastor* volume, 1816) is equally important, as a 'manifesto' of poetry as both an outcome and a prediction of an ideal community of like-minded friends – variously figured as the Hunt community or the friendship that included Mary Shelley, Byron, and Claire Clairmont – and once again Shelley includes part of this sonnet at the end of *Epipsychidion*, as the poem of passion-love resolves into one of friendship. Here is the sonnet:

> Guido, I would that Lapo, thou, and I,
> Led by some strong enchantment, might ascend
> A magic ship, whose charmèd sails should fly
> With winds at will where'er our thoughts might wend,
> So that no change, nor any evil chance
> Should mar our joyous voyage; but it might be,
> That even satiety should still enhance
> Between our hearts their strict community:
> And that the bounteous wizard then would place
> Vanna and Bice and my gentle love,
> Companions of our wandering, and would grace
> With passionate talk, wherever we might rove,
> Our time, and each were as content and free
> As I believe that thou and I should be.   (1–14; *H*)

The poem might signify the process of translation in its fantasy of a travelling-across to an ideal community of 'passionate talk' aided by a 'wizard' of this translation.

This translation participates in a beautiful poetic/historical trajectory, from Dante and his circle, to Shelley and his, to Dante Gabriel Rossetti and the Pre-Raphaelite Brotherhood of the early Victorian period. Rossetti, in his great translation of Dante's *The New Life* and the satellite poems of exchanges among members of Dante and his circle, actually quotes the first line of Shelley's sonnet in his own translation. Through this verbal link, he establishes the tradition of poetry and small groups of dissident poets.

Shelley translated one canto from *The Divine Comedy* (another, *Inferno* 33.22–75, was translated by Thomas Medwin with corrections by Shelley), *Purgatorio* 28, often referred to as 'Matilda Gathering Flowers'. This seemed to have a resonance for Romantic poets, as did *Inferno* 5, 'Paolo and Francesca'. Shelley's translation, of lines 1–51 alone, is intensely poetic, perhaps one of his best, one in which he has contrived to make a poetry in English that not only follows Dante but finds a generative source in the English as well. Consider, for example, the opening lines, in comparison, first, to Dorothy Sayers's 1955 translation:

> Eager to search, in and throughout its ways
>   The sacred wood, whose thick and leafy tent,
> Spread in my sight, tempered the new sun's rays,
> I made no pause . . .[13]

And Shelley:

> And earnest to explore within—around—
> The divine wood, whose thick green leafy woof
> Tempered the young day to the sight—I wound
> Up the green slope . . .   (1–4; *H*)

Shelley's 'within—around—' calls up a person in the midst of a situation, turning his head with the turning of the words. The sense of the tactile and ocular resistance and presence of the woods is furthered with the four accented words placed, like towering, close-standing trees, in closest proximity: 'thick green leafy woof', reinforced by the alliterative and assonantal accents: wood, whose, woof, wound.

Or consider the following weaving of sounds in Shelley – 'purest', 'hue', 'turbid', 'impure':

> Water of purest hue
> On earth, would appear turbid and impure
> Compared with this[.]   (28–30)

The most striking poetic moment, however, comes when Shelley, describing his encounter with Matilda and then addressing her, alluding both to

Milton and to Wordsworth, creates a historical trajectory from Dante to himself that marks, as a kind of palimpsest, the renewing value of Dante's canto. Here is the passage in Shelley's translation:

> I moved not with my feet, but mid the glooms
> Pierced with my charmèd eye, contemplating
> The mighty multitude of fresh May blooms
>
> Which starred that night, when, even as a thing
> That suddenly, for blank astonishment,
> Charms every sense, and makes all thought take wing,—
>
> A solitary woman! and she went
> Singing and gathering flower after flower,
> With which her way was painted and besprent.
>
> 'Bright lady, who, if looks had ever power
> To bear true witness of the heart within,
> Dost bask under the beams of love, come lower
>
> Towards this bank. I prithee let me win
> This much of thee, to come, that I may hear
> Thy song: like Proserpine, in Enna's glen,
>
> Thou seemest to my fancy, singing here
> And gathering flowers, as that fair maiden when
> She lost the Spring, and Ceres her, more dear.'   (34–51)

Shelley's allusion to Milton (observed by Timothy Webb) is an extraordinary act of 'trans-lation' because Milton, in the following passage describing Eve in Paradise (*Paradise Lost* 4), is himself imitating Dante, *Purgatorio* 28:

> Not that fair field
> Of Enna, where Proserpine gathering flowers
> Her self a fairer flower by gloomy Dis
> Was gathered, which cost Ceres all that pain
> To seek her through the world.   (4.268–72)[14]

Milton imitating Dante then gets picked up by Shelley, who then repeats the entire process, with Wordsworth's lyric 'The Solitary Reaper' (publ. 1807), which opens:

> Behold her, single in the field,
> Yon solitary Highland Lass!
> Reaping and singing by herself;
> Stop here, or gently pass!
> . . . .
> Will no one tell me what she sings?—[15]

Like Milton, Wordsworth may very well have had Dante's Matilda in mind; thus Shelley invites another poet to aid in his translation of Dante. This results in a richly intertextual situation, and raises the question: where does this poem reside? Has Shelley produced an Orphic poetry rejuvenated from time to time in history but finally without location and with an undefinable poetic agency? What emerges is a set of 'before unapprehended relations' (*Defence*) of Dante, Milton, Wordsworth, and Shelley – with little sense of the 'source' text and the 'target' text. Translation has become 'transform-ation'. Shelley's translation here in some ways anticipates the practice of his 'Ode to the West Wind', with its layerings of Dante (*terza rima*), the sonnet form, the psalms, and himself (allusions to 'Hymn to Intellectual Beauty' in stanza 4): translation practice differs little in this sense from poetic practice more generally.

Goethe

In addition to his translation from the Spanish of scenes from Calderón's play *Magico Prodigioso*, carried by strongly urbane blank verse, Shelley translated scenes 1 and 2 from Goethe's *Faust*, Part One: the 'Prologue in Heaven' and the 'May-Day Night', at a time when relatively few in England knew *Faust*. The 'Prologue in Heaven' presents a unique and fascinating discussion and presentation of Shelley's attitudes towards translation. As a footnote to the first twenty-eight lines, he provides a 'literal translation' with a subsequent explanation:

> Such is a literal translation of this astonishing chorus; it is impossible to represent in another language the melody of the versification; even the volatile strength and delicacy of the ideas escape in the crucible of translation, and the reader is surprised to find a *caput mortuum*. (H 749)

One could read this note and the accompanying literal translation following Shelley's poetic one as an exhibit of the failure of translation before 'aston-ishing' poetry in another language. With the memory of Shelley's 'violet and the crucible' in the *Defence*, this metaphor in its absurdity connotes the inherent destructiveness and near irrelevance of translation. But triangulat-ing a poetic and a literal translation with an explanatory and evaluative footnote can be said to make a different statement – that of a juxtaposition of competing choices of response to a poem, each defined not by lack or failure, but by positions from which to view the power of the third, invisible and original, version. Here is, like the Dante translation just discussed, another example of translation as a preferred dislocation. 'The poem' – in some sense Goethe's but in fact an idea of Goethe's – occupies some space between or above the two translations, each of which has a poetic validity. Compare Shelley's poetic and then literal versions of Gabriel's opening speech:

> And swift and swift, with rapid lightness,
>   The adornèd Earth spins silently,
> Alternating Elysian brightness
>   With deep and dreadful night; the sea
> Foams in broad billows from the deep
>   Up to the rocks, and rocks and Ocean,
> Onward, with spheres which never sleep,
>   Are hurried in eternal motion.   (9–16; *H*)

>   And swift, and inconceivably swift
> The adornment of earth winds itself round,
> And exchanges Paradise-clearness
> With deep dreadful night.
> The sea foams in broad waves
> From its deep bottom, up to the rocks,
> And rocks and sea are torn on together
> In the eternal swift course of the spheres.   (*H* 749, note 1)

Curiously, the second translation may have more poetic appeal than the first, in which Shelley attempts to find in contemporary lyric forms some kind of equivalent to Goethe. But the 'literal' version actually carries a poetic rhythm not based on rhymes or iambs, a rhythm in touch with 'English' that emphasizes the character of language difference, a foreground of the 'target' language as if to say: yes, this is a translation and therefore has its own idioms, grammars, and general peculiarities. Moreover, the phrase 'Paradise-clearness' ('Paradieseshelle' in Goethe's German) calls attention, through its address in English, to the immiscibility of the two languages and thus, at some level, the two poetries. It reinforces Shelley's note about the impossibility of translation while demonstrating that what results is, nonetheless, a rather beautiful presence.

At the same time Shelley insists upon the two translations together: he insists upon a reading back and forth, a kind of magic coming from this restless transport, one that seems to require a Mercury, a Bacchus, a Mephistopheles, in the strangeness of carrying-across thresholds. Shelley's translations, not particularly many in number and certainly engaging disparate literatures, work like the scattering of seeds or sparks, imagined as the outcome of his own poetry, an expansion of human transformations in the world.

NOTES

1. John Keats, Letter 159, in *The Letters of John Keats, 1814–1821*, ed. Hyder F. Rollins, 2 vols. (Cambridge, Mass.: Harvard University Press, 1958).

2. Marilyn Butler, *Romantics, Rebels, and Reactionaries: English Literature and its Background 1760–1830* (Oxford: Oxford University Press, 1982) and Jerome J. McGann, *The Romantic Ideology* (Chicago: University of Chicago Press, 1983).

3. The poems ascribed by Shelley to Homer actually belong to the anonymous post-Homeric collection today called the 'Homeric Hymns'. Like Homer's epics their verse form is dactylic hexameter. But most of the material consists of accounts of the Greek gods and goddesses. (Shelley primarily uses their Roman names.)

4. Percy Bysshe Shelley, *Relics of Shelley*, ed. Richard Garnett (London: Moxon, 1862).

5. *The Poetical Works of Percy Bysshe Shelley*, ed. William Michael Rossetti, 2 vols. (London:Moxon,1870).

6. *The Poetical Works of Percy Bysshe Shelley*, ed. H. Buxton Forman, 4 vols. (London: Reeves and Turner, 1876–7).

7. C. D. Locock, *An Examination of the Shelley Manuscripts in the Bodleian Library* (Oxford, 1903).

8. Timothy Webb, *The Violet in the Crucible: Shelley and Translation* (Oxford: Oxford University Press, 1976). For this passage in the *Defence of Poetry*, see N 514.

9. Quoted in Webb, *The Violet in the Crucible*, 126.

10. *The Homeric Hymns*, trans. Thelma Sargent (New York: Norton, 1973), 31. Subsequent references are given parenthetically in the text.

11. Quoted in Webb, *The Violet in the Crucible*, 123.

12. William Shakespeare, *The Complete Works*, ed. Peter Alexander (London and Glasgow: Collins, 1951). John Milton, *John Milton: Complete Shorter Poems*, ed. John Carey (London and New York: Longman, 1968, 1971).

13. Dante, *The Divine Comedy*, 3 vols., vol. II: *Purgatory*, trans. Dorothy L. Sayers (New York: Penguin Books, 1955), 289–90.

14. John Milton, *Paradise Lost*, ed. Alastair Fowler (London and New York: Longman, 1968, 1971).

15. William Wordsworth, *Poems, in Two Volumes, and Other Poems, 1800–1807*, ed. Jared Curtis (Ithaca, N.Y.: Cornell University Press, 1983).

7

WILLIAM KEACH

The political poet

Intelligent idealism is closer to intelligent materialism
than is unintelligent materialism.
(Lenin)[1]

Materialism and idealism

Prometheus Unbound challenges its readers to think about reality in radically unaccustomed ways. The aphorism by the Marxist revolutionary V. I. Lenin with which I begin – one of the epigraphs to Frederic Jameson's *Marxism and Form* – offers a surprising but useful point of departure for thinking about connections between style and politics in Shelley's most ambitious and experimental work. As a point of departure it should not be taken to imply some kind of hidden identity between Shelley's and Lenin's (or any other Marxist revolutionary's) beliefs about our knowledge of reality. Nor should it be taken to imply an identity between Shelley's philosophical convictions and the dialectical idealism of Hegel, to whom Lenin is primarily referring. Instead, what Lenin's aphorism recognizes is a rejection of conventional dualistic assumptions about the relation of mind and matter common to radical idealism and radical materialism. For Shelley as for Lenin, this rejection of dualism is politically as well as philosophically critical. It forms part of the conceptual basis for a range of practices that are about remaking the world of human experience by releasing its full potential as a dynamic and differentiated totality.

Most people today – even in this era of advanced neuroscience and artificial intelligence – find it hard to entertain the idea that existence is entirely a function of material forces and phenomena. They find it harder still to entertain the belief that existence is entirely a function of mental or psychic forces and phenomena. Shelley understood the claims of both positions and saw them as alternatives to the 'fatal consequences' of believing that the material realm constituted one kind of reality, the realm of mental experience and value quite another.

To grasp the poetic principles guiding Shelley's writing in *Prometheus Unbound* in relation to the political principles determining his recasting of the Prometheus myth, it is helpful to understand where Shelley was in the evolution of his basic philosophical perspective during 1818–19, the years in which he was composing his 'Lyrical Drama'. The most important point of reference in this regard is the fragmentary essay 'On Life' which Shelley drafted late in 1819. Here Shelley 'confess[es] that I am one of those who am unable to refuse my assent to the conclusions of those philosophers, who assert that nothing exists but as it is perceived' (Pr 173). This formulation, conveyed with less negative hesitation and yet more explicit qualification in A Defence of Poetry ('All things exist as they are perceived— at least in relation to the percipient', Pr 295), has come to be the foundation for accounts of Shelley as a radical and sceptical idealist. We need to acknowledge at the outset that in both versions Shelley's formulation is grammatically ambiguous in ways that are philosophically consequential. '[A]s they are perceived' can mean 'only while' or 'as long as' and also 'insofar as they are perceived' (the hard readings – existence depends absolutely and fundamentally on perception), and also 'in the way in which', 'according to how they are perceived' (the soft readings – existence depends relatively and conditionally on perception). Shelley commits himself to the idealist position that perception is constitutive of existence but leaves indeterminate the question of how foundational such constitutive perception may be. The ambiguity resonates both with the reluctance conveyed in 'On Life' ('unable to refuse my assent') and with the delimiting concession conveyed in the Defence ('at least in relation to the percipient').

Shelley advances his idealist maxim in 'On Life' by emphasizing its counter-intuitive force ('It is a decision against which all our persuasions struggle') and by linking his 'assent' to it to his previous movement in an opposite philosophical direction: 'The shocking absurdities of the popular philosophy of mind and matter, and its fatal consequences in morals, and their violent dogmatism concerning the source of all things, had early conducted me to materialism' (Pr 173). Though he goes on to characterize materialism as a 'seducing system' that 'allows its disciples to talk and dispenses them from thinking', there are good reasons for believing that the radical idealism of Shelley's later poetry and politics continued to be deeply marked by his earlier reading in the French materialist tradition (especially in Baron d'Holbach's Système de la nature and Pierre-Jean-George Cabanis' Rapports du physique et du moral de l'homme), and in the British materialist writing of Erasmus Darwin and William Lawrence. Shelley does not figure prominently in Alan Richardson's British Romanticism and the Science of the Mind, but Richardson's exploration of the importance of '"embodied" or "corporeal" accounts of mind' for British Romanticism bears provocatively on efforts to take the measure of Shelley's apparently anti-materialist poetry.[2] When Richardson observes in a note that Shelley 'uses the term "brain" more extensively than any other canon-ical Romantic poet, and in ways that reflect his interest in materialist or quasi-materialist thinkers', one senses that fresh possibilities may open up if we understand Shelley's own 'intelligent idealism' in ways that connect as well as oppose it to the 'intelligent materialism' of his own era.[3]

The point, again, is not to dissolve or explain away the differences between the undeniably idealist premises of *Prometheus Unbound* and the 'materialism' Shelley distances himself from in 'On Life'. There is too much of such dissolving and explaining away in the account offered by Kenneth Neill Cameron, one of the great materialist scholars of Shelley's work. Commenting on the passage from 'On Life', Cameron concludes that Shelley 'is not denying the existence of an external universe, but is arguing only that whatever is known is known only through the senses, and the senses disclose nothing more than sensation'.[4] This seems to me the wrong way to reconnect Shelley's version of what he calls the 'intellectual philoso-phy' with the anti-dualist materialism he had previously admired. Shelley speaks of perception, not 'sense' or 'sensation', as determining existence. In the philosophical vocabulary of Shelley's era 'perceive' and 'perception' were not limited to sensory experience but usually carried a broader and more inclusive range of meaning. Cameron's reduction of perception to sensation rules out the entire category of ideas of reflection – ideas produced by the mind's perception of its own operations – which John Locke had made a cornerstone of his epistemology. Shelley's 'perceived' stresses a kind of constitutive mental activity that includes but is not confined to 'sensation'. Paying attention to this term involves our recognizing that, for materialists as well as idealists, reality comes to exist as human experi-ence, culture, and history through acts of perception. If we were to think, as Shelley puts it with some assistance from Shakespeare, 'that the solid universe of external things is "such stuff as dreams are made of"' (*Pr* 173), we might believe that 'things' as well as 'dreams' are the 'stuff' of per-ception. And because of this we might also believe that 'things' and thoughts must be mutually determining – as at the end of 'Mont Blanc', where 'The secret strength of things . . . governs thought' (139) even as the 'universe of things' (1) depends for its existence on 'the human mind's imaginings' (143).[5]

The political implications of Shelley's distinctively inflected idealism begin to open up when we consider more fully that 'On Life' was drafted as an extension of a passage in *A Philosophical View of Reform*. Both were written near the very end of 1819 and beginning of 1820, as he was finishing *Prometheus Unbound* in its four-act form. The *Philosophical View* is driven by a conviction that human beings make their own political history, and in this sense determine their own political existence, through acts of perceiving the world and themselves. But political existence is also a function of 'material' conditions and institutions, as Shelley makes clear in his opening reference to the 'necessity of a material change in 'the existing institutions of English Government' (*Pr* 230). Later he writes of the French that they 'cleav[ed] to the external form of things' because 'Their institutions made them what they were' (*Pr* 236). Institutions exist, Shelley argues, as manifestations of the perceptions of societies that are increasingly divided between 'those whose labour produces the materials of subsistence and enjoyment' and 'those who claim for themselves a superfluity of these materials' (*Pr* 242). There is a power of necessity at work in human history as well as in the nature of things. But for Shelley the crucial political question is always how humanity, with its limited ability to know the forces and constraints of necessity, responds to these forces and constraints and distinguishes them from forces and constraints subject to human agency. It is at the conjuncture of necessity and human agency that the principle 'Nothing exists but as it is perceived' designates the parameters of historical and political as well as of epistemological and ontological meaning.

With these preliminary observations in mind, let us turn to the Preface to *Prometheus Unbound* and its indications of how Shelley wanted his readers to prepare themselves for the poetic and political challenges of his 'Lyrical Drama'. Convergences between the Preface and the prose from late 1819 that we have just been looking at are not surprising. The first four paragraphs of the Preface were written a few months before *A Philosophical View of Reform* and 'On Life', the last five paragraphs at about the same time. Shelley begins the Preface by appealing to what he calls 'a certain arbitrary discretion' in the treatment of the Prometheus narrative, and by explaining that he has no intention of attempting to 'restore' the lost *Prometheus Unbound* of Aeschylus, which contained 'a catastrophe so feeble as that of reconciling the Champion with the Oppressor of mankind' (*P* II.472). This 'catastrophe' was Prometheus' revelation of the secret concerning Jupiter's marriage to Thetis (it would result in an offspring capable of bringing about Jupiter's downfall), in exchange for his being 'unbound' by Jupiter. Prometheus must not be represented as in any way capitulating to or compromising with Jupiter – as 'unsaying his high language, and quailing before his successful and perfidious adversary'. This principle of uncompromising resistance is critical to Shelley's political analysis of the relation of reform to revolution, and to his entire conception of Prometheus as 'the type of the highest perfection of moral and intellectual nature, impelled by the purest and the truest motives to the best and noblest ends' (*P* II.473). The key features of this remarkable sentence are the word 'type' – mark, sign, emblem, especially as a figure or representation of something to come – and the six superlative adjectives Shelley deploys in specifying the content of the Promethean 'type'. Shelley's Prometheus is neither a mythical Greek deity nor a fictional human being: he is a figure of future human potential projected to the utmost degree of idealization. He is 'ideal' both in the two colloquial senses given first in the *OED* – 'Existing as an idea or archetype' and 'Conceived or regarded as perfect or supremely excellent' – and in the philosophical senses given third and fourth – 'Of, pertaining or relating to, . . . an idea, mental image, or conception'; 'Existing only in idea; confined to thought or imagination'.[6] '[C]onfined to thought or imagination' does not, of course, fit Shelley's conception of what is 'ideal' at all. For him 'ideal' names a mode of perception beyond the confines of dualistic alienation. '[I]dea' designates all existential reality as constituted through acts of perception. So when he turns immediately in the Preface from characterizing Prometheus as a poetic and political 'type' to evoking the Roman setting in which *Prometheus Unbound* 'was chiefly written' (*P* II.473), he is representing conditions and circumstances external to the text only in the sense that an 'inspiration' may be said to be external to that which it inspires. From a Shelleyan perspective imaginative inspiration and textual expiration are continuous but ineluctably differentiated moments of existence constituted through perception.

Next, as if it followed inevitably from his having moved from representing Prometheus as a 'moral and intellectual' 'type' to the circumstances in which this 'type' was conceived, Shelley turns to the stylistic experimentalism of *Prometheus Unbound*: 'The imagery which I have employed will be found in many instances to have been drawn from the operations of the human mind, or from those external actions by which they are expressed. This is unusual in modern Poetry' (*P* II.473). Here is a founding principle of Shelley's radically idealist poetics: instead of offering sensuous or material figures for mental states and processes, the writing in *Prometheus Unbound* will draw its figures or 'imagery' from mental process itself.[7] 'As suddenly / Thou comest as the memory of a dream' says Asia in addressing Spring at the beginning of Act 2 (1.7–8): the point of comparative reference for Spring's sudden descent is a double image of fleeting mental experience.

We will look more closely later at what is involved in attuning ourselves to such figurative reversals. In the Preface Shelley expands and complicates the reader's preparedness on this score by referring to 'the operations of the human mind, or . . . those external actions by which they are expressed'.

Couldn't 'external actions' accommodate most of the conventionally sensuous or physical imagery that presumably stands in contract to Shelley's 'unusual' figurative practice here? Perhaps – but we need first to consider what 'external' might mean to a writer for whom 'Nothing exists but as it is perceived.' Two later passages from 'On Life' are pertinent:

> The difference is merely nominal between those two classes of thought which are vulgarly distinguished by the names of ideas and of external objects.

> By the word *things* is to be understand any object of thought, that is, any thought upon which any other thought is employed, with an apprehension of distinction.   (*Pr* 174)

'External' for Shelley designates that aspect of perception in which the perceiving subject differentiates itself from what it perceives, from what it experiences as the object of its perception. 'External'/'internal' become designations of epistemological orientation and positioning, rather than of ontological essence. From this vantage point, what Shelley has attempted in the imagery of *Prometheus Unbound* is a radically prioritized orientation towards the perceiving subject and its distinctive modes of discourse.

From the perspective of Shelley's Preface, however, 'subject' has to mean not the individual human subject but the ideal 'type' of 'moral and intellectual' subjectivity. Shelley attempts to prepare us for entering a textual environment in which not only our common assumptions about 'imagery' but also our usual assumptions about dramatic voice and form are challenged on the basis of a strongly monistic idealism. In his powerful and influential reading of *Prometheus Unbound*, Earl Wasserman maintains that 'except for Demogorgon, Prometheus is the only reality actually present in the play, and it would be short of the truth to say that the drama takes place *in* his mind; he *is* the One Mind'.[8] We will need to return to that 'except for Demogorgon' clause. And, as I have been suggesting, there are reasons to question Wasserman's powerful account of the metaphysical 'premises' of *Prometheus Unbound*. But his argument remains compelling that all the *dramatis personae* of Shelley's text – 'except for Demogorgon' – should be grasped as representations of Prometheus' status as 'the type of the highest perfection of moral and intellectual nature'. It is not just that Jupiter is to be read as the enslaving projection of Prometheus' own capacity for hatred, and Asia as the liberating projection of Prometheus' capacity for love: all the voices are aspects of Prometheus as moral and intellectual 'type' realizing itself in a process of self-conflict and self-liberation. The philosophical proposition in 'On Life' to which this dramatic form corresponds appears in a passage that relegates individual human identity to the status of provisional discursive convenience:

> the existence of distinct individual minds similar to that which is employed in now questioning its own nature, is likewise found to be a delusion. The words, I, *you*, *they* are not signs of any actual difference subsisting between the assemblages of thoughts thus indicated, but are merely marks employed to denote the different modifications of the one mind. (*Pr* 174)

Shelley can only represent Prometheus as moral and intellectual 'type' in the necessarily delusive language of discretely individualized subjects, much as he can only theorize 'the one mind' by declaring personal pronouns to be nothing more than 'marks' of modification, 'grammatical devices'. There is no existing human language – and no possible literary form – capable of anything more than a negative and indirect articulation of what Shelley calls 'the most refined deductions of the intellectual philosophy'. The price that must be paid by a consistent idealism – and by a consistent materialism as well – is to communicate its vision of reality in a language that belies its monistic principles, that has false dualistic assumptions encoded in its rudimentary semiotic and grammatical features. *Prometheus Unbound* is therefore written, as Shelley puts it at the end of the paragraph from which I have been quoting, 'on that verge where words abandon us'.

For a writer to position himself and his readers on *this* verge is to put communication and intelligibility themselves at risk. Can Shelley's kind of 'idealism' be made 'intelligent' and 'intelligible' (to elaborate Lenin's phrase), even on its own philosophical and linguistic terms? There is plenty of evidence both in the Preface and in 'On Life' that Shelley was keenly aware of the risk – even that he conceived of the risk as a question of intelligibility. There is also plenty of evidence that he wrote as much from hope as from despair. When he says in the Preface that 'Poetical abstractions are beautiful and new . . . because the whole produced by their combination has some intelligible and beautiful analogy with [the] sources of emotion and thought, and with the contemporary condition of them' (*P* 1.474), he poses the positive but still necessarily indirect ('analogy') alternative to being 'on that verge where words abandon us'. Poetry of the kind he wants to produce depends distinctively on 'intelligible analogy', on language that corresponds but can never be identical to 'sources of emotion and thought' and their 'contemporary condition[s]'. Shelley may have been searching for readers mindful of the fact that both 'intelligent' and 'intellectual' have their historical roots in the Latin *legere*: to bring together, gather, collect; to pick out, extract; to choose, select, elect; . . . to read.

Reading as a political act

Mr Shelley can never become a popular poet. He does not sufficiently link himself with man; he is too visionary for the intellect of the generality of his readers, and is ever immersed in the clouds of religious and meta-physical speculations. His opinions are but skeletons, and he does not sufficiently embody them to render them intelligible.

('On the Philosophy and Poetry of Shelley', Gold's *London Magazine*(1821))[9]

This opinion of Shelley's relation to 'the generality of his readers' comes from a broadly positive contemporary assessment. Writing in a less generous mood the same year, Hazlitt characterizes 'The author of the Prometheus Unbound' as an 'individual instance' of 'the philosophic fanatic' entirely out of touch with common reality: 'He is clogged by . . . no earth-bound feelings, no rooted prejudices, by nothing that belongs to the mighty trunk and hard husk of nature and habit . . . It would seem that he wished not so much to convince or inform as to shock the public by the tenor of his productions.'[10] Even Shelley's most ardent and committed readers might acknowledge that *Prometheus Unbound* sometimes pushes them towards sympathy with the spirit, if not the terms, of Hazlitt's irritable response. His judgement that Shelley was capriciously playing or experimenting with 'the public' is worth pondering – not least because Shelley himself does not focus on 'the public' in the Preface. He speaks instead of intending

> to familiarize the highly refined imagination of the more select classes of poetic readers with beautiful idealisms of moral excellence; aware that until the mind can love, and admire, and trust, and hope, and endure, reasoned principles of moral conduct are seeds cast upon the highway of life which the unconscious passenger tramples into dust[.]   (*P* II.475)

Shelley's sense of his reading audience, together with our knowledge of his actual historical readership, have been explored in revealing detail by Stephen Behrendt, Michael Scrivener, Kim Wheatley, and other resourceful critics. My particular emphasis here is on how Shelley represents the possibility, activity, and circumstances of reading as crucial poetic and political issues in *Prometheus Unbound* – not just in the Preface, but within the fictional text of the 'Lyrical Drama' itself. His doing so has an important bearing on our willingness – or unwillingness – to be located on the edge of intelligibility, to occupy 'that verge where words abandon us'.

Before looking directly at Shelley's desire to communicate with 'the highly refined imagination of the more select classes of poetic readers', we should recognize that it was during the late summer and autumn of 1819, while he was completing *Prometheus Unbound* and drafting *A Philosophical View of Reform* and 'On Life', that he made his most concerted effort to reach an antithetical kind of readership. Mary Shelley (*1839*) identifies this readership:

> Shelley . . . believed that a clash between the two classes of society was inevitable, and he eagerly ranged himself on the people's side. He had an idea of publishing a series of poems adapted expressly to commemorate their circumstances and wrongs. He wrote a few; but, in those days of prosecution for libel, they could not be printed. (*H* 588)

According to Richard Holmes, Shelley projected a volume called *Popular Songs* that was to include *The Mask of Anarchy*, 'Ode to the West Wind', and 'Ode to Liberty', along with 'Lines Written during the Castlereagh Administration', 'Song to the Men of England', 'Similes for Two Political Characters', 'What Men Gain Fairly', 'A New National Anthem', '[Sonnet:] England in 1819', and 'Ballad of the Starving Mother'.[11] Of these the only ones printed in Shelley's lifetime were 'Ode to the West Wind' and the 'Ode to Liberty', both of which were included in the *Prometheus Unbound* volume of 1820 and might appear to appeal almost as much as Shelley's drama to 'the highly refined imaginations of the more select classes of poetical readers'. The others had to wait until the 1830s, when mass political agitation and Parliamentary reform opened up an audience for Shelley's poetry that he himself never experienced. So even as he was consciously aiming his most poetically ambitious work at 'the more select classes of poetical readers', Shelley was also writing – however futilely, given the political realities of the moment – for a popular audience. Even as it announces its own selective agenda, the *Prometheus* Preface recognizes the force and desirability of broad public access – in its acknowledgement of 'poems far more popular, and indeed more deservedly popular than mine'; in the claim that the 'mass of [literary] capabilities remains at every period materially the same'; in its appeal to 'that fervid awakening of the public mind' evident in the English Renaissance; in its conviction that 'Every man's mind is . . . modified by all the objects of nature and art.' Whatever we come to think about Shelley's projection of a 'select' readership, we would be wrong to follow Hazlitt and see it as motivated by either 'vanity' or 'levity'. *Prometheus Unbound* was written to 'familiarize' (the choice of verbs is telling) a 'select' group of readers with an 'ideal' vision that ought to – and someday will – be familiar to everyone.

This being said, Shelley's explicitly imagined readership still leaves us with difficult questions. From very early in his career Shelley saw himself as writing for a 'select' few – a few selected as much by the forces of class privilege as by any distinction of aesthetic refinement or political vision. He sent *Queen Mab* to the publisher Thomas Hookham in March 1813 with a letter that concludes: 'I expect no success.—Let only 250 Copies be printed. A small neat Quarto, on fine paper & so as to catch the aristocrats: They will not read it, but their sons & daughters may' (*L* 1.361). By 1817–18, when he wrote and published *The Revolt of Islam*, he appears to have developed a more hopeful sense of a self-selecting audience: 'The Poem which I now present to the world . . . is an experiment on the temper of the public mind, as to how far a thirst for a happier condition of moral and political society survives, among the enlightened and refined, the tempests which have shaken the age in which we live' (*P* II.32). This statement obviously anticipates the readership imagined in the Preface to *Prometheus Unbound* and distinguishes itself both from Shelley's worldly irony about who might read *Queen Mab* and from the different sort of self-protective irony involved in his telling Charles Ollier in 1821 'not to circulate' *Epipsychidion* 'except to the *Sunetoi*' (the cognoscenti, the initiated). In each of these instances Shelley not only anticipates but desires a special, delimited audience. If his aesthetically ambitious work is to reach a larger public readership, a 'public mind', it will be through those who share his own knowledge and refinement, if not necessarily his 'passion for reforming the world' (Preface to *Prometheus Unbound*, *P* II.475).

It needs to be made clear, since I began by quoting Lenin, that Shelley's imagining of a select audience has nothing to do with the Leninist conception of a revolutionary working-class vanguard. Shelley's idea of 'the more select classes of poetical readers' is expressive instead of the cautious, reformist side of his political thinking – of the impulse that makes him write to Peacock on 24 August 1819, a few days before he learned of the Peterloo Massacre: 'England seems to be in a very disturbed state . . . But the change should commence among the higher orders, or anarchy will only be the last flash before despotism' (*L* II.115). Thinking such as this accords well enough with an emphasis on encouraging change through 'beautiful idealisms of moral excellence', but it has little to do with the revolutionary transformation of human existence figuratively enacted in *Prometheus Unbound*. Though Prometheus' turn from disdain to compassion is pivotal, so is his unrelenting defiance in the face of Jupiter's oppression. So, too, is Demogorgon's 'power' in dethroning Jupiter and Hercules' 'strength' in unbinding Prometheus. Shelley's writing may need and appeal to cultural knowledge and skills generally found 'among the higher orders', but his political vision depends upon the eruption of volcanic forces from below that enter human existence in ways that cannot be confined to established practices of refinement and taste. What kinds of reading does *Prometheus*

Unbound imagine as being necessary to its transmission of revolutionary idealism, to its representation of acts of perception that reconstitute the world in revolutionary terms?

In this as in many respects, Act 2, with its emphasis on feminine voices and agency, is critically important. It opens with Asia's welcoming of spring and with her sister Panthea's struggle to communicate her recent dreams. As Panthea tries to speak paradoxically of a 'wordless converse' (2.1.52), Asia says – in two half-lines of blank verse that share half-lines of Panthea's speeches – 'Lift up thine eyes / And let me read thy dream' (2.1.55–6). Panthea responds with more than forty lines of words recounting one of her two dreams – the only one she can remember: Prometheus, liberated and radiant, appeared and spoke to her in a moment of passionate inter-penetration that Panthea represents in a sequence of cycling figures of evaporation and condensation. The experience of this dream, Panthea says, awakened her other sister, Ione, who imagined 'some enchantment old, / Whose spells have stolen my spirit as I slept / And mingled it with thine' (2.1.100–2). This exchange follows:

> ASIA
> Thou speakest, but thy words
> Are as the air. I feel them not . . . Oh, lift
> Thine eyes, that I may read his written soul!

> PANTHEA
> I lift them, though they droop beneath the load
> Of that they would express: what canst thou see
> But thine own fairest shadow imaged there?   (2.1.108–13)

Panthea's words recounting her dream, which we have just read, prove unreadable by Asia until they are translated into a kind of writing that (we are asked to imagine) bypasses speech altogether in a moment of visually conducted psychic transmission. What gets transmitted is a recognition of one's self in another's eyes – a double recognition, really, since Panthea interrogatively recognizes in Asia that the latter recognizes herself in her sister's look of recognition. The moment is defined by processes of reciprocal projection and mirroring that must be 'read', not spoken or heard – even though Shelley's dramatic format depends upon sustaining a fiction of speaking and hearing.

The exchange between Asia and Panthea at the beginning of Act 2 places Shelley's readers 'on that verge where words abandon us', which is where his mythic characters themselves are placed. From this verge a visionary communicative dynamic emerges that recapitulates and advances Prometheus' 'recall' of his curse on Jupiter in Act 1. At both points in *Prometheus Unbound*, acts of constitutive perceptual change are represented through a radical kind of *occupatio*, the rhetorical figure in which something is said in the process of denying that it can be said. In Act 2, reading the unsayable and unhearable works as a utopian figure – a figure deeply linked to the reflexive revolutionary utopianism that is the strongest political motivation in Shelley's 'Lyrical Drama'. Among the 'idealisms' Shelley stages for his readers is this moment of visionary reading in which a future liberated existence appears to be written 'on the verge where words abandon us', in the looks and bodies of those who dream and love. When Asia looks into Panthea's eyes and begins to see something 'dark, far, measureless,— / Orb within orb, and line through line inwoven' (2.1.116–17), she registers a condition of seeing that may stand for the reader's encounter with the lines of text themselves.

In predicating Asia's seeing 'a change' in Prometheus' existence on her act of visionary reading, Shelley may be modelling what he hopes for from his readers. He is not, I believe, pointing to a 'dialogue' between the poem and its readers of the kind that Kim Wheatley advances as an alternative to the 'paranoid' 'Satanic' stance in which Shelley confronts a hostile, antagonistic readership with his own hostile, antagonistic defiance. Wheatley argues for a Shelley who, in his later poetry, gradually writes his way towards an 'idealist' and 'reformist' stance in which the 'aesthetic' is constituted as a separate sphere from the political, and in which he can 'compose . . . a community' with readers opposed to, even frightened by, his 'passion for reforming the world'.[12] Shelley certainly imagines a community of readers, but to join in constituting this community a reader has to be willing to run the imaginative risks of defying the tyranny of things as they are, as well as of yielding to the 'all-dissolving power' of love (2.1.76). It is on these extreme and uncompromising grounds that *Prometheus Unbound* is written to be 'intelligible' to us.

Reading as radical participation

Shelley is not easy reading . . . Poets ordinarily employ material objects to represent or illustrate the phenomena of life and mental action, while Shelley does the reverse. He either makes these phenomena attributes of the material objects, or uses them to typify those things which were originally their types.
(Orestes Brownson, *Boston Quarterly Review* (1841); in CH 383, 387)

For Orestes Brownson – freelance New England transcendentalist, communitarian, supporter of the Workingmen's Party – Shelley's poetry is hard because its vision of transforming human social existence is inseparable from its radical philosophical idealism and stylistic experimentalism. The poetry is 'not easy' – but neither is it impossible, unintelligible. Although Shelley's writings 'have never enjoyed any very great degree of popularity', Brownson acknowledges in his review of Mary Shelley's 1839 edition of the *Poetical Works*, that 'his works begin to meet a merited regard' and will 'no doubt' find future readers up to the challenges the poetry poses (*CH* 382, 394). There is indeed no doubt that *Prometheus Unbound* has found readers adequate to its demands when we think of the great critical analyses of Wasserman, Curran, Hogle, and the others who comprise our era's version of Shelley's 'more select classes of poetical readers'. But what about *Prometheus Unbound* and non-specialist readers?

Shelley's 'Lyrical Drama' is accessible, I believe – not securely or comfortably possessable, but accessible – to any reader willing to work closely and curiously with the language and to imagine what the world might be like if it were true that 'Nothing exists but as it is perceived.' By way of indicating more specifically the kind of work and provisional imaginary positioning I have in mind, I want to explore four moments, one from each of the poem's four acts.

Act 1: Prometheus' opening speech

Shelley's 'Lyrical Drama' begins with a 73-line speech that will remind readers familiar with *Paradise Lost* of Satan, the 'only imaginary being resembling in any degree Prometheus' (*P* II.472). Prometheus addresses Jupiter, his oppressor and 'foe' and also the projection of his own impulses towards hatred, domination, and revenge. As 'Monarch of Gods and Daemons' Jupiter rules existence as his empire, but 'empire' is also the word Prometheus uses to designate his own realm of experience:

> Three thousand years of sleep-unsheltered hours
> And moments, aye divided by keen pangs
> Till they seemed years, torture and solitude,
> Scorn and despair,—these are mine empire.   (1.12–15)

Prometheus initially thinks that this condition of 'torture and solitude' will last 'forever!', with 'No change, no pause, no hope!' (1.23–4). But change is already underway with the first questions in his speech (1.25–9), and with the evocation of his 'torture' in detailed images that are at once visceral and visionary, corporeal and cosmic. 'The crawling glaciers pierce me with the spears / Of their moon-freezing crystals' (1.31–2) projects torture on a scale grander even than Milton's Hell. The sadistic slowness of the punishing glaciers eventually triggers slow motion in a different dimension, as 'Day and Night'

>   lead
> Their wingless, crawling Hours, one among whom
> —As some dark Priest hales the reluctant victim—
> Shall drag thee, cruel King, to kiss the blood
> From these pale feet, which then might trample thee
> If they disdained not such a prostrate slave.   (1.47–52)

The violence of Prometheus' language is disturbingly coherent, not only because the allusion to Jesus' impaled feet yields the image of those feet trampling a 'cruel King', but because – in the turning point of the speech – 'disdained' is no sooner spoken than questioned and turned into compassion: 'Disdain? ah no, I pity thee' (1.53).

In the final twenty lines of the opening soliloquy Prometheus locates one source of self-liberation in ceasing to 'hate' (1.57) and in 'recall'-ing (in every relevant sense of this word) the curse he uttered against Jupiter – that is, against the alienated and tyrannical potential in his own acts of perception. He calls upon the echoing and vibrating phenomena of physical nature to return 'that spell' (1.61), 'my words' (1.69), so that his utterance may be realigned with the change 'within' him. *Prometheus Unbound* begins with a change that is simultaneously psychic, ethical, and political – from 'No change' to 'I am changed', from the power of vengeful hatred to the power of self-revision.

Act 2, scene 3: Asia approaches the Cave of Demogorgon

Act 2 has two major functions in the argumentative development of *Prometheus Unbound*: it projects Prometheus' defiant and compassionate self-revision in Act 1 along an axis of imaginative and erotic desire, and it connects the realm of existence as constituted by the human mind's acts of perception with a hypostatized realm of being that is beyond mind, and that Shelley speculatively identifies in 'On Life' as the source of causality and necessity. After sharing liberatory dreams at the beginning of the Act, Asia and her sister Panthea follow echoic sounds to a setting identified long ago by G. M. Matthews as the 'crater of a quiescent volcano with a tall cindercone in the middle' (the stage direction for scene 3 specifies 'A pinnacle of rock among mountains').[13] Panthea recognizes the place as 'the realm / Of Demogorgon' (2.3.1–2). Asia follows with a speech that evokes simultaneously the wondrous natural setting and a sense that what she sees is but the 'shadow' of a 'Power' or 'Spirit' yet to be engaged.

Visual gives way to aural experience as Asia looks at the wall of mountains surrounding the volcanic 'vale' and hears 'a howl / Of cataracts from their thaw-cloven ravines' that 'Satiates the listening wind, continuous, vast, / Awful as silence' (2.3.33–6). The effect of comparing an 'awful' 'howl' to 'silence' is very strange; stranger still is the simile that concludes Asia's speech:

> Hark! the rushing snow!
> The sun-awakened avalanche! whose mass,
> Thrice sifted by the storm, had gathered there
> Flake after flake: in Heaven-defying minds
> As thought by thought is piled, till some great truth
> Is loosened, and the nations echo round
> Shaken to their roots: as do the mountains now.   (2.3.36–42)

Reiman and Fraistat appropriately note that this simile 'is one of the best examples of the reversal of imagery that Shelley mentions in the fourth paragraph of the Preface', when he speaks of images 'drawn from the operations of the human mind' (N 244n.2).[14] Orestes Brownson quotes this simile in his 1841 review and comments: 'Passages like these are not comprehended with the same facility as those where the imagery is drawn from objects under the immediate inspection of the senses, and where the connexion with the antitype is plain at first sight. Men are unaccustomed to look to their internal consciousness for illustrations of external existences, and those who are not habituated to reflection do it with pain' (CH 388). Brownson's reference to 'internal' and 'external' echoes Shelley's own reliance in the Preface on a conventional epistemological distinction that is shown in 'On Life' to be 'merely nominal', merely the way in which common dualistic discourse represents as ontologically distinct what are really 'two classes of thought' (N, 508). The disorienting effect of Asia's comparing an avalanche to the gathering and release of 'some great truth' is intensified by the syntactical position of 'in Heaven-defying minds' – a generalizing reference to the Prometheus we encounter in Act 1 – *before* the 'As' that grammatically structures the simile. Momentarily, 'in Heaven-defying minds' names the location of the avalanche rather than the thought process to which it is compared. The very action of reading the simile draws us, for a moment at least, into regarding the world from the perspective of radical idealism.[15]

And from the perspective of radical political change as well. Although the gathering of snow ('Flake after flake') and of truth ('thought by thought') has been interpreted as figuring the gradualism of pacifist reform, the release of violent energy at the beginning and end of the simile moves in a revolutionary direction. 'Shaken to their roots' is a literalization of the very idea of *radical*: 'nations' and 'mountains' tremble with the force of descending avalanche and, implicitly, of erupting volcano.

Act 3, scene 4: The Spirit of the Hour commemorates Prometheus' unbinding

In Act 3, which Shelley initially wrote as the final act of *Prometheus Unbound*, a vaunting Jupiter is confronted by Demogorgon and dethroned in the opening scene. This action is confirmed in an exchange between Apollo and Ocean in scene 2. In scene 3, Prometheus, now reunited with Asia, is unbound through the agency of Hercules' strength and immediately announces his intention to make a home with Asia in 'a Cave' 'Where we will sit and talk of time and change / As the world ebbs and flows, ourselves unchanged' (3.3.23–4). As they make their way towards 'the destined Cave' in scene 4, they are heralded by the Spirit of the Earth and the Spirit of the Hour, personae representing the potential emergent in physical nature and in time now that the human mind's self-emancipation has been accomplished.

In response to a one-line invitation from Prometheus – 'We feel what thou hast heard and seen: yet speak' – the Spirit of the Hour gives the longest speech in the poem (3.4.98–204, 106 lines). He or she (the Spirit's gender is unspecified) begins by recalling the 'thunder' that signalled Jupiter's fall, and then 'a change' perceived as an atmosphere permeated by and surrounding the world with erotic energy. As she floated down towards earth, the Spirit imagined a transformation in the idealized 'Phidian forms' of classical sculpture and architecture (3.4.106–21). Arriving on the earth, she was at first disappointed 'not to see / Such a mighty change as I had felt within / Expressed in outward things' (3.4.128–30). But she looked again and saw transformation in every human relationship and institution – change registered recurrently through the language of negation that Timothy Webb has shown to be peculiarly characteristic of Shelley's utopian rhetoric (clauses beginning with 'none', for instance, appear seven times in lines 137–52).[16] The signs and vestiges of oppressive authority ('Thrones, altars, judgement-seats and prisons') still exist but have become 'The ghosts of a no more remembered fame' (3.4.169), 'the tools / And emblems of [the world's] last captivity,/ . . . unregarded now' (3.4.176–9). The speech draws to a close with figures that foreground the dramatic fiction of *Prometheus Unbound* and link this fiction to old perceptual and existential illusions:

> The painted veil, by those who were, called life,
> Which mimicked, as with colours idly spread,

> All men believed and hoped, is torn aside—
> The loathsome mask has fallen[.]   (3.4.190–3)

In the space vacated by this mockery of life appears a new image of human realization:

>   the man remains,
> Sceptreless, free, uncircumscribed:—but man:
> Equal, unclassed, tribeless and nationless,
> Exempt from awe, worship, degree,—the King
> Over himself; just, gentle, wise: but man:
> Passionless? no—yet free from guilt or pain,
> Which were, for his will made, or suffered them,
> Nor yet exempt, though ruling them like slaves,
> From chance, and death, and mutability.   (3.4.193–201)

Along with the continuing language of negation (notice the '-less' and the 'un-' formations, which culminate in the notorious phrase that ends this Act, 'the intense inane'), two other features of this passage are striking.[17] First, humanity is now 'Exempt' from the mystified inequality of previous regimes of social power – 'from awe, worship, degree' – but not from those forces that stand beyond existence as constituted through acts of perception – 'From chance and death and mutability'. Secondly, while the old regimes of social power have themselves been abolished, the discourses of monarchy, slavery, and (elsewhere in the poem) 'empire' remain, transvalued through a radical collective reflexivity. 'Man' (for Shelley the feminist, the word includes 'women' as celebrated in lines 153–63) is now 'the King / Over himself' (196–7), and 'rul[es] . . . like slaves' (200) the forces of chance and necessity from which he is still not exempt. Shelley's sense that we are compelled to speak in a language that either falsifies or compromises what we most deeply know is nowhere more apparent than in his articulations of power.

Act 4: Demogorgon's final speech

'Demogorgon': he is Shelley's dramatic trope for necessity, for 'the Primal Power of the world' (Mary Shelley's 1839 note, *P* II.467).[18] Boccaccio, one of Shelley's sources, derives the name from the Greek *daimon georgos*, 'daemon of the earth'; Shelley himself would also have associated it with two other Greek words, *demos* ('the people') and *gorgos* ('fierce') (*P* II.467–9). He appears to Asia and Panthea in his volcanic cave in Act 2 as a power beyond visibility ('a mighty Darkness', 'neither limb / Nor form nor outline', 2.4.2–6), and initially beyond language except for the terms in which he is addressed and questioned ('I spoke but as ye speak', 'a voice / Is wanting, the deep truth is imageless', 2.4.112–16). Demogorgon acquires voice through the self-emancipatory agency of Asia, and subsequently of Prometheus – yet when he appears to speak at the end of Act 4, it is with 'A universal sound like words' (4.518). The simile provokes a realization that we are reading a fictive verbal approximation of ultimate power, and that this power may be represented only indirectly, as a function simultaneously of similitude and difference.

In contrast to Prometheus' blank verse at the beginning, Demogorgon speaks at the end of *Prometheus Unbound* in rhymed verse – in seven four-line *abab* quatrains, then finally in three stanzas organized into *aabccbdd ottava* sequences (the third stanza has a ninth line and concludes with a triplet). Organized through what or whose agency? Organized according to what or whose principle of formally generated meaning? 'Shelley's' is of course the answer we begin by giving. But the shaping agency of the poet in *Prometheus Unbound* has come to stand for a much more inclusive conception of human agency released from its own self-imposed bondage and capable now, in the terms of Shelley's utopian fiction, of establishing previously unimagined relations to necessity and chance.

The last stanza of Demogorgon's speech literally 'spells' out what a liberated humanity must do if, in a necessarily unpredictable future, Jupiterian oppression 'reassume[s]' its 'empire'. The stanza unfolds through a sequence of infinitive clauses and ends, riskily, by again appropriating 'Empire' as a name for freedom's self-maintaining power:

> To suffer woes which Hope thinks infinite;
> To forgive wrongs darker than Death or Night:
> To defy Power, which seems omnipotent;
> To love, and bear; to hope, till Hope creates
> From its own wreck the thing it contemplates;
> Neither to change, nor falter, nor repent:
> This, like thy glory, Titan! is to be
> Good, great and joyous, beautiful and free;
> This is alone Life, Joy, Empire, and Victory.   (4.570–8)

At the centre of Demogorgon's culminating 'spell' is a remarkably compressed invocation of existence constituted 'as it is perceived' by the mind in its struggle for self-actualization, an instance of Shelley's reflexive imagery: 'to hope, till Hope creates / From its own wreck the thing it contemplates'. Working with the terms of formal philosophy in 'On Life', Shelley says that 'Mind . . . cannot create, it can only perceive' (*Pr* 174). Demogorgon claims otherwise, stressing mind in its desiring and projective mode and in its determination to construct what it desires from the wreckage of history itself. 'Hope creates' the thought as 'thing'.

I have been suggesting that the stylistic complexity of *Prometheus Unbound* bears the impress of an authorial agency that potentially elicits from us as readers our participation in a more inclusive and collective kind of human agency. Whether or not we actually have a sense of being included – of contributing our agency in realizing the meanings of the text – is something that cannot of course be answered in advance of any reading or rereading of the poem. Thinking about *Prometheus Unbound* in such terms means temporarily inhabiting an idealism that is both intelligent and intelligible – even for readers committed to recognizing, in ways different from Shelley's own, the materiality of the work's text, context, and reception.

NOTES

1. V. I. Lenin, *Collected Works* (Moscow: Progress Publishers, 1972), 38.276. The context is Lenin's 'Conspectus' of Hegel's *Lectures on the History of Philosophy*. The English translation in *Collected Works* actually reads: 'Intelligent idealism is closer to intelligent materialism than stupid materialism.' I follow instead the less ambiguous translation that appears as an epigraph to Frederic Jameson's *Marxism and Form* (Princeton: Princeton University Press, 1971).
2. Alan Richardson, *British Romanticism and the Science of the Mind* (Cambridge: Cambridge University Press, 2001), xvi.
3. *Ibid.*, 212, n. 77.
4. Kenneth Neill Cameron, *Shelley: The Golden Years* (Cambridge, Mass.: Harvard University Press, 1974), 153.
5. See the alternate fair-copy version of these lines at the end of 'Mont Blanc', and G. M. Matthews's paraphrase (*P* 1.541, 549).
6. *Oxford English Dictionary*, 'ideal', A. adj. 1.a, b, 3.a, b, 4.a.
7. See William Keach, *Shelley's Style* (New York and London: Methuen, 1984), 42–78.
8. Earl R. Wasserman, *Shelley: A Critical Reading* (Baltimore: Johns Hopkins University Press, 1971), 257.
9. Quoted in Theodore Redpath, *The Young Romantics and Critical Opinion, 1807–1824* (London: Harrap, 1973), 361.
10. William Hazlitt, 'On Paradox and Common-Place', in *Table Talk*, ed. Catherine Macdonald Maclean (London and New York: Everyman's Library, 1959), 149.
11. *RH*, 593; Michael Henry Scrivener, *Radical Shelley: The Philosophical Anarchism and Utopian Thoughts of Percy Bysshe Shelley* (Princeton: Princeton University Press, 1982), 227–8.
12. Kim Wheatley, *Shelley and His Readers: Beyond Paranoid Politics* (Columbia: University of Missouri Press, 1999), 1–8, 109–51.
13. G. M. Matthews, 'A Volcano's Voice in Shelley', *ELH* 24 (1957), 211.
14. '[A]n external natural event', they observe, 'is compared to . . . the slow growth of new concepts in *Heaven-defying minds* until there is an intellectual revolution'.

15. See Keach, *Shelley's Style*, 76–8.
16. Timothy Webb, 'The Unascended Heaven: Negatives in *Prometheus Unbound*', in *Shelley Revalued: Essays from the Gregynog Conference*, ed. Kelvin Everest (Leicester: Leicester University Press, 1983), 37–62.
17. Everest notes the derivation of 'inane' from Latin *inane*, 'void space': 'the word in this sense is frequent in Lucretius, and see also e.g. Virgil, *Eclogue* 6.31' (*P* II.611). Compare John Locke, *An Essay concerning Human Understanding*, ed. Peter H. Nidditch (Oxford: Clarendon Press, 1975), 131 (Book 2, chap. 7, para. 10): 'Nor let any one think these too narrow bounds for the capacious Mind of Man to expatiate in, which takes its flight farther than the Stars, and cannot be confined by the limits of the World; that extends its thoughts often, even beyond the utmost expansion of Matter, and makes excursions into that incomprehensible *Inane*.' Shelley was quite capable of using the adjective 'inane' in the now familiar sense of 'silly; senseless; empty-headed'; the *OED* cites as its first example of this usage *The Cenci* 3.1.277, 'some inane and vacant smile'.
18. 'Prometheus defies the power of his enemy, and endures centuries of torture; till the hour arrives . . . At the moment, the Primal Power of the world drives [Jupiter] from his usurped throne, and Strength, in the person of Hercules, liberates Humanity, typified in Prometheus' (*H* 272).

PART III

Ideas, beliefs, affiliations

8

JERROLD E. HOGLE

Language and form

Inspired by his revolutionary visions, we sometimes forget what a verbal artist Shelley was and remains and how much that artistry is rooted in a definite theory of language. When he finally justifies his craft with *A Defence of Poetry* in 1821, Shelley sees poetry, broadly defined, as beginning when the most primitive person uses 'language and gesture' to produce 'the image of the combined effect of . . . objects and his apprehension of them'. That primal moment is poetic because it is metaphorical. It is a transfer of something (a perception, itself metaphoric in being a transfer between reception and response) into something quite different (the verbalized image). Such a theory allows Shelley to make *deliberate* poetry, the reenactment of that earlier transfer, a transformation of existing forms of language into a re-envisioning of the world as we know it. Poetic language, he writes in his *Defence*, is 'vitally metaphorical; that is, it marks the before unapprehended relations of things', making us see perceptions (as well as words) in terms of others not yet connected to them. This sense of language, poetry, and revolution as essential to each other is so crucial to Shelley's world view by the time of his mature writing that the very life of true civilization for him comes to depend on the constant renewal of language by the poetry with which it began: 'if no new poets should arise to create afresh the associations' by which a culture understands itself, he fears, 'language will be dead to all the nobler purposes of human intercourse' (*Pr* 278).

To understand Shelley, as a result, we should examine the principal elements and sources of his theory of language and how that theory is worked out in major poetic *and* prose works of his that range across his too-short career. First, however, we must recognize that his sense of language as transformative was itself transformed as he matured. In his letters to Elizabeth Hitchener in 1811, the year he was expelled from Oxford after co-authoring *The Necessity of Atheism*, Shelley maintains 'that all poetical beauty ought to be subordinate to the inculcated moral—that metaphorical language ought to be a pleasing vehicle for useful & momentous instruction' (*L* 1.98). Here the value of any composition should be judged by the ideas behind it, hardly what Shelley would say a decade later in the *Defence*, where a poet 'would do ill' to 'embody his own conceptions' in his works (*Pr* 283). This initial stance is based on his early acceptance of an empirical sense of mind and language rooted in John Locke's *Essay concerning Human Understanding* (1690) and in David Hume's eighteenth-century intensification of Locke into scepticism about what the mind can know beyond its own thoughts based on sense impressions. Shelley writes to Hitchener that Locke, despite his belief in an anthropomorphic God, '*proves* there are no innate ideas', such as a faith in divinity, prior to perceptions from the senses (*L* 1.99–100).

Words for the young Shelley should therefore name only mental *ideas*, the coalesced memories of repeated perceptions (the signifieds of language's visible signifiers, to use the terms of Ferdinand de Saussure[1]). An unknown cause animating what we keep perceiving should not be named 'God' because of a wish of the 'fancy' to believe in something like a great soul; it should instead be termed 'the *existing power of existence*' because no cause beyond that can be inferred from perceived effects. Worthwhile truth at this stage in Shelley's life is based on the correspondence of words to genuinely rational ideas and nothing else. To use signs to claim an egocentrically fashioned Godhead is to employ personification to project a 'tyrannic majesty' on 'the throne of infinitude' (*L* 1.100–1). This is the oppressive myth, in Shelley's eyes, that justifies the reigning cultural orthodoxy of monarchy, hierarchy, and Church-enforced absolutes, all constructed as earthly versions of a cosmic Chain of Being that supposedly descends from an Almighty, the locus of ultimate meaning and power.

As Shelley grew, learned from voracious reading, and wrote poetry and prose with greater sophistication, his initial literalism came to seem almost as tyrannical as the religious and political assumptions he attacked. By the time of his essay 'On Life' (1819), he finds that 'we lose the apprehension of life' as our fluid early perceptions become habitual and codified within social norms. That is because the human mind too often represses the 'freedom in which it would have acted' because of a cultural 'misuse of words and signs' where we excessively fix thoughts and feelings, as he himself used to, behind the 'painted curtain' of how we usually express them. What we take to be familiar objects are actually rigidified signs that come to suggest 'one thought which shall lead to a train of thoughts'. This process tempts us to forget the empirical fact that 'nothing exists but as it is perceived' – which means that changes in the process of perception and interpretation *can* alter what any thing (already but an object of perception) seems to be in our common understanding. Literalism has become a restriction on the liberty the mind should have to transform signifiers, and hence their signifieds, into the as yet 'unapprehended relations' that poetry can help us conceive. Until we realize all this, the older Shelley adds, we will not see that the presumed distinction between 'the names of ideas and of external objects' has been an 'education of error' that has enslaved us. Currently what we believe to be a series of objects, though they are really just ideas (including an external god), can have the effect of seeming to govern our responses and control our will externally. We can escape from that trap, if we choose, only by realizing that most distinctions in words (including 'subject' and 'object') are no more than 'grammatical devices' in language and its constructions (*Pr* 172–4).

In this more mature view, then, Shelley regards language, along with the perceptions it helps to form, as inherently transformable. This is why revolutionary thinking and poetic language can be seen, like thoughts and words, as perpetually interacting with one another for the betterment of humankind. How, then, has Shelley moved from his earlier to this later position in less than a decade, and what is the relationship between that change and the richness of development in his literary language? I want to propose answers to both questions in what follows, employing, along with moments from his prose, two of his most important poems, composed years apart: *Alastor* and *The Triumph of Life*. These narrative poems offer, among many other things, sceptical theoretical statements on the nature of poetic language. Using them, I now want to argue that Shelley's literary language, while seeming to move from the relatively loose (Miltonic blank verse in *Alastor*) to the amazingly tight (Dantean *terza rima* in *The Triumph*), really becomes more mobile, disruptive, and widely associative, ultimately achieving the metaphorical freedom he values in his efforts to dissipate our 'education of error'.

The main ingredients in Shelley's theory of language

Shelley changed his views on language between 1811 and 1819 largely because of what he read on the subject from 1812 on and how several of these texts on language suited his revisionist liberal philosophy and the empirical scepticism to which it was attached.[2] His later emphasis on the poetry at the beginnings of human thought, for example, stems from his readings on the history of language ranging from Thomas Blackwell's *Life and Writings of Homer* (1735), where any language when first 'formed . . . must be full of Metaphor', perhaps of 'the boldest, daring, and most natural kind', to Jean-Jacques Rousseau's French *Essay on the Origin of Languages* (ca. 1755), where man's 'first expressions were tropes [literally *turnings*]' because his 'first motives for speaking were of the passions', which have to be metaphorically recomposed in being translated from internal sensations to public statements.[3] Even William Wordsworth, whom Shelley (once an admirer) would later condemn for abandoning the scepticism and liberalism in his writings of the 1790s, follows Rousseau in claiming that the earliest poets set an example for the natural writing that he supposedly revives, all by 'feeling powerfully' and therefore being 'daring' and 'figurative' in their utterances.[4]

Moreover, the transformation of this primal troping into an artifice distanced from original perceptions enters Shelley's thinking from these same accounts. For Wordsworth, later poets have sought the same effect as primitive ones 'without being animated by the same passion'. They have thus made the earlier figures of speech into 'mechanical' repetitions that they employ quite *un*naturally (303–4). Shelley, however, came to see this tendency as more broadly that of language itself. He was drawn to this view partly because he agreed with Francis Bacon that words as 'the footsteps of reason' left from the past become 'the idols of the Market-place' because of the 'tacit agreement of men concerning the imposition of words and names'. This progression generates 'lines of separation' so forgetful of earlier analogies that words eventually, like weapons stolen from their makers, 'shoot back at the understanding from which they proceeded'.[5]

This argument for Shelley is easily linked to Rousseau's view that 'languages favourable to liberty' have faded during the rise of a mercantile society in which 'there is nothing to say to people besides *give money*'. There is, after all, an 'implied analogy between the alienation of speech and the alienation of capital by those who institute and control public discourse' as capitalism expands.[6] Hence Shelley in his *Defence* maintains that 'every original language near to its source is in itself the chaos of a cyclic poem', a gloriously unstable and mobile interaction among metaphors that keep changing even as they cycle back on themselves. The constraining conventions of 'lexicography and the distinctions of grammar are the works of a later age'. These, in turn, fashion 'signs for portions or classes of thought' from the original chaos. They break up the movement of metaphor and analogy into a mechanical system of fixed signs that are emptied of poetic energy – and are thus 'dead' letters (the idols of the marketplace) by comparison (*Pr* 279). To restore poetry to language for the mature Shelley is therefore to shatter the illusions of what has become conventional discourse and, by reviving the impulse of analogy *in* language, to begin projecting a future of newly emergent relationships in recombinations of words and thoughts that reanimate dead letters and ideas.

Yet this vision of language's history and future begs a nagging question. If indeed most poets, like the rest of us, begin with words as already rigidified signs of ideas, which come first: words or ideas? Again, partly owing to his reading, Shelley's mature theory offers potentially conflicting, but finally complementary, answers. On the one hand, he became convinced by Joseph Addison, Edmund Burke, and James Burnet (Lord Monboddo), among others, that thought is prior to verbalization.[7] According to his *Defence*, 'language is arbitrarily produced by the imagination' and is therefore, compared to other symbolic material, 'a more direct representation of the actions and passions of our internal being'. On the other hand, Shelley admits that language has analogy-making capacities separate from those in the imagination: 'Sounds as well as thought have relation both between each other and towards that which they represent, [so] a perception of the order of those relations has always been found connected with a perception of the order of those relations of thoughts' (*Pr* 279–80). Verbal signifiers have interactions among themselves that *first* have nothing organic to do with what they represent and *then* provide relationships among different elements through which the relations of different thoughts to each other can be perceived by thought itself.

At this moment, Shelley is leaning towards such linguists as Etienne de Condillac and Horne Tooke, for whom the activities of thinking are impossible without some arrangements of language being there already, so much so that for Tooke 'what are called [the mind's] operations are merely the operations of Language'.[8] As it happens, Shelley has already had Asia, the pantheistic historian (as well as love) of his hero's life in *Prometheus Unbound*, recount what the mythic Titan Prometheus has bestowed on humanity by emphasizing his gift of language: 'He gave man speech, and speech created thought / Which [only then] is the measure of the universe' (2.4.72–3). Thought needs the counterpart that is language in order to form itself for its own self-reflection. Although verbal signifiers are dependent on thought for any will to change, this will activate language's inherent capacity for new verbal combinations, and these in turn become the shapers of new thoughts. Just as basic creativity is metaphorical for Shelley, so his connection of thought to language becomes metaphorical. It is a transference back-and-forth between the mind and words to the point where neither is entirely independent from nor dissolved into the other.

This fundamental movement of metaphor even animates the most basic level of sense impressions as Shelley comes to see them. Like the 'Eolian harp' made analogous to the brain in a 1796 poem by Coleridge, a human being in Shelley's *Defence* 'is an instrument over which a series of external and internal impressions are driven' in which there is not only some interaction among the impressions themselves but 'an internal adjustment of the sounds and motions thus excited to the impressions which excite them' (*Pr* 277).[9] Shelley describes the same basic movement in 'On Life', where he is indebted to the scepticism in Sir William Drummond's *Academical Questions* (1805), by seeing 'an object of thought' as first 'any thought upon which any other thought is employed' (*Pr* 174).[10] Impressions are never entities at one with themselves; they are transfers of something else onto the sensorium and are even known as such only when they are transferred again, reflected on by other thoughts that are among the existing associations of ideas in the mind ('internal adjustors') that both contextualize the new perceptions and are potentially unsettled by them. In this way mental observations are like words. They refer elsewhere and thus always look back and forth for meaning to other perceptions (*or* words) from which they differ but to which they also defer, simultaneously changing and being changed by them.[11]

Only when a thought employs itself on another 'with an apprehension of [total] distinction', Shelley notes in 'On Life', do we start to believe – mistakenly – in unbridgeable differences between thoughts, words, and things (signifieds, signifiers, and referents, in Saussurean terms; *Pr* 174). We lose our apprehension of life and poetry at their most inter-relational if we choose to make such distinctions that efface the true interactions of language with thought, thought with language, words with each other, thoughts with each other, and thus minds with each other. All of these entities are signifiers in their own ways, it turns out, and none of them truly occupies a position of primacy in relation to their counterparts. Hierarchy and the many abuses that follow from it, starting with prioritizing 'things' over thoughts and thoughts over words (the way of the poet's youth), come about for the mature Shelley because humanity has forgotten about these transfer-based operations of language and thought that both make distinctions possible and put in question any truth beyond interplays of signifiers.

As it strives to restore our deep awareness of this underlying (and freer) mobility, a poet's relation to language for the older Shelley should never be merely individual. In the 'sentimental' tradition of Adam Smith, author of *The Theory of Moral Sentiments* (1759) as well as *The Wealth of Nations* (1776), the older Shelley connects all valuable expression to the fundamental subject of his essay 'On Love' (1818): the drive 'within us which, from the instant that we live, more and more thirsts after its likeness' (*Pr* 170). The at least partial reenactment of this drive in every utterance means that a poet, working against the fixed codification of language that might suppress the relational impulse of love, must use the kind of words that help him 'put himself in the place of another and of many others'. In so extending his present frame of reference to what others have said or might say, he will expand 'the circumference of the imagination [in himself and his interlocutors] by replenishing it with thoughts of ever new delight' in a 'going out of our own nature' (the very definition of 'Love' in the *Defence*) which then 'awakens and enlarges the mind [of all participants] by rendering it the receptacle of a thousand unapprehended combinations of thought' (282–3).

One exhilarating result can be the entry of such a poet, his writings, and his readers into the long historical process whereby language is frequently reinvigorated, and its tyrannies overturned, by continuous poetic trans-formation – and hence social revolution. All poems recalled in Shelley's *Defence* as achieving such a 'distend[ing]' mutation in thought and words become for him 'episodes to that great poem, which all [true] poets, like the cooperating thoughts of one great mind, have built up since the begin-ning of the world'. It is by enacting that process, not by attaining some fixed sense of an eternal Unity, that the poet for the mature Shelley 'partici-pates in the eternal, the infinite and the one'.[12] At this moment especially, Shelley is exemplifying the disruption of older language he advocates by using the 'floating' capacity of signifiers to shift these particular words from their previous contexts, once the Platonic and orthodox Christian conceptions of 'the One'. The 'eternal, the infinite and the one' now name instead a continuity of discontinuities, the ongoing disruption of settled forms of language into new analogies. By this method Shelley can affirm that poets are 'the authors of revolutions in opinion' precisely because they keep reopening 'the permanent analogy of things' in language that is for him the 'life of truth' across time (*Pr* 285–7, 279, 281).

The poetic reanimation of language's mutability is impersonal for Shelley because the metamorphic process of transference – in perception, thought, language, thought and language together, and their social consequences – is for him an eternal, albeit ever-changing, force traversing every individual and era, often forgotten yet basic to each person's mental and linguistic processes. 'It is said that mind produces motion', Shelley concludes in 'On Life', but 'it might as well have been said that motion produces mind' (*N* 509).[13] By the last four years of his life, the years of his most verbally brilliant works, Shelley has gone from seeing language as anchored strictly to its user's ideas to viewing language as the medium for enacting an ever-turning interplay between the past and present thoughts of various poetic minds.

The development of Shelley's own writing, I now want to demonstrate, parallels this progression from one theory of language to another. As Stuart

Peterfreund has shown in explaining Shelley's particular views on linguistic tropes (which are not everyone's), this poet gradually steers away from figures or images that are mostly *metonymic* (for him parts or adjacent features which point to pre-existing wholes, such as figures representing supposedly higher or deeper ideas or entities) to ones that are primarily *metaphoric* (transfers of one figure into another *and* into another, as Shelley sees them, which look forwards as much as backwards and so shift the ground of understanding, rather than hinting at a ground firmly in place).[14] As he does so, widely read as he always was, he becomes unusually intertextual – in motion across the texts of many others, as well as his own – by the standards of the poetry just preceding his, which attempted to disavow blatantly 'poetic diction', as Wordsworth called it, for what seemed a more natural 'language really spoken by men' (*Selected Prose*, ed. Hayden, 285–7).

Shelley's style also becomes what William Keach rightly values in it: more 'reflexive', more inclined to compare 'an object or action' as perceived 'to an aspect of itself', thereby making it differ from itself *within* itself.[15] This process calls attention to how the transference basic to both human perception and language makes any supposed thing 'more than one thing, as both itself and something other than itself'. These changes begin to be apparent, though only moderately, in Shelley's 1816 volume, *Alastor . . . and Other Poems*, which launches his more mature writing. But they become the driving forces, not only in 'On Life' and *A Defence of Poetry*, but in the stunning variation on the epic dream visions of Dante and Petrarch that Shelley was composing when he drowned: *The Triumph of Life*.

Caught between 'deep truths' and transformations: *Alastor*

Although it is the title poem in a collection that also includes a sonnet 'grieving' over the conservatism of Wordsworth by the time of the latter's *Excursion* (1814), *Alastor; or, The Spirit of Solitude* is composed in the blank verse that Wordsworth adapted from Milton in poems ranging from 'Tintern Abbey' in *Lyrical Ballads* (1798) to *The Excursion* itself.[16] That is because *Alastor* is largely a critical parody of Wordsworth and of other philosophic and stylistic postures to which the 23-year-old Shelley had been attached in his youth. After positing a framing Narrator in this poem – a voice already framed within a Preface that speaks from a different and highly critical position – Shelley has this primary speaker tell the story of a now deceased visionary, the poem's main character. He does so by having his Narrator pointedly recall 'There was a Poet' (50), in the manner of Wordsworth's adult speaker looking backwards in 'There Was a Boy' (1800; later the Boy of Winander episode in *The Prelude* 5.364–97).

This basic style and point of view allows Shelley to undercut the orthodoxy of *The Excursion* by taking its author's language back to a more sceptical early use of it, where the 'visible scene' was said to enter the mind of the boy (partly a younger version of the speaker) like an 'uncertain heaven received / Into the bosom of a steady lake' that reflects the uncertainty back from a different place ('There Was a Boy', 21–4). This metaphor for basic metaphoric perception is echoed in *Alastor* often, as when the dying Poet's 'influxes of sense' are described as having 'fed' the water that is thought while the latter also provides influxes of its own (641–4). At the same time, though, when his Narrator longs to penetrate mysteries of 'this unfathomable world' (*Alastor*, 18–23), Shelley uses this regression to reenact the tendency of even the early Wordsworth to press the evidence of the senses towards an external depth, 'something far more deeply interfused, / Whose dwelling is the light of setting suns' ('Tintern Abbey', 96–7). In this way Shelley critiques his own previous inclination to establish at least the mental truth behind words and other signs and to pursue this supposed inner certainty to the point of avoiding sympathies with the wider world and other people. It is this 'self-centred seclusion' for which the *Alastor* Preface castigates the Poet, and perhaps its author in earlier years, while still extolling the 'adventurous genius' of the Poet – and by implication Shelley as well (*P* 1.462–3).

The result in the language of *Alastor*, a critique still attracted to what it parodies, is a tug of war between contradictory verbal inclinations. There are broadly metonymic sequences that hope for a grounding 'signified' and restlessly metaphoric departures from that strain that pit their more sceptical fluidity against the currents that draw the Narrator and Poet towards ultimate points of origin. The insistently Wordsworthian Narrator, as much of an unreliable speaker as any figure in *Alastor*, underwrites his opening apostrophes to his muse, Mother Nature (2, 18), with a 'natural piety' (from Wordsworth's 'My Heart Leaps Up', 9) that openly projects a majestic personification into his addressee. In doing so, the Narrator approaches nature sexually, in a kind of necrophilia where he makes his 'bed / In charnels and coffins' to await her (23–4), in the hope of penetrating to 'thy inmost sanctuary' (38) now that he has exaggerated Wordsworth's maternal Nature figure enough to make her seem pregnant with ultimate revelation. Yet the Narrator also feels compelled from the start to define desire as a longing for a mutual exchange with no dominant partner. He therefore describes nature as an interplay of different elements without one of them reigning supreme, be they 'Earth, ocean, air', a 'brotherhood' (1), or 'spring's voluptuous pantings when she breathes / Her first sweet kisses' (11–12). These personifications scatter the metonymic Mother into multiple and mixed gendered metaphors, mostly of process, throughout the lines that precede and prompt the 'questionings / Of thee and thine' (26–7, where 'she' is broken up – into 'thee' and 'thine' – by a sentence that hurtles past the boundaries of one line and continues in the next, a favourite device of Shelley's that we now call enjambment). Even the 'breath' of inspiration the Narrator wants from the Mother, which ostensibly animates this interaction, is more a movement across the different strings of a lyre than it is a unified entity, despite the Narrator's quest for deep mysteries.

With one-to-one reference thus attempted yet complicated by an on-slaught of transferences, no single answer to the Narrator's search is really possible in this poem, except perhaps for his story of a Poet who turns out to be both like and unlike him. After all, 'Neither the eye nor the mind', as Shelley later writes in the *Defence*, 'can see itself unless reflected upon that which it resembles' (*Pr* 285). The story of the Poet, an inner narrative circle framed by those of the Narrator and the Preface, is this sort of mirror that both reflects and (like any mirror) partially distends the gazer. It continues the Narrator's search for origins reflexively by deflecting that quest into an analogy for the main speaker's situation. At the same time, to be the reflection they need to be for the Narrator, the Poet and his story must be even more driven towards ultimate internal and external absolutes than the Narrator finally is. Compared to the Narrator (and Wordsworth, to some extent), the Poet (like Shelley) is more of a solitary *reader* with a deeply classical education. His imbibing of many non-English and ancient 'fountains of divine philosophy' joins with each perceived 'sight / and sound from the vast earth' (68–71) to make him 'seek strange truths' by following 'Nature's most secret steps' and searching out the most 'awful ruins of days of old' where he believes he can see into the 'secrets of the birth of time' (77, 81, 107, 128). At this point *Alastor* becomes even more intertextual and allusive than it was. Wordsworthian general Nature is replaced as the object of desire, in a radical shift from one focal point to an extremely different one (what rhetoricians term a *catachresis*), by the layered vestiges of old civilizations, each one having flourished at an earlier time than the last (109–16), through which the Poet searches anxiously to find the dawn of 'meaning' (126).

True to this poem's dialectical interaction between conflicting theories of reference, however, the *topos* (or long-standing literary pattern) of 'poring on memorials' (121) reaches its ultimate form in *Alastor* in a sequence that seemingly completes the Poet's quest for secrets only by offering a dispersion of differences. In the very old ruins of 'Dark Aethiopia', where the Comte de Volney, the liberal historian–scientist, located 'the cradle of [science's] first elements' in his *Ruins of Empires* (1791), the Poet finds that 'meaning on his vacant mind / Flashed like strong inspiration' and that he now feels he grasps the 'secrets of the birth of time' (126–8). But all this occurs only because the Poet has 'gazed and gazed' on 'marble daemons watch[ing] / The Zodiac's brazen mystery', the first array of the signs of the Zodiac in ancient times (already interpreted by other figures), and on the remaining signs of 'dead men' who have left 'their mute thoughts [graven] on the mute walls around' (118–20).[17] In Shelley's most direct rendition in *Alastor* of myriad signifiers being interpreted with the hope they will lead to signifieds, the eventual 'flash' of meaning is no more than the effect of the Poet 'reading' these interplays of signs back and forth in relation to each other. The 'birth of time', in turn, results from the first encryption of the Zodiac's different figures trying to schematize large segments of temporality. If there is a deeper level than these 'memorials / Of the world's youth' (121–2), the leavings of the dead tell no tales beyond the arrangement of 'speechless shapes' augmented by 'floating shades' (123–4).

Seeking more self-completion than this point of origin offers him, however, the Poet presses on more deeply into the supposed 'cradle of civilization' to reach 'the vale of Cashmire' in northwest India (*Alastor*, 145). There, somewhat as the title character does with Luxima, the Indian maid, in Sydney Owenson's novel *The Missionary* (1811), the Poet conceives of a reflexive metonym that may be the ultimate path to 'Knowledge and truth and virtue' for him (158).[18] Now completely alone, he imagines a 'dream of hopes' that seems to him a beautiful 'veiled maid' whose 'eloquent blood told an ineffable tale', which from here on becomes the goal of his quest as he onanistically 'spread[s] his arms to meet / Her panting bosom' (150–1, 168, 183–4). This projection, even as it partially echoes some feminized ego ideals in the writings of Rousseau, is the clearest anticipation in Shelley's earlier writing of the 'miniature' he finds most of us fashioning psychologically in his essay 'On Love'. In this spectral other, he writes in that piece, we see and desire a 'prototype' of 'our entire self' stripped of 'all that we condemn or despise', a metaphoric mirror image of us that 'reflects only the forms of purity and brightness' we seek to attain as our most desired imaginary goal. Though entirely a mental construct, this is the ultimate figure to which 'we eagerly refer all sensations, thirsting that they should resemble or correspond with it' like a series of reflexive metonyms for an Absolute Selfhood (*Pr* 170).

Back in *Alastor*, to be sure, this 'veiled maid' is presented as fluidly intertexual, a 'web / Of many-coloured woof and shifting hues' (156–7). She is thus, as a complex of transfers, an unstable metaphor for the Poet ('Herself a poet') in an ever-'dissolving' form that he still wants to make the repository of all final meaning (161, 187). The *Alastor* description of her (149–88) is therefore an early example of what will become a characteristic Shelleyan mode in his poetry and prose: an onslaught of metaphors, each quite incomplete on its own, spilling frequently over the ends of lines, as though even blank verse cannot contain the possibilities. Consequently, it is the perpetual deferral of an ultimate union, as these figures lead only to other figures. This deferral is what the Poet and Narrator discover and lament when the former tries to embrace his imaginary 'prototype' and it dissolves into 'blackness' (188). Henceforth it only beckons from afar, as the point of reference for all sensations behind everything the Poet goes on to perceive, a 'fleeting shade' always pursued in substitutes, albeit 'forever lost' (209). Shelley does work in his literary language to move beyond such narcissistic obsessions carried over from the Wordsworth and Rousseau he both critiques and echoes. But the Poet and the Narrator of *Alastor* become determined from this point on to see all the remaining perceptions of the varied natural world as inadequate metonyms for 'Two starry eyes [the maid's], hung in the gloom of thought' (490), even though the Poet's course of life remains 'a bright stream / . . . fed with many-voicèd waves' (668–9). To that extent Shelley's own escape from literalism has not yet been fully achieved.

As the rest of *Alastor* recounts the Poet's fruitless voyage to find his 'prototype' beyond Kashmir at the supposed headwaters of all existence, however, Shelley does at least show, and reflect in his style, that the wages of such 'sin' – where signifiers are viewed as aiming for only one eternal signified or referent – turn out to be forms of death from an incipient sceptic's point of view. At a fairly simple level, any metaphoric reflector by which the Poet goes on to mirror, and thus redefine, himself, such as the 'well' in the deepest Edenic 'dell' he reaches (where Shelley underscores this reflexive moment with a rare use of rhyme in 454 and 457) *first* shows him his own decay in the metonym of his 'thin hair' and *then* turns his pursuit of an antitype into the image of 'Gazing in dreams over the gloomy grave', as though the Poet had trapped himself in the topos of an eighteenth-century graveyard poem (471–3).

Moreover, even when the Narrator sees the 'stream of thought' that is the Poet's journey (644) flowing beyond the latter's particular life and disappearing into an 'immeasurable void' that could be a new beginning as it 'Scatter[s] its waters to the passing winds' (569–70), any reading of that movement that views it as an end or final signified changes the waterfall into 'a storm of death', freezing it into a 'colossal Skeleton' from old Christian orthodoxy (609–11). When both the Poet and Narrator make that choice, as the Poet did when he first asked his ego ideal if 'the dark gate of death / Conduct[s] to thy mysterious paradise' (211–12), the meaning of every signifier in this poem becomes Death. Presuming an ultimate connection of every signifier to one signified for ever kills the floating potential of those thoughts or words, as when allegorical figures remain stuck in an old, tyrannical system and language becomes 'dead to all the nobler purposes of human intercourse'.

The Narrator of *Alastor* is still being critiqued on these grounds, we find, when the focus returns to him at the end of the poem, because his literalist philosophy of Wordsworthian probing remains unenlightened by the dead Poet's example. The speaker closes by lamenting the Poet's demise as simply leaving 'Nature's vast frame, the web of human things', in the fixed and emptied state of being 'not as they were' (719–20). It is up to us readers to decide if we will choose to be or not be like the Narrator and the Poet in the act of interpretation. If we make the regressive choice between the contradictory theories of language simultaneously tugging at this poem, we will find ourselves in the grip of an *alastor*, which to the ancient Greeks is either an outcast wanderer 'pursued by an avenging spirit' or 'the avenging spirit itself'.[19] That spectre has been turned by Shelley into a major target in 1815–16: the haunting old belief that signs should have fixed points of reference that are centres of truth and power. It is this 'avenging' force from the past that limits our possible self-definitions, ties us to outmoded ideologies, makes us narcissistic seekers of supposedly perfect self-images, and leaves us to wither in the ruins of dead systems even as the world keeps changing.

Striving to reopen closures: *The Triumph of Life*

After immersing himself in more non-English languages and literatures, especially as an expatriate in Italy from 1818 on, the Shelley of his last few years has even more tools – as well as strengthened philosophical and political reasons (visible in ' On Life' and the *Philosophical View*) – for a more disruptive, decentred, highly metaphorical style, compared to the stirrings of those tendencies in *Alastor*. Consequently, the moments of unleashed transference in his 1816 volume become much more the norm for him in his final burst of creativity. That is particularly so when he enacts this unsettling metaphoric freedom while deliberately constraining himself within older and already well-defined genres, all drawn from his wider reading, that come to him with settled verbal patterns presumably grounded in fixed centres and hierarchies.

Beginning at the very start of 1821, we discover, Shelley takes on this challenge again and again in the genres and schemas he chooses to transform: the Dantean *Vita Nuova* address to a deified love object in *Epipsychidion*, the tradition of the rhetorical Apology descending from Sir Philip Sidney in *A Defence of Poetry*, the Grecian–Spenserian–Miltonic development of the pastoral elegy in *Adonais* (his tribute to Keats using his subject's approach to the Spenserian stanza), and Aeschylean Greek tragedy transmuted into 'Lyrical Drama' in *Hellas*. He reflects his final theory of language most directly in verse, however, when he extends this pattern by recasting Ezekiel 1:4–28 in the Old Testament, Dante's *Purgatorio* 28–9 in his *Commedia* (1321), Petrarch's six *Trionfi* (1340–74), and even part of Wordsworth's 'Ode' on 'Intimations of Immortality' (1807) – all quite worshipful of a God he rejects – in the *terza rima* dream-vision, like Dante's and Petrarch's, that is *The Triumph of Life*.²⁰ Here Shelley, both expanding on *Alastor* and elaborating his essay 'On Life', offers his strongest figurations of how signs can be used to enslave their users. In doing so, he simultaneously shows that even these restrictions depend on the metaphoric mobility that can, if we accept it, release us from the 'error' in which 'we lose the apprehension of life'.

This poem's very use of the 'triumph' genre from Ezekiel to Petrarch, where a victory parade centred on the chariot of a conqueror gathers a horde of followers surrounding or trailing after it, guarantees that Shelley's variation will often depict the symbolic means by which power is imposed culturally and psychologically. When Shelley's dreamer-speaker first beholds the 'chariot' of Life in the 'similitude / Of a triumphal pageant', the main focus of his entire vision (86–7, 117–18), the Life this chariot carries, we find, is a self-veiling obscurity 'Beneath a dusky hood and double cape' and thus not a secure ruler of the throng surrounding it (89). Even so, its cloaking of its actually amorphous foundations, along with what it borrows from ancient Roman imperialism, gives it that apparent fixity of meaning that Shelley associates with Death in *Alastor* and the *Defence*. This Death-in-Life therefore dominates its triumphal parade as if enslaved itself, 'Crouching within the shadow of a tomb' (90). At the same time, its equally blind, and thus sheep-like, followers all repeat that pattern on their own, as many of them 'mournfully within the gloom / Of their own shadow walked, and called it death' (58–9). Like the enthroned figure of Life, which is really projected as such upon a formless obscurity, its slaves guide themselves by giving power to reflexive shades projected by each of them into positions beyond or above them. These shadows are self-images in which the enslaved mirror themselves, the way the *Alastor* Poet did, to the point where they think they must reach the depths of only these supposed absolutes or die trying. Shelley thus reveals allegories, the modes of figuration from Dante and Petrarch with which he begins this poem, to be misuses of words and signs. They are ephemeral figures that control their projectors and viewers only because such people believe they do. To the degree that this belief system provides the engine 'Of [the chariot's] rushing splendour' as it pulls 'The million' around a centre into a wild dance of forced obedience (86–7, 110), the *terza rima* stanza of the poem seems to continue the most Catholic assumptions of Dante and Petrarch themselves. At times this relentless trinity of tightly written lines does seem to enforce the old Three-in-One of God – 'past, present, future combined / In a single term', as Petrarch puts it in *The Triumph of Eternity* – and its chain-like pattern of interlocking sounds, where the middle line of each threesome rhymes with the first and third lines of the next, appears to suit the literalist inclination of the multitudes to chain themselves repetitively to a 'yoke . . . they stooped to bear' (116).[21]

At the same time, nonetheless, from the moment Life's chariot appears in Shelley's *Triumph*, the attempt of this and every other projection to be a metonym for larger essences is undermined by how these figures really operate on closer inspection. The figure of Life can cloak itself and only then seem metonymic, it turns out, because it emerges from a process that is metaphoric. 'Like the young moon' that 'Doth, as a herald of its coming, bear / The ghost of her dead Mother' as a 'dim form' within her (79–85), 'So came a chariot', we are told, containing 'a dun and faint aetherial gloom / Tempering the light' that recedes behind the immediate image (86, 92–3). Beginning with a simile, this figure is first a new appearance carrying a trace of its previous, but different, form. This metamorphosis is then transmuted further as its rising light (the new moon) becomes dimmed behind a further extension (Life's darkening obscurity, reminiscent of Milton's Death in *Paradise Lost*) in which the light is covered but not effaced, reworking the dimming of the 'mother' inside the new moon.[22]

Granted, this succession of loss/gain/loss-with-traces-of-gain, already quite intertextual, does allude to Wordsworth's 'trailing clouds of glory' in the Immortality Ode and how this glow from a half-forgotten early childhood both 'cometh from afar' and 'fade[s] into the light of common day' as 'shades of the prison house' of daily existence gradually obscure it.[23] Even so, Shelley, now more distant from *Alastor*, recasts that progression at once as a movement of changes that starts with sheer fading and rekindling rather than Wordsworth's 'God, who is our home'. The fadings can conceal what has been occurring, allowing transference to be covered over by its products, and thereby leave the transformations of life obscured behind images of arrested Life (and thus death). But there is nothing eternally prior to this basic process for Shelley, especially not in the generation of the chariot or the shape of Life. As that poetic drive declares itself more openly in the progression of this 'Triumph', in fact, the attempted self-containment of the *terza rima* stanzas and lines is increasingly broken up and forgotten. Enjambments and even slant rhymes (words that rhyme partially but not completely) abound between lines and between stanzas as well. Moreover, a continual emergence of figures transferred from fading figures, all needing other figures to rekindle their energy, ultimately belies, because it is really what animates, the multitude's devotion to graven self-images and each person's imitation of that choice in others:

> Maidens and youths fling their wild arms in air
> As their feet twinkle; now recede and now
> Bending within each other's atmosphere
>
> Kindle invisibly, and as they glow
> Like moths by light attracted and repelled,
> Oft to new bright destruction come and go . . .

> (149–54)

Not only do these tortured literalists transfer their misguided heat between each other; they also cannot be verbalized as doing so without a simile linking them to another species, all of which frantically pours across line and stanza breaks time after time, as is rarely the case in Dante and Petrarch – or Wordsworth's Immortality Ode.

In any case, Shelley soon goes on to suggest why the people in Life's train both carry out and ignore this process, and the literary language in which this explanation is couched becomes a revelation about the actual and potential poetry in all forms of self-fashioning. When the speaker in *The Triumph* is directed to look again at all the figures governed by their own shadows, many of whom are the spectres of once-living people as they were for Petrarch and Dante, he beholds 'each one / Of that great crowd' sending these shadows 'forth incessantly' in great numbers, 'numerous as the dead leaves blown / In Autumn evening from a poplar tree' – like the 'withered leaves' of Shelley's own 'dead thoughts' in writing being 'Scatter[ed]' in his 'Ode to the West Wind' (63–6) – and 'Each, like himself and each other were, / At first, but soon distorted' (*Triumph*, 527–30).

As others have seen, these leaf-like shadows recall an image from the *De rerum natura* of Lucretius, the Latin poet of the first century BC whom Shelley thought the most eloquent rebel against the 'superstitious noblemen of Rome'.[24] Seeing even spirit and perception as *material* in opposition to Roman mythology, Lucretius posited the 'image' (*simulacrum* or *lamina*) as 'a sort of outer skin perpetually peeled off the surface of objects and flying about' to produce spectres in the absence of the objects (including ghosts), reflections in mirrors, or even the perceptions we have of objects at any distance from us.[25]

Shelley's *Triumph*, eager to update Lucretius' critique, turns these simulacra into the self-images that we all pour forth. These are like 'leaves' of text, our self-constructions viewed as metaphoric performances, and we keep pouring them out as we keep projecting ourselves outwards in this poetic fashion. Yet as we construct metaphors of ourselves in order to see ourselves reflected there, we 'kill' ourselves, distorting our self-images into figures of death ('shadows' under which we cower), if we keep trying to make them always the same and like everyone else's for the sake of matching some abstract cultural Standard (such as Life, itself a deadened product of transference). The liberating irony is that we are not bound to one shadow. We all produce self-images in a series of transferences that can keep offering us new 'unapprehended relations' with the other *different* self-images around us. We 'lose the apprehension of life' if we lose this basic poetic understanding, superstitiously enslaving ourselves to a wrongly deified 'Life'. At the same time, the very process that makes this effort possible turns out to be the energy of free transformation that can save us from such self-imposed abasement, if we will let it.

The main speaker and dreamer in Shelley's *Triumph* cannot finally see this revision of his earlier view of the crowd, however, unless he turns for interpretive help, as Dante did to the Roman poet Virgil in his *Inferno* and *Purgatorio*, to an 'old root' visible near the triumphal parade (182) that is caught between past and revisionist modes of perception (hence half stuck in the ground and half rising out of it). This figure turns out to be 'Rousseau' (204), now brought forward explicitly, rather than implicitly as he was in *Alastor*, as a teacher about 'educations of error', including his own. The living Rousseau in his *Confessions* (1782) admitted to projecting 'a land of chimeras' where his desires might find their perfect objects in an ideal outside him, and therefore made his character St Preux in *Julie; ou La Nouvelle Héloïse* (1762) obsessed with a vision of his love object that kept him trapped in its shadow for years, all the while noting the mistake of such mental objectifications.[26] Consequently, a shade of the dead Rousseau, more self-aware about a life he can now look back on, is the best annotator of the figures before the main dreamer's eyes in Shelley's final poem. As such this Rousseau can be, even more fully than the Poet in *Alastor*, another intertextual set of lenses through which the narrator can articulate his own literalist tendencies and reform them by seeing them reflected more clearly in a fluid metaphor for his situation.

The Triumph of Life thus glosses its principal dream vision within itself, making a large-scale transfer the fulcrum of its own structure even more than *Alastor* did. It has Rousseau recount to the speaker, just before the whole text breaks off, his own dream about the appearance of the same parade and what brought that appearance about (308–543). The increasing rush of metaphoric recasting in the micro-details of this poem's lines

and stanza patterns – as well as its exposure of allegories as but metaphoric projections – is ultimately duplicated at the macro-level of the work.
Rousseau's dream emphatically reframes the dream that frames it so that
the new version thereby reveals, by enacting, the metaphoric basis of the
entire vision, along with Shelley's theory of poetry.

The key to Rousseau's reinterpretation, in fact, is a bold re-imaging of
metaphor in action. It thus provides a reflexive and mobile emblem for
the progression we have seen over several years in Shelley's understanding
and practice of literary language. This dream-within-the-dream opens the
way for the triumphal parade that it later rereads by first recasting the
Alastor Poet's projection of a dream maiden, partly by recalling its ancestry
in Rousseau's own sense of how 'chimerical' such visions can be and partly
by linking it to Dante's figure of Matilda in *Purgatorio* 28, who sings and
gestures a rainbow into being as she ushers in the great chariot of the
Church.[27] Shelley's dreaming Rousseau does not simply see a feminine other
as Dante does, but initially imagines 'a gentle trace / Of light' in vague
'woods and waters' interweaving with 'many sounds . . . confusing sense'
(*Triumph*, 336–41). These multiple elements, even more of a web than the
ingredients of the *Alastor* Poet's 'maid', coalesce insubstantially into a
female 'shape all light' accompanied by a 'ceaseless song' harmonizing
many more elements (352, 375–6). This figure's 'feet', clearly metrical and
thus poetic in 'the sweet tune / To which they moved', quickly 'blot / The
thoughts of him who gazed on them . . . thought by thought . . . Making the
night [of her arrival] a dream' inside this dream-within-a-dream (382–93).

Such a destructive yet memorializing movement prompts the dreaming
Rousseau to cry out 'Shew whence I came, and where I am, and why' (398),
a version of the questions asked by the Narrator and Poet of *Alastor*. The
answer to this 'thirst', though, is the shape's offer of a drink of Nepenthe
(359, 404), a draught of forgetfulness that becomes a metaphor for her
'blotting' motion obscuring previous signifiers as she shifts them towards
emerging ones. Rousseau then sees a completely new scene, with its predecessor only an unfixable memory, as though a 'wave' had erased it from
'sand'. At this point the 'new Vision' approaches that is the parade of Life,
now even more 'numerous' with shadows than it was for the main speaker
(405–6, 411, 528). As much as the shape and her motion seem to have
vanished, Rousseau's ability to see more of the 'Phantoms diffused around'
the 'chariot' (487, 469) remains subliminally connected to the shape
maintaining her 'obscure tenour' of incessant motion (427–32).

Because it has been expanded into a wider intertextuality of allusions,
this thorough transfiguration of the *Alastor* dream maiden depicts the
metaphorical impulse of poetry as Shelley has come to see it. Now he is

able to verbalize it in a series of metaphoric shifts *and* a figure of continual metamorphosis, all of which start with the most rigid and traditional modes of poetry and turn them against the ideologies and confinements they once enabled, urging us to forget those and embrace more fluid alternatives in reorganizations of lingering, but exploded, old shapes. Granted, the impulse so prominent in *Alastor* to seek ultimate answers is still prompted by the movement of metaphor, as it certainly is for Shelley's Rousseau. But the response in *The Triumph* has become what both the narrator and Rousseau behold from different angles: a large-scale canvas on which a panoply of seekers after absolutist 'shadows' are revealed to be generators and interpreters of reflexive metaphors who only choose to be oppressed by a desire to unify and obey them. Particularly once the second dream in Shelley's *Triumph* shows us a 'shaping' of the drive that dimly underlies even the parade of devotees to a deathly Life, we readers now know how illusory that construct is and how much it is based on a movement (ultimately a force of 'light') that can release us from the worship of stultified Life as readily as the same process can help us construct it. At that point we are ready for new visions of former constructs in a revitalized literary language that can help us see the old ones for what they were and hold out the hope of future alternatives. If this process is consciously recovered from cultural and psychological repression, where its 'obscure tenour' continues – or so Shelley believed as he left off writing to begin his final voyage – we will be able to give the answer to persistent, but fading, systems of power that the shade of Rousseau gives to the narrator in *The Triumph of Life*:

> 'Figures ever new
> Rise on the bubble, paint them how you may;
> We have but thrown, as those before us threw,
>
> 'Our shadows on it as it past away.' (248–51; N)

NOTES

1. Ferdinand de Saussure, *Course in General Linguistics* (1916), ed. Charles Bally and Albert Sechehaye, tr. Wade Baskin (New York: McGraw Hill, 1966), 65–70.
2. William Keach, *Shelley's Style* (New York: Methuen, 1984), 1.
3. Keach, *Shelley's Style*, 6; Thomas Blackwell, *An Enquiry into the Life and Writings of Homer* (London: Scolar Press, 1972), 41; Jean-Jacques Rousseau, *Essay on the Origin of Languages*, and J. G. Herder, *Essay on the Origin of Language*, trans. John H. Moran and Alexander Gode (New York: Ungar, 1966), 12.

4. See Shelley's 'To Wordsworth' (1815), William Wordsworth, *Selected Prose*, ed. John O. Hayden (New York: Penguin, 1988), 302. Subsequent references are given parenthetically in the text.

5. *The Works of Francis Bacon*, ed. James Spedding et al., 4 vols. (London: Longman, 1857–74), IV.433–4. For Shelley's valuing of 'Lord Bacon', see *Defence*, *Pr* 278, 280–1.

6. Rousseau, *Essay on the Origin of Languages*, 49 and 72; Stuart Peterfreund, *Shelley among Others: The Play of the Intertext and the Idea of Language* (Baltimore: Johns Hopkins University Press, 2002), 13.

7. Keach, *Shelley's Style*, 12–20, 37–41.

8. John Horne Tooke, *Epea Pteroenta, or, the Diversions of Purley*, 2nd edn, 2 vols. (London: J. Johnson, 1798), I.51. See also Keach, *Shelley's Style*, 36–41, and Peterfreund, *Shelley*, 21–4.

9. Samuel Taylor Coleridge, *Coleridge: Selected Poetry*, ed. H. J. Jackson (Oxford: Oxford University Press, 1997), 27–9.

10. For the debt to Drummond, see 'On Life' (*Pr* 173).

11. Here I am indebted to the resemblance between Shelley's theories in this area and Jacques Derrida, 'Différance', in *Marges de la philosophie* (Paris: Minuit, 1972), 3–29; see Jerrold Hogle, *Shelley's Process: Radical Transference and the Development of his Major Works* (New York: Oxford University Press, 1988), 3–27.

12. This is an often misinterpreted passage. For the dominant reading of these words for years, see Earl R. Wasserman, *Shelley: A Critical Reading* (Baltimore: Johns Hopkins University Press, 1971), 204–20.

13. The sentence is omitted in *Pr*.

14. Peterfreund, *Shelley*, 30–48.

15. What follows in these next sentences is derived from Keach, *Shelley's Style*, 79–80.

16. See *N* 92, including n.1; William Wordsworth, *The Poems*, ed. John O. Hayden, 2 vols. (London: Penguin, 1977), I.357–62, II.35–289.

17. See Constantin Chasseboeuf, Comte de Volney, *The Ruins; or, Meditations on the Revolutions of Empires*, tr. anon. (New York: Eckler, 1926), 148.

18. See the first sighting of Luxima in Owenson's *The Missionary: An Indian Tale*, 3 vols. (London: Stockdale, 1811), I.153.

19. Michael Ferber, *Critical Studies: The Poetry of Shelley* (New York: Penguin, 1993), 24.

20. For being the first to detail all these main sources for *The Triumph*, we remain indebted to Harold Bloom's *Shelley's Mythmaking* (1959; repr. Ithaca, N.Y.: Cornell University Press, 1969), 220–75.

21. *The Triumphs of Petrarch*, tr. Ernest Hatch Wilkins (Chicago: University of Chicago Press, 1962), 108.

22. See *Paradise Lost*, 2.666–80, in the Norton Critical Edition, ed. Scott Elledge (New York: Norton, 1975), 45–6.

23. 'Ode: Intimations of Immortality from Recollections of Early Childhood', in Wordsworth, *The Poems*, ed. Hayden, I.525–6 (lines 65, 61, 68, 77). The citation from this poem in the next sentence is from line 66.

24. The first careful study of such echoes throughout Shelley's poetry was Paul Turner, 'Shelley and Lucretius', *Review of English Studies*, n.s., 10 (1959), 269–82; Preface to *The Revolt of Islam (Laon and Cythna)*, *P* II.44.

25. Lucretius, *On the Nature of the Universe*, tr. R. E. Latham (Baltimore: Penguin, 1951), 131.
26. Jean-Jacques Rousseau, *The Confessions of Jean-Jacques Rousseau*, tr. J. M. Cohen (Baltimore: Penguin, 1954), 398; Rousseau, *La Nouvelle Héloïse*, ed. and tr. Judith H. McDowell (University Park: Pennsylvania State University Press, 1968), part 1, letter 5.
27. Dante, *The Divine Comedy*, tr. Laurence Binyon, in *The Portable Dante*, ed. Paolo Milano (New York: Viking, 1969), 332–49.

9

PAUL HAMILTON

Literature and philosophy

Thinking beyond Platonism

Considered from a philosophical point of view, Percy Shelley's writings are most intriguing because they so signally look both backwards and forwards in the history of philosophy. First of all, they draw on materialist and empiricist traditions in philosophy from which Romanticism is usually thought to have distinguished itself. Secondly, Shelley's thought anticipates those more modern materialisms that displace the individual subject as the starting point for speculation, substituting instead the larger, impersonal vistas of our social and natural being. Both kinds of thinking are expressed as much through his poetry, and the way it is written, as through his discursive prose, and the arguments it sets out.

Shelley was aware that his thought pointed before and after, a speculative habit which in any case he attributed to characteristically human self-understanding. In his fragment 'On Life', he plots his transition from an early belief in materialism to the 'intellectual system', a philosophy that sounds idealist, but, as we shall see, actually is not. The philosophical characterization, however, most often given to Shelley has been that of Platonist. This is fair enough, provided a wide enough view of Plato is taken.[1] Shelley is never straightforwardly idealist, but nor is Plato. The later Plato of the *Timaeus* describes the drives and forces of a Demiurge whose orderly deployment of original matter creates out of chance effects or necessity the perfect originals of everything. Necessity is 'persuaded' by the Demiurge to see in a random possibility the best example of something. The 'principle' of a future member of our universe is recognized. Creation is as dependent on a chance material occurrence as it is on a subsequent rational selection.[2] Only afterwards, for the purposes of distinguishing general and individual terms, are these 'principles' or 'forms' of things abstracted from particularity and relocated in the ideal world – a postulate that, unfairly, became synonymous with Platonic thought.

In the earlier *Ion*, a comparable interaction of original productivity and rational interpretation this time explains how human, not universal, artefacts are made. The protagonist of the *Ion* discovers, to his chagrin, that to be inspired is to be possessed beyond his individual, professional control. Plato thus privileges an unconscious origin for our own creativity.[3] In both cases, cosmic and individual, the collusion of reason and necessity constructs a philosophical dialectic. Its interactive give and take of mind and matter, consciousness and unconsciousness, design and chance, virtue and occasion is best figured ironically. This is achieved in myth. The irony comes from conceding that fiction gets closer than truth to evoking the life productive of our powers to describe it. Plato's famous examples of the Myth of the Cave and the Myth of Er in *The Republic* respectively imagine what it would be like to be able to look at knowledge and at life in the round, rather than from inside them as we are actually obliged to do. For Shelley, this totalizing fantasy becomes accessible in that permanent mutability to which, in *A Defence of Poetry*, he attributes poetry's powers of historical survival. The triumph of life, title of Shelley's last, unfinished work, can only be witnessed by reading a poem defined as 'the very image of life expressed in its eternal truth' (*Pr* 281).

No doubt most of Shelley's readers quickly advance beyond Arnold's conception of him as a writer longing for impossible ideals and, in stock Platonic fashion, lamenting the pathos of those second-hand experiences of the good and beautiful, which, aesthetically, he is obliged to make suffice (*Arnold* 1.237). Some of Shelley's statements do, superficially, suggest that this state of philosophical abjection is the one to which as an artist he is consigned. The benighted nightingale singing in solitude to cheer itself up, the poet to whom life is thorns on which he bleeds, the excruciating dilemma of the lover in *Epipsychidion* all suggest a Platonic cliché. Confined to a world of Becoming and generation, the poet longs, impossibly, for a life of Being and eternity. He avails himself of the neo-Platonic rehabilitation of art as the medium that, artfully bypassing our epistemological difficulties, puts us in immediate contact with the perfection we cannot make a permanent part of a life constitutionally in flux: 'The One remains, the many change and pass' (*Adonais* 460). Shelley's elegy for Keats gains the general application all such individual poetic commemorations have sought by, in this case, mourning our tragic condition, our tragically conflicted state.

This reduction of Shelley to a caricature of Platonism is best countered by remembering Geoffrey Matthews's successful insistence on the importance of context when considering generalizations about Shelley based on any of his striking quotations.[4] Thus, in the context of *A Defence of Poetry*, the charming obscurity of the nightingale matches poetry's power to suggest audiences still to come, and to puzzle or reproach its contemporaries for the obscurity in which their reception shrouds its progressive impulse. It sings, after all, to cheer 'its own solitude', to people its environment with response, to produce that quintessential Platonic requirement for thought – dialogue. This is hardly a sentimental lingering over epistemological defeat. The same is true of the 'glorious Phantom' illuminating Shelley's age at the end of 'England in 1819' (13; N). The phantom's apparent disqualification from real, effective intervention allows it to set new standards for political embodiment still to come. The pathetic figure scratched by briars in the 'Ode to the West Wind' is calculated to represent the unavoidable but suspect sentimentalism of any radical intelligentsia that advocates its own dissolution in the interests of the more democratic processes which, in justice, ought to prevail. The poet is levelled by a political imperative that must feel like an overwhelming natural process. The implication, though, is that he can still reasonably hope for a natural variety to emerge from this natural necessity, one capable of a new, perhaps more miscellaneous growth out of the equality of opportunity for which his distinctiveness has been sacrificed. Again, a hopeless poetic velleity for a perfect world turns into a classic exposition of the difficulties of living a political vanguard's self-destructive, trans-individual mission in terms that are still recognizably human. *Epipsychidion* arguably plays out the same loss of self or 'little death' in the language of courtly love, the idiom of Dante and Petrarch, but historicized, brought up to date by the visible strains imposed on the poem by the tensions of an erotic sensibility typical of Shelley's own milieu.

Finally, the Preface to Shelley's *Prometheus Unbound* specifically warns us against confining his literary aspirations to the tragic model of Aeschylus he has just transformed. Instead Shelley uses Plato to explain his historicizing revision of Aeschylus, by reference to an overall project 'to produce a systematical history of what appear to me to be the genuine elements of human society' (P II.475). In this context, then, the poet at the end of *Adonais* embarks neither upon some supernatural voyage, nor on an allegorical crossing of a divide he is philosophically prohibited from bridging. He does not, in other words, set off for a Platonic heaven, an immutable world of archetypal forms where he too will be immortalized. The 'abode where the Eternal are' is more like an adaptation of the creation myth of the *Timaeus*. The originality of the poet attunes him to a 'Power' beyond his individual control: 'He is made one with Nature: there is heard / His voice in all her music' (370–1). He both dies and survives through that perpetual openness to reinterpretation by which poetry commits its individual gains to common usage, and the poet's distinctive idiom to the renovation of language generally. Unlike the Rome in which Keats is buried, the eternal abode represents an acceptance of the creative challenge to be revived in new forms, however impersonal or naturally levelling these may seem, like the indifferent flood in which the mythic Adonis returns to fertilize the banks of the Nile. To accept such radical seasonal transformation is better than to be monumentalized in those crumbling original forms, however inalienable or memorable they may seem, belonging to a particular individual, ideology, or era.

The Platonic model providing an alternative here to Aeschylean tragedy is not simply the opposition of Being and Becoming, setting an unobtainable ideal world against a natural world whose imperfections are overcome only in poetry. Above all, Plato practised dialogue, inviting as a procedural requisite the contestation of any opinion put forward. Socrates is, famously, the midwife of truth, and truth only comes to light after a hard labour, elicited from another person by the skill of Socrates.[5] Philosophy becomes a conversation in which the audience is as important as the speaker, in which truth emerges dialectically, and in which the discovery of ignorance rather than of facts is the incremental gain from every exchange. In Shelley's more Romantic and therefore historicizing idiom, the inadequacy of every approximation on which poetry seizes announces a comparable philosophical challenge. Socrates does not just tell us what he knows, perhaps because an unscripted coming to know something, the process of identifying the best principle among others, repeats his view of how truth gets established in the first place. Socrates' ironic surrender of philosophical authority to his pupil reappears in exaggerated form when Shelley struggles to write in ways that invite judgements whose principles have still to be 'acknowledged'.

Shelley's poet can be surprised now at the meaning of what he produces, because its generous authority exceeds his own good or bad intentions, and because it expresses less his own spirit than the 'spirit of the age'. These local failures to control poetry may personally disadvantage the poet, and much of Shelley's narrative art, from *Alastor* onwards, conjures up figures interestingly expressive of this self-lacerating dilemma. But poetry's destiny to be fully realized only through a succession of future audiences exculpates its poet from contemporary charges of obscurity. This is one charge to which *A Defence of Poetry* replied, reassuring Shelley against the neglect of his peers. The gap, however, between poetry's success as a midwife of the truth to be recognized by future audiences and that for which the poet can take personal credit now, acquiring poetic fame and reputation, is as disturbingly wide as the historical gap to be crossed by the poet's voyage at the end of *Adonais*. But this poetic instability allows Shelley's reader not only to be persuaded to find the possibility of change lurking in established certainties and opportunities for reform hiding in ostensibly immutable social taboo or institution; the same reader is also confronted with the emotional and psychic disturbance that accepting such change would incur. Sometimes the barriers to retaining a personal interest in an achievement that has been entrusted to the radical creativity of future audiences appear insurmountable. Socratic equanimity about the transfer of authority dovetails with an indifference that surely has surrendered all rights of ownership? Individual expression disappears if it can be re-described by Shelley as only one more 'modification' of the world-soul or 'the one mind' (*Pr* 174). But then that agony gets into the poetry too, and adds further pathos to its characteristically self-transcending success.

Dialogue, as used by Enlightenment philosophers from Hume to Diderot, is a sophisticated instrument of scepticism. But in Plato it describes a metaphysical principle as well as a philosophical method. It applies to the world-creating give and take between reason and necessity as much as it does to the relation between Socrates and one of his respondents. It invokes the compromise between internal, individual creativity and the 'external influences' of circumstance which, insists Shelley, contribute in equal measure to literary production. But, most strikingly, the Platonic matrix allows our determinations of what exists to remain provisional, relativizing both existence's claims to brute materiality and our supposed power to order such chaos into coherent experience. Our understanding is subject to an answering universe whose power is nevertheless furthered by the roles our understanding creates for it to play. Its performances may then give us cause to revise our understanding, and the dialogue continues without an obvious conclusion. We usually excuse such philosophical irresolution as poetic. 'Plato', wrote Shelley, 'was essentially a poet' (*Pr* 280). By creating the form of dialogue, Nietzsche would similarly argue, 'Plato, the thinker, arrived by a detour where he had always been at home as a poet.'[6] Any attempt to bypass dialogue and fix this ongoing dialectic in one of its polarities, whether that be in 'thought's empire over thought' or in a single manifestation of 'necessity', is doomed to failure. Necessity, after all, is the 'mother of the world' in *Queen Mab* and the nemesis of the arch-conservative, Zeus, in *Prometheus Unbound* because it is naturally generative and projective of futures others may want to prevent from happening.

So, within Shelley's Platonism lie not only dangers for the coherence of an individuality we seem humanly wedded to, a personal uniqueness in which poetic ambition appears to have a distinctive investment. The opposites of individuality – chance, necessity, mutability, everything we cannot take credit for – themselves conform to a benign intention, a higher poetry working on a cosmic scale, in which reality's repeated surpassing of itself once more patterns forth the nature of poetry. The opposite problem then arises, the difficulty, that is, of finding a universal description of things escaping poetic anthropomorphism. Shelley's writing in poetry and prose often implies that natural evolution is politically radical. Nature's lack of respect for individuals and establishments looks callous. Its indifference to the personal can nevertheless be understood as actually conforming to the most glorious but nevertheless self-defining sacrifices of humanity: 'Thou hast a voice, great Mountain, to repeal / Large codes of fraud and woe' (80–1). Power may 'dwell apart', as 'Mont Blanc' has it (96), but there is a reward for the readiness of Shelley's poetry to make of personal extinction a symbol of a poem's possible future increase in as yet untold receptions. Shelley's poetry sets inhuman targets of self-sacrifice and sympathy, and the pay-off is to find beckoning in nature's power to frame our knowledge of it an invitation to poetry, to quintessential human expression. Nature can then become the expressive vehicle of a loyalty to species and environment whose pathos surpasses personal interest. Shelleyan scepticism of conventional religious claims to individual immortality discovers ample recompense in the poetic needs of a materialism evoking the 'everlasting universe of things'. Poetry, deprived of any 'necessary connection with consciousness or will', rediscovers its identity as the discourse most likely to succeed in describing our grounding outside our powers of measuring that grounding (*Pr* 296). Once more, the ostensible triumph of life becomes a poem, and so we can tolerate our personal relegation within the impersonal process of which our personality consists. Once more, also, the pattern of redirecting an earlier Enlightenment materialism to describe a much more modern philosophical preoccupation leaps out of Shelley's theoretical deployment of poetic anachronism.

Refuting Deism: Shelley and materialism

Shelley's philosophical affiliations, therefore, are wide-ranging and suggestive by any standards, but for an English Romantic poet they are quite unusual. His philosophical reading and theorizing from very early in his career address primarily the preceding tradition of the *philosophes*: Voltaire, Holbach, Condorcet, and the thinkers associated with Diderot's great project of an Encyclopaedia. These were French Enlightenment philosophers; behind them lay Spinoza, and behind him, Lucretius. Their atheism, materialism, and republicanism were meat and drink to the author of tracts such as *The Necessity of Atheism* (1811), *A Refutation of Deism* (1814), and *Proposals for an Association of Philanthropists* (1812). To Shelley's interest in this group must be added his abiding preoccupation with

Rousseau, the destabilizing critic at their Enlightened heart. In tandem with his use of the *philosophes* goes his conspicuous awareness of their British contemporaries, the great empiricists, Locke, Berkeley, and Hume (and behind them, Bacon, rather than Hobbes). As a rule, other main Anglophone British Romantic poets only read enough of the *philosophes* in order to use them as a foil for their own ideas concerning human creativity. Coleridge and Hazlitt produced sustained critiques of Helvétius, Rousseau, and others; they held the Lockean tradition in contempt or as something from which, in its influential updating by David Hartley in his *Observations on Man* of 1749, it was important to escape. In *The Excursion*, a copy of Voltaire is enough to telegraph to Wordsworth's reader the dilemma of the Solitary. Anything associated with a *philosophe* and his philosophical *confrères* immediately invoked a cabal, like the one demonized by the Abbé Barruel and Edmund Burke, supposed to be responsible to a considerable extent for the destruction of the *ancien régime* in France and the Terror that followed. Any philosophical attractiveness about the French tradition only disguised the infectiousness of French terrorism. This violent contagion was conspicuously used by Wordsworth, Coleridge, and others to account for the despondency into which early sympathizers with radical political change in France were bound to fall when the awful, Jacobinical consequences of their laudable approval of political emancipation unfolded. Lack of serious philosophical engagement with French materialist writings, even while refuting them, could therefore be defended. Shelley, though, thought it 'still doubtful' if the causal connection between French philosophy and the French Revolution was proved, but in any case tended to criticize the philosophers from the left, not the right (*Pr* 67). His use of Holbach's *Système de la nature* in *Queen Mab* appears uninhibited by these reservations.

Karl Marx was sarcastic about the materialism of both the French and the British empiricist traditions. The materialism of *philosophes* and Lockeans was 'Cartesian': a system of ideas whose standards of coherence tended to override the anticipated appeal to reality for corroboration and legitimation.[7] For that luminous student of the philosophical Enlightenment, Ernst Cassirer, this disadvantage was in fact a commendable lack of dogmatism and presumption in describing the world. To this extent, the semiotic bias of the *philosophes*, in which relations between ideas take priority over matters of fact, shows exemplary modesty. For Cassirer, a thinker like d'Alembert has no metaphysical pretensions, and his system accordingly allows a conception of nature as the ultimate arbiter, free of our conceptualizations, at liberty to take its own course, leaving it to us to change our sciences to match its variety. By contrast, Holbach exhibits 'the turn towards mechanism and materialism', his necessitarianism imposing contemporary standards of knowledge on a material in all likelihood capable of exceeding them.[8] Now in *Queen Mab*, Shelley's first long poem, he notoriously borrows from Holbach, principally on the subject of necessity. In this regard, it might be worth remembering the Platonic meaning of necessity, which, in the *Timaeus*, lies closer to arbitrariness than determinism. Nevertheless, Holbach's world-picture was taken by various literary luminaries – Voltaire, Rousseau, Goethe – to present nature as a mechanical system emptied of human interest and belonging. Shelley's advocacy of Holbach is still unusual and surprising.

But one way of explaining the attractions for Shelley of the impersonality and apparently dehumanized version of nature offered by Holbach's philosophy might be its affinity with Shelley's desire, from an early age, to escape from the ideological contamination he saw to be inherent in current cosmologies. As is well known, his principal target was Christianity, or, as he understood it, Christian interference in the strictly logical business of making sense of the world. The main offenders here, he thought, were as much Deism as revealed religion or fundamentalism. If anything, Deism, with its attractive latitudinarianism or theological broadmindedness and its undoctrinal reliance on teleological arguments for God's existence from the design visible in nature, was the more pernicious of the two. Hume, Shelley clearly assumed, had, in his *Dialogues on Natural Religion*, shot down the fashionable theological arguments of Deists as different as the radical John Toland and the liberal Anglican churchman William Warburton. Shelley's writings against Deism seem fuelled by a kind of intellectual outrage at the fact that those who were well aware of the impossibilities besetting Christian revelation nevertheless went on to keep the religious beast alive through a further series of sophisms. In *A Refutation of Deism*, written late 1813 to early 1814, he allows the Deist in his dialogue to refute a doctrinaire Christian, but then hands over to this discredited individual the task of demolishing the Deist's own arguments by perversely assuming an atheism he, the Christian, obviously does not profess in order to attack Deist arguments from design.

Certainly, there is some clever avoidance of censorship going on here. In the mouth of a self-professed Christian, the atheistic arguments become sheer strategy, an invitation to avoid the awful atheistical consequences of his abandonment of Christian doctrine. The economy of the dialogue, in which no one is allowed to be a self-professed atheist, as Shelley was, saves the author from charges of blasphemy. But the disingenuous Christian's atheistical arguments against the Deist are presented as devastating. The Platonic format allows Shelley, dramatically at least, to contrive to humiliate the Deist more than the Christian by showing the irresistible force of the arguments used against him to carry the day, irrespective of the character of the antagonist who uses them. Even a Christian can defeat a Deist. In passing, the Christian looks pretty silly when he mounts an attack based anyway on the ruins of his own theological position. Predictably, Shelley makes the Christian's Pyrrhic victory as crushing as he can. His strategic success against the Deist must be self-defeating if, simultaneously, it adds to the sense that his own position is irretrievable.

But Shelley was opposed to any ideological trimming when it came to closing on nature in an adequate philosophical or poetical manner. Deism was perhaps the most conspicuous and accessible contemporary form of the attempt to impose a tendentious teleology, or explanation by reference to a design or purpose, on nature. Shelley consistently asserts that our beliefs that certain things are the case owe their conviction not to will, the source of intentions rationalizing teleology, but to sensation, and to our combinations and classifications of agreements or disagreements concerning ideas derived from sensations. This classically Humean stance appealed to Shelley for several reasons. First of all it obviously aligned itself with the liberal notion that people should not be persecuted for their beliefs. They were not responsible for them. Beliefs were a product of the circumstances generating the sensations on which their beliefs were founded. But those circumstances could include the human mind itself. Hume allowed for ideas of reflection, abstract and conceptual products of observation of the course taken by our mental faculties. The same epistemological economy – no ideas without prior impressions/sensations – is enforced here. We can be impressed by our own capacities to frame ideas, and derive ideas from those impressions. This happens in just the same way that we receive experiential content from sensations thought to come from a real world existing outside the mind. Hume's empiricism encourages the introspection Shelley's poetry so enjoys. At the same time, Hume's ideas of reflection expose the mental sources of supposedly external forms of organization. Certainties such as causality and personal identity had no necessary foundation in external fact, but, for Hume, are produced by reflecting upon regularities in the patterns of our ideas.

Deism was a particularly important target for Shelley because it contrived an afterlife for religious dogmatism: false belief in a divinely expressive order of nature actually dependent on the way in which we perceived things – actually signifying what in *The Triumph of Life* is called 'thought's empire over thought'. Deism was as pernicious, to him, as Christianity because the new dogmatism instituted as the eternal order of things whichever prejudices happened to appeal to it most. Shelley's defence of vegetarianism, now no longer seen as cranky but as integral to his thought, targets the way in which any argument from design suppresses obvious competitors.⁹ We can adopt various diets, and deduce their propriety from our possession of means facilitating the dietary ends we have chosen. Different foods, some meat, some vegetable or dairy, may suit our metabolism. We need an additional argument, though, to justify our preference for this chain of means and ends over that one. In *A Vindication of Natural Diet*, Shelley draws the parallel with the putative author of Ecclesiastes, Solomon, who possessed a thousand concubines and pronounced life to be 'vanity'. He might, Shelley reasonably supposes, have realized that because he was able to have a thousand lovers that did not necessarily mean it was the best thing to do. His disillusion with life might have been less wholesale, limited to an incompatible partner perhaps, if his undoubted sexual means had been ruled by the monogamous preferences of Shelley's own day. It is mistaken, though, to understand Shelley's argument as primarily directed against 'debauchery'. Rather, in the context of the rest of his thought, he is more likely to be suggesting that the possession of a capacity does not conclusively argue its propriety. Just because you can do something does not mean you should do it. He is refuting the sufficiency of arguments from design. These arguments are used to keep any establishment or hegemony in place – religious, political, ethical, cultural – because the existence of a means designed for an end appears to justify the end – if you attribute enough authority to the designer. But justification of the designer requires another argument. The apparent crankiness of Shelley's preference for vegetarianism is evident in his lists, culled from John Newton, proving the longevity of vegetarians. Formally, though, in terms of his argument's structure, to adduce such evidence, however implausible, in fact shows that there is a utilitarian debate still to be had when the variety of our human capacities is exposed and the nonsense involved in tracing them back to a single, divine designer or intention demonstrated. To that extent, Shelley's claims for vegetarianism are perhaps also calculated to provoke his opponents to concede the inconclusiveness of arguments from design.

Hume, then, is used by Shelley in *A Refutation* at one end of the argument as a source for describing the infinite recess inherent in Deistic thought: from God's perfection, why not deduce an intention for which God himself was designed to design this universe, and so on? At the other, mundane end, Hume's utilitarian belief that good and evil are distinguished in terms of the pleasures and pains they incur shows the inadequacy of purely teleological arguments from design to justify anything. We are designed in such a way as to have the means of doing all sorts of things; so the possession of various capacities does not supply reasons for distinguishing between them. Shelley is often thought to be anti-utilitarian, in a stereotypical way, like Hazlitt, say. But in *A Defence of Poetry*, poets give the lead to utilitarians. Shelley employs the same principle he brought against the argument from design, showing that a utilitarian calculus of pain and pleasure cannot provide the qualitative assessment needed to decide between different goods. The difference is that the utilitarian imperative is not refuted, only refined, although no variety of enlightened self-interest can stretch to accommodate Shelley's poetic sympathies.

Shelley's *A Refutation*, however, also brings in Spinoza's *Tractatus*, and, getting away from designer theology altogether, uses Spinoza's pantheistic identification of nature as the power of God under another name to talk about the true sufficiency of nature to any ideas we might have of it (*Pr* 137). Now, like Holbach too, Shelley finds matter instinct with motion, 'infinitely active and subtile. Light, electricity and magnetism are fluids not surpassed by thought itself in tenuity and activity . . . The laws of motion and the properties of matter suffice to account for every phenomenon, or combination of phenomena exhibited in the Universe' (*Pr* 133). We should remember that this active universe is conjured up in the context of an anti-teleological argument, a Godless Spinozism. Then we can see how Shelley's poetry and philosophy might aim to uncover a being circumscribing any specific purposes we enjoy within it, although only available to us as something directing itself through our limited ends.

We can use matter instrumentally, and we can have an idea of it existing beyond our uses as well, but neither of these characterizations is in itself sufficient. Hence the conundrums of 'Mont Blanc': 'Power dwells apart', but the mountain's power is consonant with human purposes. Neither entirely outside nor inside our purposeful containments, the mountain gets itself represented in contradictory ways. Its power to specify our peculiar human take on nature, our human divisions of experience, produces a complementary sense of a 'silence and solitude' resisting our meanings. At the end, the poem's language recalls Pascal's existential terror, diametrically opposed to Deism, that human experience might be bounded by 'vacancy', void, nothing, and so rendered nugatory by that overwhelming comparison.[10] But, without needing to bet with Pascal on the truth of Christianity, the poem has rhetorically allayed this fear through its 'imaginings' of a mountain unsusceptible of, certainly, but also characteristically productive of the divisions of experience. Maybe vacancy isn't the frightening thing; terrifying, rather, is the idea that vacancy is occupied by things we can make little sense of, 'silence' and 'solitude', instead of being the arena in which 'power' becomes manifest?

Neither teleology nor an opposite nihilism will do, Shelley's poem argues. Its language of a nature in the perpetual process of reinterpreting itself recalls Schelling's near contemporary *Naturphilosophie* and looks forward to Heidegger's ontology.[11] Mont Blanc discloses itself by renewing the human sense of a vocation of self-surpassing and self-historicizing. Poetry convinces Shelley that, ironically, we express ourselves most adequately when least definitively: in terms not bound by present interpretations but also awaiting activation by future audiences and circumstances. In this way is manifested 'the secret strength of things / Which governs thought'. Being ('the secret strength of things') is primary, not as an alternative to thought but as what voices the restrictions necessary for thought to be possible, and which is characteristically known in this limited way. 'Nothing exists but as it is perceived' (*Pr* 174).

Shelley's adage echoes Hume's predecessor, Bishop Berkeley, who, in his *Principles of Human Knowledge*, asserted of 'unthinking things' that 'their *esse* [being] is *percipi* [to be perceived]'.[12] But the meaning of 'Mont Blanc' is rather that existence situates perception. Existence shows that we can only perceive it, but at the same time it makes us aware that to be known in this way is only one of its aspects. The dimension we cannot know is not some essence beyond knowledge, but precisely the forgoing of that possibility in order to make *our* knowledge conclusive. Sometimes Shelley writes as if we could get direct access to 'the intense inane', as it is called in *Prometheus Unbound*. At other times, it remains the sense of being determined to know things in the human way we do, not as the sense of anything different or of a mystic abandonment of our defining limitations. Prometheus, certainly, is not human, but a Titan. His retreat from our world with his female counterpart, Asia, genders and orientalizes an out-of-life experience in a manner that feminist and post-colonial critics have rightly suspected. Barbara Charlesworth Gelpi worries when Shelley becomes preoccupied with 'the mother's immanence in language, not in woman's fulfilment through the use of language'. Nigel Leask is similarly anxious that Shelley 'disperses . . . dialogic energy' in the interests of a 'lyrical abstraction' required to celebrate Asia's overcoming of (in the figure of Jupiter) 'the self-proclaiming universalism of Western truth'.[13] This Heideggerian overcoming of subjectivity through an exotic female principle is clearly tempted by stereotypes as well.

Back in the world not of Titans but of humans, to rebuild not escape the human is the task: 'to hope, till Hope creates / From its own wreck the thing it contemplates' (*Prometheus Unbound* 4.573–4). This activity can look depressingly repetitive, as it does at the end of *Hellas*, depicting a human race bound to the treadmill of a human history perpetually recording cycles of mastery and slavery. Then the temptation is to fable another dispensation, the temptation of religion, which enervates our confidence that we can seize the historical occasion to re-make ourselves in a better image than the supposedly divine one we inherit and betray.

The refutation of Deistic teleology dominates the polemical aspects of Shelley's thought, testified to by his early use of Hume and Holbach, and confirmed by inadvertent parallels with Schelling and anticipations of Heidegger. He attacked the reduction of nature to human purposes, followed by the passing off of that reduction as the immutable character of nature itself. This, he thought, was a source of political conservatism. Equally, he suspected the consignment of everything not susceptible to materialist reduction to 'immateriality', or some realm lying outside our subjectivizations of nature. From this unlimited, heavenly perspective we would stand in need of redemption from what characterized us as a species. This, he thought, was the source of religious prejudice. Both prejudices, political and religious, locked each other in place. As with Schelling at such points, his Spinozism kicked in, and he argued that our ignorance of the power of God is co-extensive with our ignorance of Nature (*Pr* 137). Now he no longer sounds like a Humean empiricist or utilitarian, although his initial starting point was a Humean scepticism of beliefs that nature was an external reality in whose evident design our privileged station could be clearly deciphered. Mont Blanc speaks an altogether more difficult and challenging language than the Deistical one, yet, at the same time, its nature frames our different human purposes and gives us a sense of their historicity. It does so without itself being anything other than the fuller articulacy both of our relativism and of our destiny continually never to gain admittance to a different, absolute dispensation. 'God', Shelley wrote in an early letter, is 'a synonime for the *existing power of existence*' (*L* II.101).

Shelley's philosophy of 'life'

Shelley therefore expresses the philosophical stance he carves out here in various ways. His use of Plato crystallizes less in the expected theory of an ideal world containing the prototypes of what we experience, rather in the dialogic form of writing that was also a Platonic legacy. In the dialogue, argued Nietzsche, the (Aeschylean) tragic insight of the Greeks finds a refuge after its historical moment has passed. That dramatic environment allows for the surrender of individual interest to a wider, self-destroying one, but in a form in which such otherwise intolerable expansion can be borne. Socrates' delegation of his own authority to the discoveries of his interlocutors is perhaps what inspires Shelley's own relinquishings of individual authority to further a radical historicism. That historicism fuels his attacks on establishments of all kinds, and generates a view of nature free of the teleology or immutable purposes used by conservatives to justify their permanent retention of power. Nature's politicization, though, is caught in a poetry whose eschewal of Wordsworthian or Coleridgean symbols of divinity or 'something ever more about to be' in favour of those of necessity or arbitrariness risks a special kind of difficulty. The language used by a writer to reveal his determination by larger forces or to expose the untimeliness of his own choice of words must be calculatedly and suggestively provisional. The themes Shelley adopts call for a reader to see round his obscurities of expression or fallibility of characterization in order to glimpse his lucid historicization of the limitations to which he is restricted. But these restricted, over-taxed expressions are all he has to work with, and, if they do not evoke a kind of poetry of anticipated revival, they have failed. Readers can be encouraged, though, by the fact that Shelley's detractors usually miss the force of his tactics and are uninterested in the exigencies to which his radicalism is forced.

Evidently, it is difficult to separate out Shelley's philosophy from the medium in which it is written, just as it is difficult to dissociate his poetry from the philosophical position it is used to express. While this has appeared as a disadvantage to many in the past, it has also fitted Shelley better than most Romantics to the linguistic turn of the continental philosophy so influential on recent Anglophone literary theory. F. R. Leavis and T. S. Eliot argued that Shelley's incorrigibly interactive metaphors, in which vehicle and tenor become interchangeable – or in which what something is a metaphor of reconfigures our notion of the thing it is likened to – rendered his thought incoherent, sundering it from the literal basis required by any theory of meaning. 'Loose clouds', in Shelley's 'Ode to the West Wind', are shed 'like Earth's decaying leaves' (16; N), a figure made sense of, though, by reference to the meteorological involvement of 'heaven and Ocean' (17) – not a tree in sight. Or, in a more structurally minded example, the poet is like a skylark to the extent that the skylark's song escapes reduction to any meaning that would make a strict comparison between the two work. Both poetry and skylark's song have to re-conceive each other, or generate a dialogue, for the alien perfection of the bird's music to offer a future for the poet in which 'The world should listen then—as I am listening now' ('To a Sky-Lark', 105; N). Not that the poet would then be skylarking, but he would be in dialogue with his proper audience.

Saussurean theories of meaning do not, of course, make the foundational demand, contrary to Shelley's practice, that meaning be founded on a literal basis. For Saussure and his followers, the meaning of any word is differential, dependent for its sense upon its place within the vocabulary of a language, its signification never ultimately confirmed. Pragmatically, we settle for what works, but the potential to follow 'harmonious' semantics into a kind of 'madness', as in Shelley's 'To a Sky-Lark', remains. The superior harmonies correct any complacency that our own communication is ever fully realized, and the 'madness' corroborates the extreme provocation to current standards that complete communication would represent. Shelley's insistently figurative renderings both of his poetic art, and of the philosophical aspirations it deferred to future audiences imagined to be worthy of their reception, made him an excellent choice with which to illustrate the new grammatology. The enhanced elasticity Derrida and his followers attribute to linguistic meanings, postponing indefinitely any final pronouncement on what any individual word signifies, reformulates the avowed provisional quality of so much of Shelleyan utterance.

Shelley's great, final, perhaps unfinished poem, *The Triumph of Life*, became the key text for the Yale critics – Geoffrey Hartman, Harold Bloom, Paul de Man, J. Hillis Miller – in the flagship book for the deconstructive criticism that claimed to take its cue from Jacques Derrida's philosophy. Although Derrida contributed an essay to the book, his thought now appears only partially reducible to the virtuoso exercises in close reading by which the Yale critics sought to use Shelley to show that 'literary language foregrounds language itself as something not reducible to meaning'.[14] Equally partial, though still helpfully suggestive, are the applications of the book's readings to Shelley's own thought. Leaving aside for the moment the questions of whether or not the poem corroborates that thought, we can claim the following.

In the fragment 'On Life', Shelley makes clear that his 'intellectual system', to which he turned in reaction to the 'shocking absurdities of the popular philosophy of mind and matter', allows him access to a concept of life (*Pr* 173). Life, here, becomes, like Hartman's language, the kind of thing that, because you can never get outside it, escapes any of your attempts to say what it is. Again the question is whether we should experience this ineffability as oppression or 'triumph' over us, or as a final validation of poetry's survival of, indeed increase from, historical change. Great poetry, according to Shelley's *Defence*, wears its period characteristics as a mask facilitating its inspirational performances on later historical stages. Where these characteristics are doctrinal or ideological – a dogmatic theology in Shelley's example of Milton – subsequent historical interpretation can bring out the great poem's resources for refuting its local prejudices. We have already noticed the agonies that Shelley's poet suffers owing to the fragility of the ties of ownership to a poetic creation so flagrantly in possession of a future beyond his or her control. But this letting-go, this relinquishment of individual rights, does seem, for Shelley, to be a Platonic condition of ultimate philosophical credibility.

'Life' is approached in Shelley's new philosophy, his 'intellectual system', not by establishing 'new truth' or 'additional insight' – for how could we add anything to life? – but by leaving in their place a 'vacancy' (*Pr* 173). The importance of 'vacancy', which we have seen demonstrated by 'Mont Blanc', is to make space for the characteristically projective and retrospective being of human life. In 'On Life', Shelley immediately proceeds from this claim to another claim about the nature of language. He describes linguistic signs as 'standing not for themselves but for others'. Rather than possessing a proper meaning, they function 'in their capacity of suggesting one thought, which shall lead to a train of thoughts' (*Pr* 173–4). This view partly echoes eighteenth-century theories of the association of ideas, as formulated from Locke to Hartley, theories very influential on the psychological speculations of the preceding generation of English Romantics. But present in Shelley's formulation is also the idea that the meaning of a word depends not on a referent, but on the word's position within a larger system or structure, a reckoning we make but do not state whenever we use the word. This certainly sounds akin to a proto-Saussurean view of language, leading to succeeding claims that it is the spaces between words that take on significance. But in the context of Shelley's thinking, the spaces are coloured in as pasts and futures, and the abandonment of present, fixed meanings is always a calculated affront to any establishment of the day that has a vested interest in keeping things this way. As Jerrold Hogle, a critic very obviously writing in the wake of the Yale achievement, asserts: 'no analysis of Shelley's writing should separate transposition from his radical social programme'.[15]

According to 'On Life', the psychological equivalent of 'vacancy' is 'reverie'. In reverie, we are relieved of the popular need to distinguish mind and matter. In reverie we may appear, therefore, to lose our bearings, but part of the meaning of reverie is that we become lost in what is most ours, a loss which is thus also a kind of finding or self-discovery. In such loss, Shelley thinks, we experience 'an unusually intense and vivid apprehension of life' (*Pr* 174). Rousseau has preceded him in this thought in his *Reveries of a Solitary Walker*, so it is puzzling to remember immediately that Rousseau is also the victim chosen by Shelley to narrate a large part of *The Triumph of Life*. There is no easy solution to the conundrum of why Shelley makes his precursor in apprehending life its outstanding casualty. Why should Shelley be consistent? Couldn't he have changed his mind between the 1819 endorsement of Rousseauian reverie in 'On Life' and the 1822 presentation of a Rousseau provoking the narrator's spontaneous 'O Heaven have mercy on such wretchedness!' (*The Triumph*, 181)? But why should the narrator necessarily have got it right? This is a Rousseau who heroically has bequeathed all to the future – 'A thousand beacons from the spark I bore' (207). Plato, interpreted not as the poet of *A Defence* but as an idealist now forced to know his bodily existence rather than be permitted to abstract himself philosophically into an ideal realm of values, is an obvious contrast. He is very different from this Rousseau whose insistent physicality, suffering what he wrote, steeped in 'the joy and woe' Plato avoided, qualifies him to comment on the failure of others to accept their incorporation in a progressive necessity (life) their purposes can never frame. Those in authority of any kind command only 'thought's empire over thought' (211). Yet to surrender that authority is to appear, like Rousseau, to be decayed. However, Rousseau is also described as 'overcome / by [his] own heart alone' (240–1). Earlier in Shelley's writings, this verdict would suggest a 'license' that would 'incapacitate and contract' (*Proposals for an Association of Philanthropists, Pr* 67). *The Triumph*, though, may inadvertently be conceding that for Rousseau himself, 'heart' is precisely that natural universal that binds people together in a just society, irrespective of their individualizing characteristics. In Shelley's thought too, to be ruled by 'a secret correspondence with our heart' is also to feel bound by authentic community in 'patriotic' enthusiasm (*Pr* 170).

Arguably, then, the character given to Rousseau in *The Triumph of Life* surrenders his individuality in different ways. The first surrender is philosophically and politically exemplary, the second abject and disabling. There are a couple of concluding comments worth making on this definitive Shelleyan dilemma. The first concerns Shelley's own theory of individuality as expounded in another fragment, 'On Love', probably written a year or so before 'On Life'. In 'On Love', it is argued that we discover within ourselves an 'ideal prototype' of human perfection. But this image of ourselves purged of all deficiencies quickly turns into a love object: our 'antitype', or 'an understanding capable of clearly estimating' our potential to transcend our characteristic limitations. We typically fall in love with an ideal version of ourselves: the recognition of what we want to be creates erotic wanting as well. And 'want' also maintains the connection with 'lack' or 'absence', problematizing erotic self-definition. Desire only exists when there is something wanting, so, on Shelley's definition, what I am is constitutionally missing from my make-up. But only when that specular possibility is considered can I be treated ethically, or as I deserve: for 'the great secret of morals', as *A Defence* has it, is also 'love' (*Pr* 282). I am revealed not by what I already possess but by a response to what I am capable of as a human being. We grow enamoured of anything upon which we can project a reflection of ourselves that enhances us so justly. But we have imagined this responsive creature, otherwise *we* could not take credit for the liberality of its estimation of us. The fate of the Poet in *Alastor* represents the dangers of narcissism inherent in such a model of identity. But Rousseau, in *The Triumph of Life*, represents the contrary trials besetting us when we entrust the definition of our best self to something not present, to 'the invisible and unattainable point to which Love tends' (*Pr* 170), to a future audience's reception of those qualities presently unrealized. As should be obvious now, Shelley's individual shares the fate he assigns to poetry.

The second comment concerns the community into which this selfless citizen is to be received. The puzzling anonymity or impersonality that each of us, when understood most generously, takes on has many parallels before and after Shelley, from Rousseau's General Will to the Freudian Unconscious. The defining community that Shelley cites in *A Defence of Poetry* is a Machiavellian republic. This society, too, needs to be poetically energized, 'renewed' by 'bringing back the drama to its principles' (*Pr* 286). The dialogue unmasking our personal possibilities is here less a poetic idealism and more a piece of hard-headed political realism. Political participation, Machiavelli's requisite for civic virtue, is only maintained by a dramatic interest, which makes each citizen feel that they are in dialogue with the whole. Like Rousseau's 'state of nature', this touchstone has to be continually updated. Patriotic loyalty, a willingness to serve the state whose interests we let shape our better civic-minded selves, and the idea of fulfilment through public service follow. Such generous self-surrenders both realize poetry in action and accord politics the unscripted, responsive virtues it needs to possess in order to retain its mandate. Shelley wrote that 'the true poetry of Rome lay in its institutions' (*Pr* 287). The renewal of political excitement, vital for sustaining that republican life, is to be achieved on the model of poetic regeneration central to Shelley's thought.

NOTES

1. The classic reference book here is James A. Notopoulos, *The Platonism of Shelley: A Study of Platonism and the Poetic Mind* (Durham, N.C.: Duke University Press, 1949). Notopoulos distinguishes three strands in Shelley's Platonism: 'direct' and 'indirect' influences, based on reading and tradition, and a 'natural' Platonism or openness to 'the identity in difference', under which my chapter subsumes the other two (4, 28).
2. Plato, *Timaeus*, 46d–48.
3. Notopoulos surmises that Shelley 'probably' read the *Timaeus* in 1810–11.

4. G. M. Matthews, *Shelley*, Writers and their Work, no. 214 (London: Longman, 1970).
5. The classic discussion is in the *Theaetetus*, 149a.
6. Friedrich Nietzsche, *The Birth of Tragedy*, tr. Walter Kaufmann (New York: Random House, 1967), sec. 14.
7. Karl Marx, 'The German Ideology', in *Selected Writings*, ed. David McLellan (Oxford: Oxford University Press, 1977), 179.
8. Ernst Cassirer, *The Philosophy of the Enlightenment*, tr. Fritz C. A. Koelln and James P. Pettegrove (Princeton: Princeton University Press, 1951), 55–6.
9. The intellectual rehabilitation of Shelley's vegetarianism is completed in Timothy Morton, *Shelley and the Revolution in Taste* (Cambridge and New York: Cambridge University Press, 1994).
10. Blaise Pascal, *Pensées*, no. 206 in *Pensées et Opuscules*, ed. Léon Brunschvicg (Paris: Librairie Hachette, n.d.): 'Le silence éternal de ces espaces infinis m'effraie' ('the eternal silence of these infinite spaces terrifies me').
11. Martin Heidegger, *Schelling's Treatise on the Essence of Human Freedom*, tr. Joan Stambaugh (Athens: Ohio University Press, 1985).
12. George Berkeley, *The Principles of Human Knowledge*, ed. G. J. Warnock (London: Fontana, 1962), 66, 109.
13. Barbara Charlesworth Gelpi, *Shelley's Goddess: Maternity, Language, Subjectivity* (New York and Oxford: Oxford University Press, 1992), 27; Nigel Leask, *British Romantic Writers and the East* (Cambridge: Cambridge University Press, 1992), 150.
14. Harold Bloom, Paul de Man, Jacques Derrida, Geoffrey H. Hartman, and J. Hillis Miller, *Deconstruction and Criticism* (London: Routledge and Kegan Paul, 1979). The quoted remark is from Hartman's Preface, viii.
15. Jerrold E. Hogle, *Shelley's Process: Radical Transference and the Development of his Major Works* (New York and Oxford: Oxford University Press, 1988), 15.

10

TIMOTHY MORTON

Nature and culture

Within you without you

'And the time will come when you see we're all one / And life flows on within you and without you.' Thus concludes George Harrison's song 'Within You Without You'.[1] 'Nature' and 'culture' are often opposed to each other. We commonly talk about the difference between 'nature' and 'nurture'. In Shakespeare's *The Tempest*, Prospero calls Caliban the slave a devil on whose nature nurture could never stick (4.1.188–9).[2] Nature and culture, however, are not necessarily as different from one another as the colonialist Prospero thinks. For example, 'culture' can mean the growth of a plant, or of bacteria in a laboratory, or 'cultivation', as in 'agriculture'. Rather than a chasm, it is as if there were a loose and slippery continuity between the two terms.

For Percy Shelley, nature and culture were coterminous. In the antihomophobic essay 'A Discourse on the Manners of the Ancient Greeks Relative to the Subject of Love', he puts it succinctly: 'Man is in his wildest state a social being' (*Pr* 220). *A Defence of Poetry* is as much a biological treatise as it is a poetic and philosophical one, and life and language turn out to be deeply intertwined within it. The essay begins with a strong thesis on the organic, embodied nature of consciousness. Shelley advocates an anti-dualist idea of the mind as embedded in nature. This mind interacts with its environment like an 'Aeolian lyre' played by the wind:

> poetry is connate with the origin of man. Man is an instrument over which a series of external and internal impressions are driven like the alternations of an ever-changing wind over an Aeolian lyre which move it by their motion to ever-changing melody. But there is a principle within the human being, and perhaps within all sentient beings, which acts otherwise than in the lyre and produces not only melody alone but harmony, by an internal adjustment of the sounds or motions thus excited to the impressions which excite them. It is as if the lyre could accommodate its chords to the motions of that which strikes them in a

determined proportion of sound, even as the musician can accommodate his voice to the sound of the lyre. (*Pr* 277)

There is a continuity between the mind and its environment. Thoughts are simply patterns made by the clash and harmony of different kinds of 'note' played by the influence of the environment. Moreover, the ability of the mind to produce harmony is another kind of continuity, an 'accommodation' of the mind to its world. Notice how Shelley suggests extending the capacity for harmony to 'all sentient beings'. Poetry, on this view, is perfectly natural.

It is an all-encompassing mimetic theory. 'In the youth of the world', declares Shelley, 'men dance and sing and imitate natural [that is, 'surrounding'] objects' (*Pr* 278), and they do so later too. It is only that one of the 'natural objects' to hand is the future, which poets call into being in the present. Poetry, therefore, is both supremely mimetic and utterly revolutionary. Poets' 'thoughts are the germs of the flower and the fruit of latest time' (279); poets are 'mirrors of the gigantic shadows which futurity casts upon the present' (297). Thus the 'accommodation' of mind with world is in no sense an acquiescence with the status quo, with all the attendant political implications. That would be to prioritize the world over the mind, and Shelley's view does not do that, though it does not do the opposite either. 'Nature' here does not mean the status quo, as it might in William Wordsworth's *The Excursion*, with its prefatory remarks on how the 'external' world is 'fitted' to the mind (63–8); William Blake remarked caustically 'You shall not bring me down to believe such fitting & fitted I know better & Please your Lordship'; Shelley may have agreed.[3]

It is not simply nature and culture that are joined here: the very ideas of inside and outside have fused and thus the difference between them has vanished. Distinguishing between 'inside' and 'outside' is fundamental to any metaphysical system.[4] For Shelley the mind was inseparable from its world, as it was for some of the progressive brain scientists in the Romantic age. In 1796, Samuel Taylor Coleridge had proposed the radical idea that humans were 'organic harps', though subsequently he retreated from the materialism and pantheism implied in his suggestion even in the inscription of the idea itself ('The Eolian Harp', 44–8).[5] It is actually difficult to label Shelley's and Coleridge's Aeolian metaphor as a result either of materialism or of idealism, since in the image mind and world interpenetrate to such an extent. In the name of a non-theistic (some have said pantheistic) view, the harp simile revises a strong and varied tradition of imagining people as fleshly instruments both in Pythagorean and Neoplatonic philosophy and in Christian liturgy and poetry, which accounts for the image's spiritual resonance.

The harp image evokes the idea that human beings in some sense *are* their environment. It is common to think that humans are intrinsically different, separate, cut off from their world. There are various political reasons for this, not the least of which is the sense that current social conditions are insurmountably awful. But for Shelley, the mind is not just formed by the ambient medium in which it finds itself, but interacts with this medium so as to reform it in turn. In a strong sense this is an *ambient* idea of the mind, and, as we shall see, of poetry itself. In this respect, Coleridge's 'The Eolian Harp', with its imagery of the harp's 'soft floating witchery of sound' (20), its sense of 'the one life within us and abroad' (26), and its contemplation of the environment in which the poem is being written, is certainly the prototype of Shelley's writing:

> How exquisite the scents
> Snatched from yon bean-field! and the world so hushed!
> The stilly murmur of the distant sea
> Tells us of silence.   (9–12)

By 'poetry' Shelley means something much more fundamental than just endstopped lines of verse. He means the very capacity of sentient beings to synthesize sense impressions and ideas, which for him are made of sense impressions in the same manner as chords are composed of individual notes. If nature and culture are not just similar but part of the same phenomenon, and if both indicate a kind of 'aroundness' – they surround, even permeate, sentient beings – we need a word like 'ambience' to suggest this, a word that is not itself caught up in any metaphysical baggage about differences between culture and nature.

Shelley's poems contain many images of forms of ambient 'aroundness', images that stand in both for culture and for nature. It is often radically ambiguous which one they represent. Consider this passage from *Laon and Cythna*, later renamed *The Revolt of Islam*:

> The starlight smile of children, the sweet looks
> Of women, the fair breast from which I fed,
> The murmur of the unreposing brooks,
> And the green light which shifting overhead,
> Some tangled bower of vines around me shed,
> The shells on the sea-sand, and the wild flowers,
> The lamplight through the rafters cheerly spread,
> And on the twining flax—in life's young hours
> These sights and sounds did nurse my spirit's folded powers.
>
> (2.1.667–75)

Laon, the revolutionary, is describing his infancy: literally, the culture that 'nursed' him. Shelley does everything he can to evoke a sense of ambient space – or more precisely a nestling *place* that is not objective and punctual (it is not a point in Cartesian space), but which includes perception and inter-subjective experience ('the sweet looks / Of women, the fair breast from which I fed'). This place is more like Plato's *chora*, an enveloping 'Receptacle' that contains each thing in the universe; or Aristotle's idea of *periechon*, literally that which 'goes around' things.[6]

Western philosophy has gradually drained the idea of place of its living quality, reifying and reducing it to a series of zero-dimensional points in an empty void. For Laon, however, the world has become a lactating breast. Laon's words reduce distinctions between inside and outside, causing them to interpenetrate. The very first phrase, 'The starlight smile of children', brings together near and far, objective and subjective, in a vigorous mixing of opposites. 'Sweet looks' hesitates between seeing and tasting. Since philosophy has tended to see the former as more objective than the latter, the image, a synaesthetic pun, means to blend subject and object. If 'culture' is metonymically present in 'lamplight' and 'rafters', 'nature' exists along-side it in the series of phrases that includes 'The shells on the sea-sand, and the wild flowers'. This is paratactic syntax – the bare listing of phrases side by side. Parataxis heightens the energy of the stanza, conveying a sense of a surrounding yet unbounded world – the list could go on for ever. Light does not transcend the things of this world, nor does it strike them and bounce off them. Instead light gets caught up in things. It is inter-twined with objects, refracted and tinted as 'starlight' or 'green light'. It is 'spread' through the wooden beams of the house and glows on the flax. The flax almost assumes the quality of incarnated, concrete light, seeming to complete the series.

This light is *almost* meaningful – it appears in smiles, it is 'cheerly spread'. Likewise, sound, present as a 'murmur', is a 'white noise', a minimal onomatopoeic hum that does not mean something in particular, but does not mean absolutely nothing either. Shelley is reminding us, as did the composer John Cage in the twentieth century, that sound is just noise to which we pay attention, which we pull into the foreground. The 'visual onomatopoeia' of the glowing charm of light, and the sonic trace of murmurs, indicate that what counts as meaning (culture) and what counts as nonmeaning (nature) have become as arbitrary as the difference between foreground and background. Above all, let us note the openness of Shelley's imagery. The murmuring streams continue without 'repose' (rest) and the same may be said for the patterns of light, and for the list of phenomena in general. This is not the self-contained, heavy, obscure, and minatory organic world of reactionary 'tradition', but the free-floating and friendly space of democratic values. Nevertheless, it *is* a place, even if that place is not very localized. Shelley is throwing down the gauntlet to those ideologues who spin reactionary cultural webs in which to catch the modern subject, nostalgic for a world they may never have actually inhabited. Why should such ideologues have a monopoly on fantasy images of 'culture'?

Of course, we should be aware that this is a risky enterprise. In the modern period, the 'aesthetic', 'literature', and 'culture' have often come to evoke some soothing 'in-between' state that would, like a healing ointment, massage the fractured contours of our world without dealing with the sources of the fracture. It is simply that progressive politics can take encouragement in the play of ambiguity and difference, the tricksterish quality, in Shelley's particular form of this language – its shifting lights, its compelling but non-authoritative charm.

Future readings of Shelley will need to take account of how persistently difficult it has been to appreciate his work from a normative modern standpoint. Certain forms of poetry, including Shelley's, commonly use the surrounding world figuratively, as a sounding board or echo chamber for actions or thoughts. Rocks resound with grief, trees sigh with melancholy. One could describe this as the 'pathetic fallacy', like the Victorians and the modernists, a misattribution of emotions to natural phenomena – the sea does not really 'rage'. Yet the tradition is noble and long, stretching back at least as far as Plato's Orphic ideas about language and poetry, let alone the actual myth of Orpheus, who calmed the animals with his singing. It is as if Shelley literalizes such figures, taking the so-called pathetic fallacy very seriously. In the reformed worlds of *Queen Mab* and *Prometheus Unbound*, it is not just 'as if' nature is transformed along with political and cultural change; it really *is* transformed. And it is the task of poetry to receive the impressions of the surrounding environment just as the mad poet in Plato's *Ion* receives inspiration from elsewhere (a god, heaven, some realm beyond this one). As Shelley puts it, poetry 'is . . . the interpenetration of a diviner nature through our own; but its footsteps are like those of a wind over the sea, which the coming calm erases, and whose traces remain only as on the wrinkled sand which paves it' (*Defence*, Pr 294). Shelley's figure here is in fact the inverse of the pathetic fallacy. Shelley ascribes environmental phenomena to the human subject.

We shall be returning in a later section to Shelley's literalization of the pathetic fallacy. But it is high time that this poetic tendency be re-evaluated. Scholarship could start by generating some value-neutral terms that would describe what occurs in Shelley's rhetoric which could fall under the heading of the pathetic fallacy. These terms would be based on chiasmus, since that figure is one of contrary motion. (The late work of the phenomenological philosopher, Maurice Merleau-Ponty, attempts to account for the embeddedness of consciousness in its environment via the idea of chiasmus – indeed, 'the chiasm' is his name for the enfolding of the subject in the world.[7]) Shelley as it were takes the 'inside' to stand for the 'outside', and vice versa. The crisscrossing pattern of 'inside-out' and 'outside-in' causes the environment to represent the figure, and the figure to represent the environment (the pathetic fallacy again).

In the long narrative poem *Alastor*, a radical poet seeks the essence of a vision but somehow ends up missing it, dying in isolation and misery amidst a vast and sublime natural landscape. The Poet becomes overwhelmed by his surroundings. In the imagery, his body ('frame') is an Aeolian harp that the elements no longer play:

> Even as a vapour fed with golden beams
> That ministered on sunlight, ere the west
> Eclipses it, was now that wondrous frame—
> No sense, no motion, no divinity—
> A fragile lute, on whose harmonious strings
> The breath of heaven did wander—a bright stream
> Once fed with many-voicèd waves—a dream
> Of youth, which night and time have quenched for ever,
> Still, dark, and dry, and unremembered now.   (663–71)

As we have seen, Shelley found the image of this ambient instrument very compelling – it is the founding image of his *Defence of Poetry*. The Poet in *Alastor*, however, in becoming 'one' with nature, has missed what it means to be human. His absorption in nature is death rather than life. Shelley describes this state precisely as one of 'repose' (621, 641), the after-dinner slump of the tyrant – unlike Laon, the Poet's life has reached a fixed point. We could read *Alastor* as an allegory about how to think nature and culture together. If our sense of nature does not include notions of sympathy and solidarity with other beings, as the Preface states, we will die a lonely death. Appreciating nature is not just a matter of gawping at a rock formation, but of helping to build a more just world.

Scholarship has often distinguished sharply between 'political' and 'apolitical' forms of Shelley's verse, specifically viewing the 'political' poetry as not 'poetic'. It is evident, however, that Shelley's explicitly political poetry bears a strong awareness of environment in a way that bears upon his precise understanding of poetics. In an age before environmental art, Shelley was experimenting with floating balloons 'filled with knowledge' over the Irish Sea, inserting radical pamphlets into the clothes of passing babies being carried in the streets of Dublin, and sending radical messages in bottles down the Bristol Channel (*RH* 149–50). In an age of political paranoia, the bottles were considered worthy of investigation by the secret service (*RH* 168). Shelley's sonnet to the balloon imagines the space of contact between people as the vast space of the sky:

> Bright ball of flame that through the gloom of even
> Silently takest thine etherial way
> And with surpassing glory dimm'st each ray
> Twinkling amid the dark blue depths of Heaven,
> Unlike the Fire thou bearest, soon shalt thou
> Fade like a meteor in surrounding gloom,
> Whilst that, unquenchable, is doomed to glow
> A watch-light by the patriot's lonely tomb.
>
> ('To a Balloon, Laden with *Knowledge*', 1–8)

Ballooning was associated with philosophical speculation in general, and (French) revolutionary philosophy in particular.[8] The first aeronautic writing offered a radically displaced view of the earth, as if seen by extraterrestrial beings.[9] Rather than embodying a sense of 'here', of home and hearth, Shelley's imagery of the star or meteor presents nature (and culture) as decentred, unfamiliar, elsewhere. Shelley figures enlightening knowledge as a spark or star that persists within the vastness of space. The space of nature has become the 'gloom' of political oppression. The figurative logic is of concentric containers: the knowledge is a ball of light contained in the balloon, itself contained in the sky. Each container in turn becomes the contents of the next, in a flip-flopping transition between figures and grounds. The 'tomb' of the patriot itself is also a figure for the persistence of other points of view. Derived from Godwin's essay on sepulchres, the tomb is surely the mute reminder that by 1812 the ghosts of the English Revolution (Hampden, Sidney, and Russell) have not yet been put to rest. Shelley's sense of culture is not a solidification of whatever is the case, but a shading of the not-yet, or as he puts it in the *Defence of Poetry* the shadow of the future cast into the present. This shadow haunts our world. The environment, for Shelley, can be virtual, not just 'real' in an empirical sense. It does not have to be simply 'what is the case'; otherwise, Shelley's figuration of nature would slip into Burkeanism or Alexander Pope's 'Whatever is, is right' (*Essay on Man*, 1.294).[10] The environment can include the possibilities of 'what if', a conditional, subjunctive quality. This is crucial to his oppositional, and specifically republican, politics.

The sonnet 'On Launching Some Bottles Filled with *Knowledge* into the Bristol Channel' is about an actual event in Shelley's life. He placed texts such as the *Declaration of Rights* and *The Devil's Walk* into bottles and floated them out towards Ireland. The Home Office put him under surveillance for it. The sonnet represents the container itself contained by the 'surrounding roar' of the Irish Sea:

> Vessels of Heavenly medicine! may the breeze
> Auspicious waft your dark green forms to shore;
> Safe may ye stem the wide surrounding roar
> Of the wild whirlwinds and the raging seas;
> And oh! if Liberty e'er deigned to stoop
> From yonder lowly throne her crownless brow
> Sure she will breathe around your emerald group
> The fairest breezes of her west that blow.   (1–8)

Liberty's 'brow' is 'crownless' and her 'throne' is 'lowly'. Shelley confronts the republican dilemma of producing an iconoclastic icon, an image that is compelling but lacking a trace of feudalism. Liberty is associated with a direction in an environment – the (American?) West – and assumes the qualities of an environing wind. Ambience clinches the sequence of images, dissolving the problematic figure of Liberty into the surrounding world. Shelley thereby establishes a new way of generating figures in relation to their environments.

In 'Ode to the West Wind' Shelley figuratively produces the theory of this disseminative practice:

> Make me thy lyre, even as the forest is:
> What if my leaves are falling like its own!
>
> . . . .
> . . . Be thou me, impetuous one!
>
> Drive my dead thoughts over the universe
> Like withered leaves to quicken a new birth!
> And, by the incantation of this verse,
>
> Scatter, as from an unextinguished hearth
> Ashes and sparks, my words among mankind!
> Be through my lips to unawakened Earth
>
> The trumpet of a prophecy!   (57–69; N)

The energy of the west wind plays in the open space between the penultimate and last stanza. Here the syntax is pulled open by the poem's very form, such that Shelley conveys his favourite cultural space of the not-yet, the pregnancy of political possibility: what the republican Machiavelli would have called *occasione*. Black marks are mixed with blank space. Likewise, in the general imagery of the ode, the interpenetration of environments, and of self and environment, is reflected in the way in which each element becomes the metaphorical vehicle for each other one. Clouds become like leaves (16), the sea becomes like the land it reflects (33); at the conclusion, the poet's thoughts become like the dead leaves with which the ode began. By extension, the wind becomes the poet. 'Interpenetration', indeed any compound prefixed by 'inter', were Shelley's favourite words. In the 1790s, the London Corresponding Society had established forms of political association based on the formation of cells that divided once they reached a certain size, cells that disseminated knowledge and calls to action such as universal suffrage. It was an internet without computers. Pitt's government undermined the LCS. Shelley's poetics mimics the virtual form that such political movements had to assume.

Shelley's phrase, 'By the incantation of this verse', produces an illocutionary statement, in other words, a statement that enacts its own meaning *in* rather than *through* itself, such as 'I now pronounce you man and wife.'[11] Illocutionary statements are necessarily context specific. I cannot pronounce my fellow passengers on the bus to be man and wife; I need to be a priest in a church conducting a marriage ceremony. In other words, illocutionary statements depend upon their environment to be valid. We may conclude that Shelley is declaring a faith in his 'verse' as a validating environment for his radical illocutionary prayer: an ambient poetics, indeed.

Shelley's vegetarianism: the politics of human nature

Shelley's ideas about poetry were one way in which he collapsed differences between nature and culture, outside and inside. Another way was his interest in food. Food comes from the 'outside', from the environment, and passes into the 'inside': it is prepared, cooked, eaten. Some ecological writers talk about nature in the abstract, and so does Shelley. The image of the mountain in 'Mont Blanc' crystallizes the very idea of freedom (80–1). But Shelley was also interested in concrete nature: in animals, plants, and what humans do to them, and with them. When we think about food as a function of our place in an environment, we necessarily involve ourselves in a metabolic model of interaction with that environment. Food is gathered, produced, eaten, and taken into the stomach, digested and excreted, thus altering the very environment from which it was harvested. It is not quite right to think of this as a circular process, since this metabolic process alters the very world from which we took the food.

Shelley the vegetarian was keenly interested in what we take into and what we leave out of our stomachs: how we modify our world, or not.

Indeed, Pythagoreanism was an ancient view of metabolic interconnected-
ness, in the doctrine of the transmigration of souls. Shelley's essay 'On the
Devil and Devils' plays this view in a burlesque that mixes high morality
with the gross body, wondering 'What became of the Devils after the death
of the pigs [in the Gadarene Swine episode of the gospels], whether they
passed into the fish [on hurling themselves over the cliff], and then by
digestion, through the stomach, into the brain of the Gadarene Ichthyopha-
gists [fish-eaters]' (*Pr* 271). Moreover, food imagery demonstrates one way
in which Shelley's depictions of social transformation always entail environmental, global transformation. The very ambient medium changes in response to human oppression and revolution, such that the diet of animals is
said to change. In *Queen Mab* an extended ecotopian passage celebrates the
dawning of a new age:

> The lion now forgets to thirst for blood:
> There might you see him sporting in the sun
> Beside the dreadless kid; his claws are sheathed,
> His teeth are harmless, custom's force has made
> His nature as the nature of a lamb.   (8.124–8)

The Daemon of the World, a compressed version of *Queen Mab*, revises
that poem's vegetarian passage, replacing 'no longer now / He slays the
lamb that looks him in the face' (8.211–12) with 'no longer now / He slays
that beast that sports around his dwelling' (2.153–4). The sense here is of
animals precisely as an aspect of the surrounding environment. As elsewhere
in his work, Shelley revises Isaiah 11, where the lion lies down with the
lamb, superimposing it upon a revision of Greek and Latin representations
of the Golden Age.[12] In this as with other figurative topics, Shelley's early
didactic masterpiece *Queen Mab* provided a template that he reused
throughout his life. In *Prometheus Unbound*, the liberated world is figured
in the image of kingfishers eating vegetarian food: 'two azure halcyons
clinging downward / And thinning one bright bunch of amber berries'
(3.4.80–1). Even animal diet has changed. Is this just a decorative poeticism,
or is it a symptom of something more substantial in Shelley's thinking? The
question pertains to Shelley's development of the chiasmus of environment
and subject (one moment of which, as we have seen, has been labelled the
pathetic fallacy). Let us consider it a little further.

It is fashionable in some circles no longer to believe in something called
human nature. It has become hard to see just how radical and powerful
human nature was when it was first proclaimed by the lineage that began
with the radical Dutch philosopher Spinoza and his followers in the seventeenth century. Whether human nature is a product or is innate has been

subject to debate. But we should recall that ideas of human nature have not always been foundationalist. Nowadays it is possible to forget that the idea of human nature can actually support the idea that social reality is a construct, a form that can be reformed, deformed, and un-formed – if we want to. Postmodern theory is really a continuation of Enlightenment philosophy, though some would say that it extends it to the point at which it crumbles into nothingness. Shelley himself quoted swathes of Spinoza, and signed *The Necessity of Atheism* with that philosopher's neat flourish, 'Q.E.D.' (*Pr 39*).

There is a tendency in some scholarship to see Shelley in particular, and Romanticism in general, as critically departing from the Enlightenment and journeying towards this nothingness. But from another point of view, Shelley and his cultural moment simply make the Enlightenment reflect upon itself. Questioning and critique are intrinsic to ideas of human nature. Once you have a sense that there is something beyond or behind our current forms of representing ourselves, you are bound to start wondering both why this essence or substance is unavailable in those current forms, and whether you have got the right idea of it. Why should this be seen as sheer nihilism? Why does thinking carry on at all, unless it emerges from wishes to avoid pain and seek pleasure in whatever form? Even an extreme nihilist still believes in something, or they would not be an 'ist' at all.

The Romantic period marked the beginning of 'isms' of all kinds both in art and in politics. These 'isms' (from Romanticism itself to postmodernism) have been more or less attempts to create a manifesto and a cultural and political form that would change the world, or perception of it, in some fundamental way. Shelley was a great practitioner of 'ism'. He had a strong idea of what poetry was for and was prepared to use it. He also had strong ideas about how to think and live, which affected his art. One of these was atheism. Another was vegetarianism.

Vegetarianism is based on the idea that humans have a certain nature which has become socially distorted, but which can be un-distorted, to the benefit of society and the natural world. To study Shelley's practice of vegetarianism is to see how committed he was actually to *embodying* a revolutionary attitude, as Timothy Clark puts it (see Further Reading). This is what Marxist thinkers call *praxis*: a fusion of theory and practice such that action can have a reflexive quality, and reflection can have an activist quality. In praxis, things that appear opposite come together, as in the rhetorical figure of chiasmus: the revolution can be eaten, while eating becomes revolutionary. Shelley would have felt right at home in mass activist movements such as anti-globalization, which combine reflection and action.

The word 'vegetarian' had not even been invented by the time Shelley became one – the preferred term was 'Pythagorean', after the vegetarian practices recommended by the Greek philosopher ('vegetarian' was coined in 1842, two decades after Shelley's death). Shelley was not alone in the Romantic period in practising a form of vegetarianism that was ethical, political, medical, and even in some sense spiritual (despite the fact that he was technically an atheist) all at once. He wrote two essays on vegetarianism, *A Vindication of Natural Diet* and the 'Essay on the Vegetable System of Diet'. Moreover, vegetarianism appeared in an expansive array of his prose and poetry. Shelley became a vegetarian as early as his time in Oxford, and it is possible that in 1811 he met Dr William Lawrence, a biologist who made very significant early contributions to materialist theories of evolution and the body which had a profound influence on Mary Shelley in writing *Frankenstein*. Lawrence himself was a vegetarian. Shelley cared so much about vegetarianism that he lent his favourite book on the subject, Joseph Ritson's *An Essay on Abstinence from Animal Food as a Moral Duty*, to Basil Montagu, his lawyer in the custody trial for his children. Shelley and his first wife, Harriet, practised vegetarianism in their house in Grafton Street, Dublin, in 1812. In 1812–13 he lived at Bracknell, near Windsor, in a vegetarian community of sorts that included Harriet, Lawrence, John Frank Newton, Mrs Harriet Boinville, Dr William Lambe, and even the reluctant Thomas Jefferson Hogg. Shelley practised the diet late into his short life. Beyond Shelley's vegetarian circles, it is possible that there were thousands of vegetarians in England alone in the Romantic period. Vegetarians belonged to all classes. People were becoming very interested in a practice that fused mind, body, society, and the natural world. My research has identified seventeen writers on vegetarianism who were not, it seems, themselves practitioners (twenty including Rousseau, Hegel, and Schopenhauer).[13] Add to this numerous groups, and eleven writers on animal rights who were not explicit vegetarians or writers on the subject.[14] The result is a list of forty-nine figures in total, excluding groups. We can only assume that this is the tip of the iceberg.

Vegetarianism undermined the normative hierarchy between humans and other sentient beings: the eater and the eaten. Symbolically, it also undermined the hierarchy among humans themselves. It was associated with the levelling politics of the French Revolution. In feudal times, it was the king and the upper classes who ate most of the meat; and nothing much had changed in capitalism. To eat a diet of vegetables was a form of solidarity, an eschewal of class distinctions as well as species ones. Vegetarian rhetoric in the period is often connected to pro-feminist and anti-slavery rhetoric. These forms of politics radicalized the Enlightenment idea that old-fashioned social structures warped human nature out of true. On what basis? Ultimately, for Shelley, it is the notion that 'all sentient beings' may be just that: sentient, or 'poetical' in the largest sense. Shelley was not a crass utilitarian – but he was a utilitarian (*Defence*, *Pr* 292–3). It was utilitarianism, for instance in Jeremy Bentham, that suggested ways of imagining animal rights. The idea of utility, of maximizing happiness and minimizing suffering, is based on sentience.

Vegetarianism became popular at the very beginning of the construction of modern, middle-class ideas of 'body image'. (Before the Romantic period, it had been the purview of English Revolutionary radicals and mystics, but had grown more widespread in the eighteenth century.) To have one at all was a significant development, an aspect of nascent consumerism, that other great leveller. The middle-class body image was and still is lean, mean, and flexible, *comfortable* rather than *luxurious*. It was supposed to be balanced: not too thin and not too fat, ready to take up a variety of positions in the modern workplace. While Mary Shelley was writing *Frankenstein*, Percy ate vegetarian food and Mary recorded the amounts in grams (*MSJ* 1.142). The recorded weights are suitably French and revolutionary, but also indicate a utilitarian attitude to food, in anticipation of modern concepts of food as 'nutrition' rather than 'flavour'. In the Romantic period, vegetarianism was not only against cruelty; it also expressed anxieties about the idea of sheer enjoyment, in a complex response to the history of imperialism and its oppressive production of sugar and spice. For Shelley, eating meat had a direct effect on mental as well as bodily ease. A quotation from Samuel Rogers's *The Pleasures of Memory* (1792) appears, without citation, in *A Vindication of Natural Diet*. Rogers laments 'time misspent and comfort lost', and wonders whether if memory persisted after death, it would 'realize the hell that priests and beldams feign' (note z, 'said to have been written on a blank leaf of this Poem').[15] This is to literalize the idea put about by Satan in *Paradise Lost* that 'my self am hell' (4.75), in his great proclamation of subjectivity and interiority (such proclamations endeared him to Shelley).[16]

Of course, the idea of body image is not really 'balanced': it has given rise to special forms of pathology such as anorexia and bulimia. This is the dark side of fusing nature and culture, of naturalizing social practices such as eating. But vegetarianism is potentially a way of communing with other beings in the warmth of fellow feeling, not just an aspect of modern bourgeois control-freakery. It has a trace of working-class sensibility in it, a point not lost on some of the radical working-class readers of Shelley such as Richard Carlile. And yet, vegetarianism as delineated by Joseph Ritson and Shelley (one of Ritson's biggest fans) takes on the whole the form of a *negative* identification with other beings, refraining from harming them rather than seeking positive kinds of mutual satisfaction. Nevertheless, we could at least declare that vegetarianism is haunted by the possibility of a wider solidarity between beings often thought to be separate. Such is the utopian aspect of an 'ecological' praxis that seeks to see and embody nature and culture as two aspects of the same thing.

Natural culture, 'cultural' nature

There are other ways in which Shelley fuses nature and culture. These ways blend the one into the other on one level, while preserving the distinction between them on another. Shelley was not entirely concerned to undermine the difference between nature and culture: they could come in useful as metaphysical terms, and as figures for certain kinds of ideas – ideological shorthand.

It is easy to recognize this when we consider those things that Shelley considered 'unnatural'. If humans *are* their environment, and culture is nature, how can anything be unnatural? Nevertheless, some things are more natural than others. We must be very careful to distinguish different ways of seeing nature and culture as the 'same'. For instance, without a sufficiently strong view of nature as malleable and impermanent, the idea that social life has a biological basis becomes the kernel of fascism. Scholarship must confront those moments in Shelley in which nature becomes something suspiciously solid and metaphysical.

In the *Defence of Poetry*, Shelley is careful to say that thoughts are harmonies with the impressions made upon the mind by its environment. There is no account of how thought may be dissonant with its world, but the very notion of harmony implies that some psychic tones are appropriate while others are not. Shelley's classic image of the unnatural is that of the tyrant. For Shelley, a despotic hierarchy was not part of the natural order of things. Throughout his life, from his earliest work, Shelley employed a topos of 'blood and gold', an extended metonymy for the 'unnatural'.[17] 'Blood and gold' stands for the horrors of war (killing and profiteering); slavery (purchasing the labour of slaves); the business of killing and selling animal flesh. Sometimes it is literalized: in *Laon and Cythna*, the tyrant's misrule permits human flesh to be sold openly in the street: 'They weighed it in small scales' (10.19.3955–63).

Shelley was open to the idea that all forms of eroticism and love contained a natural essence. The essay on homosexuality establishes that it is only 'superstition' (Enlightenment code for ideology) that makes Greek homoeroticism less palatable 'than the usual intercourse endured by almost every youth of England with a diseased and insensible prostitute' (*Pr* 223).

A form of culture ('manners') appears as entirely part of a malleable nature. There is a sense here of Shelley taking away with one hand what he gives with another. On the one hand this is a symptom of his circumspection about homosexual language, an attempt to induce his reader to tolerate its possibility. On the other hand it is a way of maintaining the category of the natural evacuated of specific ideological determinants ('superstition') – except for the ideology that nature is not determined. Universalism was the name of the game. Shelley's texts on love augment the thesis of Adam Smith's *Theory of Moral Sentiments*, declaring that compassion is natural for sentient creatures. It is natural to put oneself in the shoes of another, or as Shelley phrases it: 'The great secret of morals is love, or a going out of our own nature and an identification of ourselves with the beautiful which exists in thought, action, or person, not our own' (*Defence*, Pr 282–3).

When Shelley uses 'nature', it is frequently code for that which is beyond prejudice. It is through bitter disappointment that he so fiercely attacks Wordsworth, whom he saw as having fixed the horizons of his thinking, addressing him as 'Poet of Nature'.[18] (It is ironic that Wordsworth himself at significant moments in his poetry diverged from Shelley's version of him, and indeed can be seen as having formulated an anti-essentialist poetics of his own.[19]) Martin Heidegger, the saint of deep ecology, would never have approved of Shelley, since Heidegger's view is that nature is, precisely, prejudice ('pre-understanding'). This prejudice has a determinedly environmental quality, surrounding the subject with what is handy and homey. Heidegger extends this idea that some things are simply 'around', unquestionably to hand, to the notion that history is *destiny*. He thus provided one of the most toxic social regimes in the history of humanity with the convenient sense that the German Reich was as inevitable as knowing that one's shoes go on one's feet, not on one's head. Shelley was peculiarly sensitive to how much a politics based on an Enlightenment opposition to 'custom' and 'superstition' needed a sense of environment to counteract the compelling image of nature as the rightness of established authority.

In all this, Shelley inherits the ideas of the radical Enlightenment: that there is no god, or that humans can get along quite well without one, even if one existed; that humans, like other sentient beings, possess a basic goodness that enables them to feel and act with sympathy and love; that the natural order of things has no place for tyrants. As argued above, we should be careful to differentiate between ways of undermining distinctions between biological and social being. For example, Shelley does not think of culture in its touchy-feely sense, as the second nature of an embracing and authoritative tradition. Nor does he construe culture in the prototypical way in which Edmund Burke, who had reacted fiercely against the French

Revolution, opposes radicalism to the weight of tradition, the power of accumulated organic layers; an idea that leaves a trace in the nationalistic strain of Heidegger's idea of a surrounding *Umwelt*. Instead, Shelley's fantasy of ambience is closer to French (and American) revolutionary notions of *civilisation* and liberty – open, rational, and flexible ideas of the world that surrounds us.

How to convey a sense of cultural and/or natural 'space' that did not bear the seal of aristocracy or monarchy? The difference is between seeing nature and culture as *essence* – as existing in an abstract transcendental principle, such as 'humanity' or 'liberty' – and seeing them as *substance* – as forms of embodied *thing*, concrete, tactile, enveloping. *Civilisation* tends more towards essentialism, while German ideas of *Kultur*, and related English ideas of 'organic community', are more substantialist. In Shelley's time, essentialism was on the side of radicalism, while substantialism was usually reactionary. The essentialists, if they were poets like Shelley, faced a problem: how to generate images of something transcendental, even iconoclastic?

While Prometheus is being tortured by the tyrant Jupiter, nailed to the mountainside at the beginning of Shelley's psychodrama, the environment is sickened and denatured. The Earth, a female personification, speaks:

> I am the Earth
> Thy mother, she within whose stony veins,
> To the last fibre of the loftiest tree
> Whose thin leaves trembled in the frozen air,
> Joy ran, as blood within a living frame,
> When thou didst from her bosom, like a beam
> From sunrise, leap—a spirit of keen joy!
> And at thy voice her pining sons uplifted
> Their prostrate brows from the polluting dust,
> And our almighty Tyrant with fierce dread
> Grew pale—until his thunder chained thee here.
> Then—see those million worlds which burn and roll
> Around us: their inhabitants beheld
> My spherèd light wane in wide heaven; the sea
> Was lifted by strange tempest, and new fire
> From earthquake-rifted mountains of bright snow
> Shook its portentous hair beneath Heaven's frown;
> Lightning and Inundation vexed the plains;
> Blue thistles bloomed in cities; foodless toads
> Within voluptuous chambers panting crawled;
> When Plague had fallen on man and beast and worm,
> And Famine, and black blight on herb and tree;
> And in the corn, and vines, and meadow-grass,

Teemed ineradicable poisonous weeds
Draining their growth, for my wan breast was dry
With grief; and the thin air, my breath, was stained
With the contagion of a mother's hate
Breathed on her child's destroyer—aye, I heard
Thy curse, the which, if thou rememberest not,
Yet my innumerable seas and streams,
Mountains, and caves, and winds, and yon wide air,
And the inarticulate people of the dead,
Preserve, a treasured spell.   (1.152–84)

Jupiter is a figure for tyranny, which Shelley sees as having usurped the natural harmony of things: as a titan, Prometheus ruled before Jupiter did. Jupiter's reign affects the very air. Cities and meadows alike, culture and nature, become infected with 'blue thistles', 'Famine', and 'Plague'. These symptoms of tyranny are dispelled when Prometheus revokes his curse and Jupiter is deposed, suggesting that they do not belong to the category of the natural.

The Earth, however, speaks whether or not she is infected with unnatural symptoms (compare the utopian speech, 4.370–423). Is this extraordinary speech of an articulate Earth a glaring instance of that bane of modern poetics, the pathetic fallacy? In a sense, the world is a reflection of the conflict between tyrant and titan. Since, however, these characters are allegorical figures for political and philosophical states and views, they themselves are not the tenor for which the imagery of natural catastrophe is a vehicle. Moreover, since the Earth herself is an allegorical figure, we cannot tell which chicken came before which egg. We are certainly dealing with pathos, but it is impossible to decide upon whether it is fallacious, even if we wanted to.

Prometheus' defiant curse (1.262–301) is recorded in the environmental substance like a message on a tape or wax cylinder. The Earth is Prometheus' analogue medium of communication. But when we focus upon a certain aspect of the environment (cities, meadows), the Earth ceases to be 'environmental' and becomes an object of blessing or curse. The distinction between object and subject depends upon a sense of environmental background. Once this background comes into the foreground, we can no longer distinguish between subject and object. Thus Shelley's Orphic poetics ('Language is a perpetual Orphic song', 4.415) erases not only the distinctions between subject and object, but also more fundamental ones between figure and ground. If nature is to culture as ground is to figure, then it has become impossible to tell the difference between the two. This is what the image of the Earth implies, as a recording substance that can speak. In a chiasmus, its 'culture' or speech is natural, while its 'nature' as a medium for recording speech is intrinsically cultural.

The use of chiasmus should alert us to the presence of ideology. Shelley's Earth incarnates the compelling fantasy of republicanism and, to some extent, democracy. She embodies the idea that open and equal communication is possible in a neutral medium – the model that John Thelwall called *conversazione*, and which Jürgen Habermas calls the 'ideal speech situation'.[20] Here it is the globe of the earth itself; elsewhere it is a dome or an assembly chamber. But the features remain the same. The communication environment is only temporarily dysfunctional, stained with oppressive impurities and tyrannical 'noise' that can be eliminated like so much tape hiss. The question arises: to what extent is the apparently neutral medium in fact stained? Is its neutrality either a disguise for ideological orientations, and/or is that neutrality itself a form of ideological orientation? Culturally speaking, is the collective space we inhabit really unmarked by any particular (political) interest?

By the 1840s, Karl Marx attacks this notion of a neutral social space. Writing on Rousseau, Marx undermines the idea of 'culture' as 'natural'. He discovers that the supposedly neutral medium of contact is a reflex of the notion of abstract value. This is the idea that the extra labour energy used by the capitalist to produce a profit appears to hover somewhere above, beyond, beside, or around actual commodities. Somehow we find it almost impossible to refer this abstract value back to the workers who produced it rather than to the capitalists who claim to own it. Abstract value is crucial to the operation of capitalism and its ideological forms. The noble savage in the jungle, Rousseau's essential man, turns out to be the self-made man in the concrete jungle.[21] Anthropology was the new ideology. In this light, Marx asserts that the level playing field created through ideas of liberty and equality is more level for some than for others.

We should have seen this coming. The Earth, as a fantasy thing (is 'object' quite the right word?), is, inconsistently, the substantial incarnation of an essence (of abstract liberty and sympathy). Such an incarnation is paradoxical. Like Milton the republican iconoclast, Shelley was plagued with giving body to the disembodied. In seeking to provide an iconic image to serve an iconoclastic ideology, Shelley is in trouble. Neither 'nature' nor 'culture' will do the trick.

Green Shelley: forwards to nature

The sonnet 'Ozymandias' is a succinct example of how Shelley saw nature and culture as two sides of a whole:

I met a traveller from an antique land,
Who said: Two vast and trunkless legs of stone
Stand in the desert. Near them, on the sand,
Half sunk, a shattered visage lies, whose frown,
And wrinkled lip, and sneer of cold command,
Tell that its sculptor well those passions read
Which yet survive, stamped on these lifeless things,
The hand that mocked them and the heart that fed;
And on the pedestal these words appear:
'My name is Ozymandias, King of Kings:
Look on my works, ye Mighty, and despair!'
Nothing beside remains. Round the decay
Of that colossal Wreck, boundless and bare,
The lone and level sands stretch far away.   (1839)

The haunting close of the poem manages to link the desert with the tyrant's oppressive power, as elsewhere in Shelley's work. Somehow, though we are not told how exactly, that oppression has resulted in this desert. For Shelley, a just society would have persisted, not decayed. Tyranny undermines itself such that 'Nothing beside remains' – a scorched earth policy perhaps, or the result of an ecological catastrophe brought on, as we now understand the Sahara to have been brought on, by human hands. The too open, vast, empty horizontal space contradicts the bald assertion of the toppled vertical, the I of Ozymandias.

Just as Paul Foot famously dubbed Shelley 'red', it is quite appropriate to talk of a 'green Shelley'. Some ecocritics see green as an alternative both to reactionary blue and radical red. This is surely letting the ideological finger paint carry us away. What particular shade of green was Shelley? Deep, or as they say, shallow? This distinction must be treated with care, since it is itself a product of 'deep ecology', a view promoted by Arne Naess, Bill Devall, George Sessions, and others such as the 'monkeywrenching' Dave Foreman and the neoromantic Julia Butterfly Hill. Deep ecology suggests that what is required is a deep personal, even spiritual transformation. It is a quintessentially 'Romantic' form of ecology, if by that we mean that it wishes to engage politics at the level of subjective feelings, desires, and positions, rather than objective phenomena. In the words of the Woodstock festival attendee, if we think hard enough, maybe the rain will stop. Somehow, if we refine our subjectivity properly, the ecological catastrophe will disappear. Alternatively, perhaps some drastic action is required, in a reactionary, anti-intellectual spirit. Both responses are aspects of the same syndrome.

Hegel gives an elegant analysis of this Romantic political view when he describes the syndrome of the 'beautiful soul' in *The Phenomenology of*

Spirit. For the beautiful soul, a chasm exists between the subject, who possesses all the 'right' ideas, and a degraded reality. All dressed up with nowhere to go, the beautiful soul is stuck in a predicament. In order to maintain his or her world view, he or she must *preserve* the very chasm they also wish to abolish.[22] While being critical of the beautiful soul, we should be aware that it is a symptom of the machine against which it is raging. As Marx says of religion, it is a cry of the heart in a heartless world, 'the sigh of the oppressed creature . . . the soul of soulless circumstances'.[23]

Like an arrogant teenager, the beautiful soul assumes itself to be pure and its world to be corrupted. It reaches for two solutions to the split between impure and pure realms: quietism and activism; some would say terrorism, but one person's terrorist is another person's guerilla. There are certainly elements of 'beautiful soul syndrome' in Shelley. As a form of Romantic consumerism, vegetarianism is just such a syndrome – if we eat the right food, the suffering will cease: 'diet for a small planet', as the title of Frances Moore Lappe's book puts it.[24] Scholars have argued that Shelley was a deep ecologist before his time (see Ralph Pite's essay in Further Reading). But Shelley was also determined to see social problems as at the root of ecological problems. He manages to interweave the categories of nature and culture in ways that differ from deep ecology – which ironically preserves a gap between self and world even as it insists upon the lack of such a gap.

The beautiful soul may want to regress, scratch away the surface of modern life to reveal the pulsing reality underneath; or it may want to transform things in a progressive way. Deep ecology is profoundly reactionary. It inherits the atavism of some Romantic-period thinking, which wishes to wind society back to a mythical golden age. Shelley, on the other hand, posited his golden age in the future. His cry was not so much 'back to nature' (the title of one of his friends' vegetarian books is *The Return to Nature*) as 'forwards to nature'. For Shelley, even primitive, indigenous societies were subject to oppression and misery (*Queen Mab* 8.70–81, 145–97). In the truest sense, the state of nature *had not happened yet.*

Shelley was involved in a land reclamation project in Wales, on behalf of the working poor (*RH* 165, *IP* VII.327). Producing more land to produce more food does not sound like the practice of one committed to deep ecology, whose tenets include the idea that the world is heavily overpopulated. Such a Malthusian idea would have struck Shelley as obscenely reactionary. Yet Shelley was also interested in using the land more productively by farming potatoes instead of cattle, carefully taking notes on Humphrey Davy's *Elements of Agricultural Chemistry* (see *Pr* 87, *RH* 576).[25] This view unfortunately put him on the ruling-class side of an imperialist mission to feed the colonial subject and the working class, a mission strengthened by Thomas Malthus himself. Shelley did borrow from Malthus the tricolon of war, disease, and famine, a figure he uses throughout his oeuvre. But unlike Malthus, for whom these three are necessary evils, he saw war, disease, and famine as temporary and 'unnatural' phenomena that could be mitigated or even abolished.

It is difficult to speculate like Marx as to whether Shelley would have become a fully fledged socialist had he lived a little longer, though this is exactly what Marx's daughter held as the trajectory of Shelley's career.[26] It is, however, remarkable to read the following sentence from Marx's writing on the interconnection between history and nature: 'in certain writers the real production of life seems to be primeval history, while the truly historical appears to be separated from ordinary life, something superterrestrial. With this the relation of man to nature is excluded from history and hence the antithesis of nature and history is created.'[27] We have seen the extent to which Shelley would have agreed with this proposition.

Just how he would have agreed, however, remains ambiguous. On the one hand, 'history' is 'natural' insofar as it is based on biological processes that subtend it and which revolutionaries must uncover. Criticizing German liberals who 'look for the history of freedom beyond our history in the primeval Teutonic forests', Marx asks: 'how is the history of our freedom different from the history of the wild boar's freedom if it is only to be found in the forests?'[28] Shelley's valuation of nature is neither atavistic nor localist, but it does sometimes separate nature and history; in the essay 'On the Vegetable System of Diet' it is precisely the 'wild boar' that is more noble than the domesticated pig (*Pr* 93).[29] On the other hand, Shelley's 'nature' can often be fully 'historical': starvation is not a force of nature, but a social symptom, and to fight against it is to grasp it as such. The latter position seems more like a Marxist one. Shelley's depictions of a transformed earth of reason, delight, and satisfaction suggest, like Sebastiano Timpanaro, that nature is not eternal, just very rigidified. Such rigidity is nature's least natural aspect. Shelley's ecological writing softens calcified *destiny* into workable *history*. Marx explicitly approved of Shelley on rights. We have, however, discovered a subterranean connection between the two writers' ideas of nature. This discovery suggests that there exist wellsprings in seemingly barren fields such as 'nature' and 'humanity' into which we may yet tap.

NOTES

1. The Beatles, *Sergeant Pepper's Lonely Hearts Club Band* (EMI Records, 1967).
2. William Shakespeare, *The Complete Works*, ed. Peter Alexander (London and Glasgow: Collins, 1951).

3. William Blake, *The Complete Poetry and Prose of William Blake*, ed. David V. Erdman (New York: Doubleday, 1965; revised 1988), 667.
4. Jacques Derrida, 'Violence and Metaphysics', in *Writing and Difference*, tr. Alan Bass (London and Henley: Routledge and Kegan Paul, 1978), 79–153 (151–2).
5. Samuel Taylor Coleridge, *The Complete Poems*, ed. William Keach (Harmondsworth: Penguin, 1997).
6. Edward Casey, *The Fate of Place: A Philosophical History* (Berkeley: University of California Press, 1997), 41, 48, 55; Leo Spitzer, 'Milieu and Ambiance', in *Essays in Historical Semantics* (New York: Russell and Russell, 1948; repr. 1968), 179–316.
7. Maurice Merleau-Ponty, *The Visible and the Invisible*, tr. Alphonso Lingis (Evanston, Ill.: Northwestern University Press, 1968 (French edn, Paris: Gallimard, 1964)), 7–11.
8. Jane Stabler, *Burke to Byron, Barbauld to Baillie, 1790–1830* (Basingstoke and New York: Palgrave, 2002), 132–40.
9. Barbara Maria Stafford, *Voyage into Substance: Art, Science, Nature, and the Illustrated Travel Account, 1760–1840* (Cambridge, Mass.: MIT Press, 1984), 434–5.
10. Alexander Pope, *The Poems of Alexander Pope: A One-Volume Edition of the Twickenham Text, with Selected Annotations*, ed. John Butt (London and New York: Routledge, 1963; repr. 1989).
11. J. L. Austin, *How to Do Things with Words* (Oxford and New York: Oxford University Press, 1962), 147.
12. See, for example, a note to Miss Hitchener (*IP* 1.152); *Proposals for an Assocation* (*Pr* 61); *Queen Mab* 8.70–87 (this includes the other Isaian image, that of the baby 'sharing his morning's meal / With the green and golden basilisk / That comes to lick his feet', 85–7); *Laon and Cythna* 5 (5.50.2161–2, 51.2242–56); the cancelled final stanza of *An Ode Written October 1819, before the Spaniards had Recovered their Liberty*; *The Cenci* 2.3.151–2; *The Witch of Atlas* 97–104; the note on the final chorus of *Hellas* (*Pr* 334); *Prometheus Unbound* 4.404–5.
13. Anon., *Bruce's Voyage to Naples* (1802), William Blake, Henry Brougham, James Burnet (Lord Monboddo), John Taylor Coleridge, William Godwin, David Hartley, Benjamin Robert Haydon, Thomas Jefferson Hogg, James Henry Leigh Hunt, Thomas Medwin, Benjamin Moseley, Thomas Love Peacock, Horace Smith, Thomas Taylor, John Trelawny, Thomas Trotter.
14. Robert Browning, Church of Swedenborgians in Salford (Henry Cowherd), the 'Newton-Boinville' set in Windsor (Harriet de Boinville and her family, the Newtons, the Shelleys, and others), Richard Phillips's family, Harriet Shelley, John Tweddell, Members of the Vegetarian Society (founded 1847), and, of course, by necessity, the emerging working class; Samuel Taylor Coleridge, William Cowper, Henry Crowe, Thomas Lord Erskine, Rev. C. Hoyle, James Montgomery, John Lawrence, Anon. in *The Medusa* (radical underground newspaper), Samuel Jackson Pratt, Mary Wollstonecraft, Thomas Young.
15. Samuel Rogers, *Poems* (London: T. Cadell and W. Davies, 1814).
16. John Milton, *Paradise Lost*, ed. Alastair Fowler (London and New York: Longman, 1968, 1971).

17. For example, *Queen Mab* 3.46–9, 3.147–68, 4.168–71, 4.190–5, 6.103–21, 7.98–9, 7.170–86; *Laon and Cythna* 8.18.3352–60, 12.4459–61; *Charles the First* 1.58–65; *The Witch of Atlas* 185–92; *The Triumph of Life* 285–7.

18. Percy Bysshe Shelley, 'To Wordsworth', 1 (1816); William Wordsworth, *Selected Prose*, ed. John O. Hayden (New York: Penguin, 1988).

19. Timothy Morton, 'Why Ambient Poetics?', *The Wordsworth Circle* 33.1 (Winter 2002), 52–6.

20. Jürgen Habermas, 'Disourse Ethics: Notes on Philosophical Justification', in *Moral Consciousness and Communicative Action* (Cambridge, Mass.: MIT Press, 1990), 43–115.

21. Karl Marx, 'On the Jewish Question', in *Selected Writings*, ed. David McLellan (Oxford and New York: Oxford University Press, 1977, 1987), 56–7, and *Grundrisse*, ibid., 345–6.

22. Georg Wilhelm Friedrich Hegel, *Hegel's Phenomenology of Spirit*, tr. A.V. Miller, analysis and foreword by J. N. Findlay (Oxford: Oxford University Press, 1977), 383–409.

23. Karl Marx, 'Towards a Critique of Hegel's *Philosophy of Right*: Introduction', in *Selected Writings*, ed. McLellan, 64.

24. Frances Moore Lappe, *Diet for a Small Planet* (New York: Ballantine Books, 1971).

25. Bodleian MS Shelley Adds. e.6, 172–55 (rev); Bodleian MS Shelley Adds. e.2–3, 6–7; Tatsuo Tokoo, 'The Contents of Shelley's Notebooks in the Bodleian Library', *Humanities: Bulletin of the Faculty of Letters, Kyoto Prefectural University* 36 (December 1984), 1–32.

26. Edward Aveling and Eleanor Marx Aveling, *Shelley's Socialism: Two Lectures* (London: private circulation, 1888; repr. London: Journeyman Press, 1979), 16.

27. Karl Marx, *The German Ideology*, in *Selected Writings*, ed. McClellan, 173.

28. Karl Marx, 'Towards a Critique of Hegel's *Philosophy of Right*', in *Selected Writings*, ed. McClellan, 65.

29. Clark's edition of Shelley's prose (*Pr*) contains the misreading of 'bear' for 'boar'. E. B. Murray and I have independently verified that the MS of the essay reads 'boar'.

COMPLETE WORKS

The Poems of Shelley, ed. Kelvin Everest, and Geoffrey Matthews, 3 vols. (London and New York: Longman, 1989–).

The Complete Poetry of Percy Bysshe Shelley, ed. Donald H. Reiman and Neil Fraistat, 4 vols. (Baltimore and London: Johns Hopkins University Press, 2000–).

The Prose Works of Percy Bysshe Shelley, ed. E. B. Murray, 2 vols. (Oxford: Clarendon Press, 1993–).

Paperback editions

Shelley's Poetry and Prose, ed. Donald Reiman and Neil Fraistat (2nd edn of Norton Critical Edition; 1st edn ed. Donald Reiman and Sharon B. Powers) (New York and London: Norton, 2002 (1977)).

Shelley's Prose: Or The Trumpet of a Prophecy, ed. David Lee Clark (1954, 1966; London: Fourth Estate, 1988).

THE LIVES OF SHELLEY AND HIS CONTEMPORARIES

Cameron, Kenneth Neill, *The Young Shelley: Genesis of a Radical* (London: Victor Gollancz, 1951).

Carlson, Julie, 'Coming After: Shelley's *Proserpine*', *Texas Studies in Language and Literature* 41 (Winter 1999), 351–72.

Cox, Jeffrey, *Poetry and Politics in the Cockney School: Keats, Shelley, Hunt and their Circle* (Cambridge and New York: Cambridge University Press, 1998).

Holmes, Richard, *Shelley: The Pursuit* (London: Weidenfeld and Nicolson, 1987).

Robinson, Charles, *Shelley and Byron: The Snake and Eagle Wreathed in Fight* (Baltimore: Johns Hopkins University Press, 1976).

Trelawny, Edward John, *Recollections of the Last Days of Shelley and Byron*, ed. David Crane (London: Robinson, 2000).

RECEPTION

Allott, Miriam, 'Attitudes to Shelley: The Vagaries of a Critical Reputation', in *Essays on Shelley*, ed. Miriam Allott (Liverpool: Liverpool University Press, 1982), 1–38.

Behrendt, Stephen, *Shelley and His Audiences* (Lincoln: University of Nebraska Press, 1989).

Bennett, Andrew, 'Shelley in Posterity', in *Shelley: Poet and Legislator of the World*, ed. Betty Bennett and Stuart Curran (Baltimore: Johns Hopkins University Press, 1996), 215–23.

    Romantic Poets and the Culture of Posterity (Cambridge: Cambridge University Press, 1999).

Dunbar, Clement, *A Bibliography of Shelley Studies: 1823–1950* (New York and London: Garland, 1976).

Foot, Paul, *Red Shelley* (London: Sidgwick and Jackson in association with Michael Dempsey, 1980).

Jones, Lilla Maria Crisafulli, 'Shelley's Impact on Italian Literature', in *Shelley: Poet and Legislator of the World*, ed. Betty Bennett and Stuart Curran (Baltimore: Johns Hopkins University Press, 1996), 144–57.

Kaufman, Robert, 'Legislators of the Post-Everything World: Shelley's Defence of Adorno', *English Literary History* 63.3 (Fall 1996), 707–33.

    'Intervention and Commitment Forever! Shelley in 1819, Shelley in Brecht, Shelley in Adorno, Shelley in Benjamin', *Romantic Circles Praxis* (May 2001); http://www.rc.umd.edu/praxis/interventionist/kaufman/kaufman.html.

    'Aura, Still', *October* 99 (Winter 2002), 45–80.

O'Neill, Michael, '"A Storm of Ghosts": Beddoes, Shelley, Death, and Reputation', *Cambridge Quarterly* 28.2 (1999), 102–15.

Pottle, Frederick A., 'The Case of Shelley', *Publications of the Modern Language Association of America* 67.5 (1952), 589–608.

Rossington, Michael, 'Commemorating the Relic: The Beginnings of the Bodleian Shelley Collections', *Bodleian Library Record* 18.3 (April 2004), 264–75.

Webb, Timothy, *Shelley: A Voice Not Understood* (Manchester: Manchester University Press, 1977), 1–32.

Wheatley, Kim, *Shelley and His Readers: Beyond Paranoid Politics* (Columbia: University of Missouri Press, 1999).

DRAMA

Cox, JeffreyN., *In the Shadows of Romance: Romantic Tragic Drama in Germany, England, and France* (Athens: Ohio University Press, 1987).

Curran, Stuart, *Shelley's Cenci: Scorpions Ringed with Fire* (Princeton: Princeton University Press, 1970).

    Shelley's Annus Mirabilis (San Marino, Calif.: Huntington Library, 1975).

Gladden, Samuel, 'Shelley's Agenda Writ Large: Reconsidering *Oedipus Tyrannus; or, Swellfoot the Tyrant*', in *Reading Shelley's Interventionist Poetry, 1819–1820*, ed. Michael Scrivener, *Romantic Circles Praxis* (May 2001); http://www.rc.umd.edu/praxis/interventionist/toc.html.

Morton, Timothy, 'Porcine Poetics: Shelley's *Swellfoot the Tyrant*', in *The Unfamiliar Shelley*, ed. Timothy Webb and Alan Weinberg (forthcoming).

Rossington, Michael, 'Shelley, *The Cenci* and The French Revolution', in *Revolution in Writing: British Literary Responses to the French Revolution*, ed. Kelvin Everest, Ideas and Production series (Milton Keynes and Philadelphia: Open University Press, 1991), 138–57.

'An Historical Note on the Cenci Story and the Sources of Shelley's Knowledge of It', in *The Poems of Shelley*, ed. Kelvin Everest and Geoffrey Matthews, contributing eds. Jack Donovan, Ralph Pite, and Michael Rossington, 3 vols. (London and New York: Longman, 1989–), II. 713–863, 865–75.

'Shakespeare in *The Cenci*: Tragedy and "Familiar Imagery"', in *Shakespearean Continuities: Essays in Honour of E. A. J. Honigmann*, ed. John Batchelor, Tom Cain, and Claire Lamont (Basingstoke and New York: Macmillan and St Martin's Press, 1997), 305–18.

Simpson, Michael *Closet Performances: Political Exhibition and Prohibition in the Dramas of Byron and Shelley* (Stanford: Stanford University Press, 1998).

Wasserman, Earl, *Shelley's 'Prometheus Unbound': A Critical Reading* (Baltimore: Johns Hopkins University Press, 1965).

Woodings, R. B., '"A Devil of a Nut to Crack": *Shelley's Charles the First*', *Studia Neophilologica* 40 (1968), 216– 37.

'Shelley's Sources for Charles the First', *Modern Language Review* 64 (July 1969), 267–75.

NARRATIVE

Behrendt, Stephen C., Introduction, in Percy Bysshe Shelley, *'Zastrozzi' and 'St Irvyne'* (Peterborough, Ont.: Broadview Press, 2002).

Chandler, James, *England in 1819* (Chicago: University of Chicago Press, 1998), 483–554. (On Shelley and history.)

Finch, Peter, 'Monstrous Inheritance: The Sexual Politics of Genre in Shelley's *St Irvyne*', *Keats-Shelley Journal* 48 (1999), 35–68.

Rajan, Tillotama, 'Promethean Narrative: Overdetermined Form in Shelley's Gothic Fiction', in *Shelley: Poet and Legislator of the World*, ed. Betty Bennett and Stuart Curran (Baltimore: Johns Hopkins University Press, 1996), 240–52.

PHILOSOPHY AND POLITICS

Cameron, Kenneth Neill, *The Young Shelley: Genesis of a Radical* (London: Victor Gollancz, 1951).

Shelley: The Golden Years (Cambridge, Mass.: Harvard University Press, 1974).

Clark, Timothy, 'Shelley after Deconstruction', in *Evaluating Shelley*, ed. Timothy Clark and Jerrold E. Hogle (Edinburgh: Edinburgh University Press, 1996), 91–107.

Dawson, P. M. S., *The Unacknowledged Legislator: Shelley and Politics* (Oxford: Clarendon Press, 1980).

Duffy, Edward, *Rousseau in England: The Context for Shelley's Critique of the Enlightenment* (Berkeley: University of California Press, 1979).

Hoagwood, Terence A., *Skepticism and Ideology: Shelley's Political Prose and Its Context from Bacon to Marx* (Iowa City: University of Iowa Press, 1988).

Scrivener, Michael, *Radical Shelley: The Philosophical Anarchism and Utopian Thought of Percy Bysshe Shelley* (Princeton: Princeton University Press, 1982).

POEMS AND POETICS

Butler, Marilyn, 'Myth and Mythmaking in the Shelley Circle', in *Shelley Revalued*, ed. Kelvin Everest (Leicester: Leicester University Press, 1983), 1–21.

Carothers, Yvonne M., '*Alastor*: Shelley Corrects Wordsworth', *Modern Language Quarterly* 42 (1981), 21–47.

Clark, Timothy, *Embodying Revolution: The Figure of the Poet in Shelley* (Oxford: Clarendon Press, 1989).

Cronin, Richard, *Shelley's Poetic Thoughts* (New York: St Martin's Press, 1981).

Curran, Stuart, *Poetic Form and British Romanticism* (New York: Oxford University Press, 1986). (See index entries under 'Shelley, Percy Bysshe').

de Man, Paul, 'Shelley Disfigured' in *Deconstruction and Criticism*, ed. Harold Bloom et al. (New York: Seabury Press, 1979), 39–73.

Essick, Robert N., '"A Shadow of Some Golden Dream": Shelley's Language in *Epipsychidion*', *Papers on Language and Literature* 22 (1986), 175–85.

Hamilton, Paul, *Percy Bysshe Shelley* (Plymouth, Devon: Northcote House, 2000).

Hogle, Jerrold, *Shelley's Process: Radical Transference and the Development of His Major Works* (Oxford: Oxford University Press, 1988).

Jones, Steven, E., *Shelley's Satire: Violence, Exhortation, and Authority* (DeKalb: Northern Illinois University Press, 1994).

Keach, William, 'Obstinate Questionings: The Immortality Ode and *Alastor*', *The Wordsworth Circle* 12 (1981), 36–44.

Maddox, Donald L., 'Shelley's *Alastor* and the Legacy of Rousseau', *Studies in Romanticism* 9 (1970), 82–98.

McGann, Jerome, 'Shelley's Veils: A Thousand Images of Loveliness', in *Romantic and Victorian*, ed. W. Paul Elledge and Richard L. Hoffman (Cranbury, N.J.: Fairleigh Dickinson University Press, 1971), 198–218.

Peterfreund, Stuart, *Shelley among Others: The Play of the Intertext and the Idea of Language* (Baltimore: Johns Hopkins University Press, 2002).

Walker, Constance, 'The Urn of Bitter Prophecy: Antithetical Patterns in *Hellas*', *Keats-Shelley Memorial Bulletin* 33 (1982), 36–48.

Wasserman, Earl, *Shelley: A Critical Reading* (Baltimore: Johns Hopkins University Press, 1971).

Weisman, Karen, *Imageless Truths: Shelley's Poetic Fictions* (Philadelphia: University of Pennsylvania Press, 1994).

THEMES IN SHELLEY

Gender, sexuality, and love

Gelpi, Barbara Charlesworth, *Shelley's Goddess: Maternity, Language, Subjectivity* (New York and Oxford: Oxford University Press 1992).

Ulmer, William A., *Shelleyan Eros: The Rhetoric of Romantic Love* (Princeton: Princeton University Press, 1990).

Ecocriticism

Dawson, Paul, ' "The Empire of Man": Shelley and Ecology', in *Shelley: Poet and Legislator of the World*, ed. Betty Bennett and Stuart Curran (Baltimore: Johns Hopkins University Press, 1996), 232–9.

Morton, Timothy, *Shelley and the Revolution in Taste: The Body and the Natural World* (Cambridge and New York: Cambridge University Press, 1994).

'Shelley's Green Desert', *Studies in Romanticism* 35.3 (Fall, 1996), 409–30.

Pite, Ralph, 'How Green Were the Romantics?', *Studies in Romanticism* 35.3 (Fall 1996), 357–73.

Orientalism, colonialism, imperialism

Leask, Nigel, ' "Sharp Philanthropy": Percy Bysshe Shelley and Romantic India', in *British Romantic Writers and the East: Anxieties of Empire* (Cambridge and New York: Cambridge University Press, 1992), 68–169.

Makdisi, Saree, *Romantic Imperialism: Universal Empire and the Culture of Modernity* (Cambridge and New York: Cambridge University Press, 1998), 122–53.

Morton, Timothy, 'Trade Winds', in *The Poetics of Spice: Romantic Consumerism and the Exotic* (Cambridge and New York: Cambridge University Press, 2000), 39–108.

Rossington, Michael, 'Shelley and the Orient', *Keats-Shelley Review* 6 (1991), 18–36.

Translation

Webb, Timothy, *The Violet in the Crucible: Shelley and Translation* (Oxford: Oxford University Press, 1976).

INDEX

CAMBRIDGE COMPANIONS TO LITERATURE

CAMBRIDGE COMPANIONS TO CULTURE

The Cambridge Companion to Modern German Culture edited by Eva Kolinsky and Wilfried van der Will

The Cambridge Companion to Modern Russian Culture edited by Nicholas Rzhevsky

The Cambridge Companion to Modern Spanish Culture edited by David T. Gies

The Cambridge Companion to Modern Italian Culture edited by Zygmunt G. Barański and Rebecca J. West

The Cambridge Companion to Modern French Culture edited by Nicholas Hewitt

The Cambridge Companion to Modern Latin American Literature edited by John King

The Cambridge Companion to Modern Irish Culture edited by Joe Cleary and Claire Connolly